CW00793906

Corporate Governance
and Accountability

Corporate Governance and Accountability

Richard C. Warren

Liverpool Academic Press

© Richard C. Warren 2000

First published in Great Britain by Liverpool Academic Press

A CIP catalogue for this book is available from the British Library

ISBN 1 903499 02 X
The right of Richard C. Warren to be identified as the author of this work
has been asserted by him in accordance with the Copyright, Designs and
Patents Act 1988.

All rights reserved. No part of this publication may be reproduced, stored in
a retrieval system, or transmitted in any form or by any means, electronic,
mechanical, photocopying, recording, or otherwise without prior permission
of Liverpool Academic Press, 12, Caldbeck Road, Croft Business Park,
Bromborough, Wirral, CH62 3PL.

Typeset by Bitter & Twisted, N. Wales

Printed and Bound in Great Britain by
Athenaeum Press Ltd, Newcastle upon Tyne

Contents

Acknowledgments

This project was initiated with the help of two colleagues formerly in the Department of Business Studies at the Manchester Metropolitan University, Julia Clarke and Monica Gibson-Sweet. It was completed with the support of Ajit Warren and the forbearance of Hera, Jazparl and Bebe Warren. I would like to thank Professor Nigel Healey, Head of Department for giving me research time to work on this project. I would also like to thank Blackwell Journals for permission to reproduce some of the material in my articles previously published in *Business Ethics: A European Review*.

To Jean and Frank

Introduction

'... as the representative social institution of our society the corporation in addition to being an economic tool is a political and social body; its social function as a community is as important as its economic function as an effective producer.'[1]

It could be said that all western management thought is simply footnotes upon the writings of Peter Drucker[2]. This book will take up one of his concerns expressed in the seminal work on the modern corporation published in 1946, *The Concept of the Corporation*. This is the relationship of the corporation to society and the need to understand the company as an important social institution. It is important to realize that the company is a public institution and not just a private arrangement created by contract; it cannot, therefore, be fully determined by economic factors alone, but is, importantly, also partly determined by political and social factors. Sometimes these political and social factors can become more deterministic in shaping its destiny than the economic factors. This tends to be the case when the legitimacy of business institutions is called into question. In these circumstances, the normal economic determinants of business practice can be superseded by political events and the environment of business practice can change radically. Sometimes a new set of institutions for the conduct of business can emerge and so, in a sense, the form of the company and other business practices can be said to evolve. The primary focus of this study will be on the company form, that is its legal code of governance. Although business activity is regulated in many ways by laws, taxes and codes these aspects are beyond the scope of this exposition. The new politics of corporate governance is about balancing economic performance against social accountability.

The term 'the evolving company' is not intended to imply a Darwinian foundation to business practice, but the metaphor of punctuated evolutionary change following a crisis of survival and the need to adapt to new conditions of existence seems to be an appropriate one for the description of these processes. These changes are not always in a progressive direction (politically, socially or ethically); if the new institutions of business are not found to adequately serve the needs of society, they will probably be called into question again and further adaptation and change will become necessary. The relationship between business and society is a complex phenomenon and is likely to require a multi-disciplinary approach to understand its full ramifications. This book is an analysis and a synthesis of the new politics of corporate governance and draws upon economics, management, law, politics, ethics, and sociology to examine the representative institution of business in our society, the company. An analysis will be made of how its legal form has changed over the years in response to social drivers and political imperatives. Then a synthesis will be presented of the various perspectives that are trying to shape the debate about the future trajectory of the company form.

The legal form of the company has developed over the past two hundred years from the incorporation of private property in simple joint stock companies to the complex architecture of the transnational companies that span the world today. In the UK, in 1999, there were 3.7 million businesses; 1.14 million of these were companies registered at Companies House, and 2,450 had their shares publicly traded on the London Stock Exchange. The setting up of a Modern Company Law Review in 1998, by the Department of Trade and Industry, is an indication that the legal institutions of business are coming under increasing pressure from a range of internal and external stakeholders wanting the company in particular to demonstrate greater responsibility and more accountability. This book will attempt to track the nature and course of these developments and try to understand the present situation and then attempt to give some insights into how companies may be expected to develop in the future. It is highly probable that, in the advanced economies, a new institutionalization of the company form will slowly emerge, representing a new compact between business and society.

The perspective of the study, although multi-disciplinary, in many aspects is perhaps, in the final analysis, predominantly political, because it is the relationship of the company to society that is the major focus of the analysis. Most studies of the firm are from either an economic or managerial perspective, either looking at the factors which determine the economic outcomes, or the problems of managing these factors to obtain success, however this is defined. The economic perspective tends to examine the company according to rational decision-making criteria, and the management perspective takes a more observational and pragmatic approach. The political view presented here will examine the company from the angle of its relationships and examine how these affect its institutional form and function. In this respect, a major theme of the study will be to examine to what extent the corporate form changed in response to socio-political factors as well as economic factors.

The importance of socio-political factors in the operational strategies of business firms is apparent to most consumers today. The controversy surrounding genetically modified (GM) foods in recent times is a real sign that consumer pressure has come of age and is a potent force that companies will have to deal with. In times of increasing voter apathy in politics are consumers now more passionate about what they buy than about how they vote? Do consumers look to companies for a response to their problems today more than they do towards politicians? If the slogan 'you are what you consume' is taken seriously then this could be the beginning of an important watershed in democratic societies. Consumer activism in the twenty first century could be what political activism was in the twentieth century. And yet, many people, it would seem, have an uneasy relationship with companies. In the UK, a Mori poll published in the *Financial Times* indicated that the public approval rating for big business was at a 30-year low, with only 25% of the public considering it a 'good thing' for large companies to make profits. Over 70% of people in the survey were concerned that companies should behave 'ethically'. In 1999, the amount of money investors put into 'ethical investments funds' has doubled in size[3]. Many people are now demanding that companies deliver what they want and need, champion their causes, put resources and computers in their schools and help to rejuvenate their inner cities. Most companies in response have developed policies on corporate social responsibility. The debacle of Shell over the sinking of the Brent Spar has no doubt been uppermost in the minds of many large company directors. The chief executive of BP Amoco, Sir John Browne, has made several public declarations that his company needs to win and retain public trust, and that, in order to do this, he will maintain an open dialogue with the public and make the company's activities more open to scrutiny. A quick reading of the report and accounts for many large companies will reveal that transparency, accountability and sustainability have become the slogans of the 1990s. Many companies are publishing environmental and social reports alongside their mandatory accounts and some have actively welcomed independent auditors and pressure groups such as Greenpeace as verifiers of their statements. The infamous slogan of Du Pont, the US chemical company, in the face of its detractors is now 'don't trust us, track us'. The failure of a company to take swift action in the face of consumer pressure can be enormous; it is much harder for managements to get these decisions wrong than right. In the case of GM foods, the supermarkets acted overnight in response to consumer concerns, and the government was forced to follow in their wake as concern over the environmental impact of these crops mounted. The US firm Arco has been forced to sell its interests in Burma because of the pressure from the western consumer lobby in response to the Burmese military dictatorship's persecution of democratic opposition parties and human rights abuses. For many companies, the attention that has had to be devoted to social responsibility issues is proving to be costly and time-consuming. Over 93% of companies now allocate some of their marketing budget to social responsibility issues.[4] What was once perhaps a public relations stunt is now a serious business strategy and has become a major recipient of company resources. Shell, in 1999, spent £15 million on a relaunch of its social and environmental policies[5]. The campaigns and issues begun by the Body Shop in the 1980s have become the concern of many other companies (Granada, Coop Bank, Tesco, ASDA, etc.) in the 1990s. The causes firms champion must now be ever greater, ever more substantial and ever more original. Small wonder that one of the most important functions in the boardroom of today is public relations. A fundamental change is taking place in the relationship between business and society and it needs to be charted and understood.

To gain an understanding of the issues involved also requires some historical perspective regarding the development of the company form. Incorporated joint stock companies were the result of a long political debate about the growth and the dependability of business enterprises two centuries ago. We will briefly review this debate as it progressed in chapter 1, and some of the concepts necessary to understand this process will be identified. Peter Drucker's *The Concept of the Corporation* was an attempt to understand the nature of the corporation in post-war America and this study will pick up that concern and assess the position of the company in the UK at the end of the millennium. The question of the legitimacy of companies will be the subject of analysis in chapter 2, and the question will be posed: are we experiencing a new legitimacy crisis at the moment? The drivers of change pushing upon the company will be the topics of discussion in the next three chapters. The present position regarding the structure and practices of corporate governance will be briefly outlined in chapter 3, together with some of the criticisms made of the present system. The debate about the need of management to pay more attention to the stakeholders in the company will also be reviewed. The Department of Trade and Industry's review of company law, mentioned above, is in progress and a wide range of interested parties have submitted proposals for changes to be incorporated into a new framework of legislation due in 2001. The question of stakeholders is, in the view of the steering committee in its own consultation document, said to be 'at the heart' of its deliberations. Chapter 4 will examine some of the demands that are being made for firms to become socially responsible and consider some of the methods companies are using to make themselves more transparent and accountable in this respect. Chapter 5 focuses upon the environmental issues that have become a pressing concern for all companies in the 1990s which are likely to become even more important in the next century. It will also look at the growing interest in the relationship between companies and human rights, and examine how this issue has moved up the agendas of many consumer pressure groups. Sir Geoffrey Chandler, chairman of Amnesty International's UK Business Group, writing on behalf of a wide range of interest groups in a letter published in the *Financial Times* put the matter this way:

Society needs to know what companies are doing to uphold human rights, protect the environment and help to tackle world poverty. In exchange for the legal privilege of limited liability, companies should disclose comprehensive information on their social and environmental performance alongside their financial results.[6]

The suggestion is that all companies adopt the Social Accountability (SA 8000) as a standard framed by the Council on Economic Priorities, which will align a company's policies with various human rights conventions in areas such as child labour, health and safety and freedom of association. However, the burdening of companies with a raft of social responsibilities will have to take into account the developing nature of commerce in an increasingly global market place. In chapter 6, the characteristics of the so-called 'informational age' will be outlined, and the implications for the company form explored. The future trajectory of the company form is likely to be partly determined by the political perspective that is taken of the right to hold, use and dispose of private property: is it to be an absolute right inalienable in the face of other competing values, or is it to be a social right dependent upon the acceptance on the part of property holders of certain community and environmental obligations. It may also be partly determined by they extent to which companies are expected to contribute to the maintenance and generation of trust and wider social relationships in society, now often called social capital. Putting these two dimensions together, in an analytical sense, gives rise to four possible scenarios for mapping the future trajectory of the company form. Each of these scenarios will be outlined in turn in the next four chapters, and the leading protagonists of these perspectives will be identified. Chapter 7 will examine the radical communitarian agenda for the transformation of the company. Chapter 8 will consider a more reformist version of this approach. Chapter 9 will outline the liberal agenda for restoring the shareholders' control of company operations. And finally chapter 10 will consider whether the corporate form and the large company in particular are likely to be superseded by other sorts of business organizations and mechanisms of coordination. An evaluation is made of these four trajectory scenarios in the final chapter, and a stab at predicting the most likely course of events (probably recklessly) is attempted in the conclusion. The overall purpose of this book is one of orientation, to measure the strong currents that the ship of business enterprise is having to negotiate as it enters the uncharted waters of the new millennium.

References

[1]   Drucker, P., (1964), *The Concept of the Corporation*, New York, Mentor, p 122.

[2]   To borrow a phrase from A.N. Whitehead, 'All western philosophy is simply footnotes on Plato'.

[3]   Hertz, N., (1999), 'Better to shop than vote', *New Statesman*, 21st June, p7.

[4]   Ibid.

[5]   Ibid.

[6]   *Financial Times*, 'Review of company law should uphold social responsibility', 8.6.99.

chapter one

The Company Form

'Society, therefore, is from its beginning a mitigation of ownership. Ownership in the beast and in the primitive savage was far more intense a thing than it is in the civilised world today. It is rooted more strongly in our instincts than in our reason.'[1]

Introduction

This chapter aims to give a brief account of the evolution of the company form. The company form needs to be distinguished from the structure of the organisation which makes the company a purposive actor in the social world. The form of the company is its legal and institutional licence to operate in society which is in essence a relationship between the company and society. The company form is a device that has arisen over time to protect and utilise the property of one or more people in the pursuit of business. Most importantly, it allows the owners of this property, in advance, to declare that their liabilities for the success or failure of the business are limited and to what extent the business is to be regarded, for legal purposes, as a distinct legal personality that is separate and independent from the owners of the shares in the company. The chapter will also give some indication of the growth and scope of the corporate economy and some comparative figures from the USA and Europe. Companies are today centres of great power and this will be considered, together with the justifications offered about why this power is rightly held by the owners of company property. To be able to explain these changes in company form some concepts and a theory are developed which will attempt to show these historical developments as an evolutionary process.

A brief history of the company and its growth in the economy

A company is a group of people who share responsibility for a commercial venture. Historically, business was conducted by individuals on their own account at fairs and in towns. Some merchants in the crusades began to share the risks of these ventures by collaboration. In Italy, some maritime traders began to call themselves *compagnie* when they traded and took bread together (cum-panis). British merchant adventurers of the 16th and 17th century are the forerunners of the modern companies of today. In order to undertake long trading missions they gained government approval as corporate bodies and in return for paying taxes had the monopoly of trade in a particular region. They also issued shares to finance these trading ventures and were the founders of joint-stock companies and the early stock exchanges. For example, the British East India Company was chartered in 1600 by Queen Elizabeth 1 on behalf of merchants who were sending out a trading venture to India.[2] Over the next 250 years it became a joint-stock company and came to dominate trade between India and the rest of the world. Its head office was in London and a chairman and board of directors presided over an intricate combination of interests including overseas investors, ship-owners, traders and plantation owners. However, after loosing out on some of its trading activities in China and Singapore, this bureaucratic company with its own army began to decline in profitability. After the Indian Mutiny in 1857, its charter was dissolved and its administrative functions in India were taken over by the British government.

The industrial revolution in Britain and the growth of a trading empire started up a more extensive set of trading relationships in the world than had been known since the 15th century. Most of the businesses involved in this trade were small, and company form was not important except to the large colonial trading companies such as the East India Company, British East Africa Company and the Hudson Bay Company. Britain's leading position in the world economy at this time meant that it had a key position in the flow of international trade and investment which later lead to the City of London becoming the leading centre of financial capital until it was overtaken by the USA after the second world war.

The creation of companies as an institution for doing business is a fundamental step in the development of a capitalist society and did not necessarily happen by design or by pre-planning but by an emergent process when a number of factors in the social milieu of the UK came to be in place. One of the best interpretations of this early train of events is to be found in the article by G. D. H. Cole called, 'The Evolution of Joint Stock Enterprise'.[3] Cole claims that the development of the joint-stock enterprise is the outstanding achievement of modern capitalist organisation. Although company laws differ between different countries, the essential institution of the joint-stock company remains the same and has become, in all capitalist societies, its central and representative institution in the same way that the craft guild was in medieval society. However, as Cole points out, capitalism did not invent the joint-stock form; this was legally recognised and in existence well over a hundred years before the industrial revolution.

Early on in the 18th century the joint-stock company was regarded with great suspicion because of the scandals over the spectacular fraud of the South Seas Bubble Company and other incidents of a similar kind. In 1711, Lord Robert Harley hatched a scheme which put together all those holding government debt (£9m) into a company that would exploit the supposed riches of trade with South America. The South Sea Company was a sham and the directors had little experience of this trade but it set off a speculative frenzy and a further 190 'bubble' schemes were started up in the period 1719-20, raising a total of £220m. But when the 'bubbles' burst the stock market prices of these companies fell to about 15% of their former levels, causing a political scandal and the setting up of a Parliamentary committee of enquiry to investigate these companies. Serious corruption and accounting irregularities were uncovered which lead Parliament to pass the 1720 Bubble Act, which limited the granting of the joint- stock company form. The Act stipulated that unless firms were incorporated by Royal Charter or private Act of Parliament, they had no right either to transfer their shares or have more than six partners. For some time this effectively put the brake on the growth of the joint-stock company and threatened the development of capitalist enterprise. The only companies created during this period were those sanctioned by an Act of Parliament. However, in various cases and amongst businessmen in general the inconvenience of not allowing the company a distinctive legal personality began to weigh heavily. The transference of shares between investors was hindered and bringing actions against a number of individuals in a court action was cumbersome and liable, when mistakes were made in naming the said individuals, to lead to the frustration of the court action. Moreover, the development of industrialism and the need to raise larger amounts of capital from a wider range of investors meant that not treating the company as a collective actor was undermining the economy.

The common law, slow as it is to adapt to change, did eventually respond to the requirements of the time and, by degrees, the courts, through making distinctions and the creation of new precedents, began to allow for 'representative actions' whereby companies were allowed to be represented in court not by the entire body of the shareholders but through a representative individual as standing for the whole company. Another influence in the battle to obtain legal recognition for the company was when bodies of commissioners were set up in the 18th century to make and administer the river improvements and road improvements needed at that time. The organisations founded for this purpose were in turn used when railway companies were founded and later still the gas and water companies. The form they took was the joint-stock company as laid down by special resolution of Acts of Parliament. Each company was defined as a separate legal entity and to it exceptional powers were granted. For administrative convenience as the number of these bodies to be created and debated on the floor of the House of Commons increased it was deemed necessary to define a procedure which simplified the process. This was found in the form of the creation of legislation by 'reference to clauses' in previous Acts so that it was unnecessary to pass through a new Act. This method of legislation by reference to previous Acts helped to standardise the structure and operation of the statutory companies and so enabled the courts to develop a set of rules and procedures that applied to them in general. However it would be quite a while before this set of procedures about public utilities would be applied to private property interests. The industrial revolution with the growth of factories and the development of machinery lead to the increase in business organisations which began to be run by professional managers and clerks. Railway companies began to develop businesses that had to be run and coordinated across countries and continents. Prior to these large companies the only other large organisations had been armies and churches. Consequently, aspects of organisation and control often reflected these antecedents, for example, railway uniforms and officer titles for operatives and managers, and the requirements of discipline and obedience from the railway servants to their stationmasters. The financing of the railway companies was only possible by joint-stock company methods and limiting the liability from the Act of 1855 became the norm for many kinds of business enterprise.

In 1834 Parliament began the process of the recognition of the joint-stock company some ten years after the repeal of the Bubble Act, which had halted their development since the time of that scandal. An Act was passed enabling the Crown by Letters Patent to grant unincorporated companies the right to sue and be sued in their own names. However, this procedure was so cumbersome that some ten years later a further Act was passed which enabled companies to obtain a letter of incorporation without either a grant of Letters Patent or by special Parliamentary resolution. This Act of 1844 was the start of the joint-stock institution because it recognised all joint-stock companies which registered under it as incorporated bodies and so gave them a legal personality under the law. Under this Act and its amendment Act in 1847 many new companies were created, but they were not yet limited in liability. The granting of this privilege was again many years in the making.

The issue of whether the partners in a business should be fully liable for the debts of that business was a topic of constant debate over many years. The argument for limited liability was won in 1855 when a new Act gave businesses the same standing as the utility companies and the right of limited liability for their shareholders, which when amended and consolidated became the foundation of the Companies Acts in 1862. This granting of limited liability for those companies that sought to apply for it broadened very considerably the expansion of capitalist development after its enactment. Nevertheless, it took some time for the knowledge of these privileges to become widely known and to be taken advantage of by investors. These reforms of company law between 1825 and 1862 helped to create the stock exchanges in major provincial cities: Manchester 1836, Liverpool 1836, Glasgow 1844, Edinburgh 1844, Leeds 1845, Bristol 1845, Birmingham 1845, and Leicester 1845. These stock exchanges were not, however, fully exploited as a source of new finance for business until much later in the century, and much of the finance raised for UK industry continued to come from family wealth and retained profits.

The size of firms in Britain remained fairly small during the competitive phase of 19th century capitalism until the creation of the joint-stock company. Hobson noticed that a rise in the number of company floatations after the 1862 Companies Acts had allowed companies to issue shares on the stock market.[4] After 1862, over 24,000 companies were registered in the following twenty-five years. After this time Britain also began to experience a long-term decline in the number of large family-owned enterprises. At the turn of the century the largest firms were railway, dock and canal companies which were floated in the stockmarket. Large firms existed prior to the 20th century; the capital of the Rothschild's Banks has been estimated at over £20 million in 1863. Railway companies were the first giant firms of the industrial age, 19 in the UK had capital in excess of £3 million, when the nearest large firms had capital of less than £500,000.[5] The increase in the size of firms tended to coincide at around the turn of the century. Many factors contributed to this: technical innovations, expanding markets, improved communications, intense competition, government regulations, entrepreneurial activity, and, perhaps most importantly, the investment opportunities opened up by the stock market.

Cole claims that the great advantage of the joint-stock form is that it allowed the combination of an extreme individualistic theory of property with the power and control of a corporate organisation: '...individual turned into association: yet in such a way that the individual remained, and the hero of business romance could wield his battle-axe not merely with the strength of ten, but with the assimilated vitality of ten thousand shareholders.'[6] Over time both heroes of business, the entrepreneur and the investor, became ever-more subordinate to the manager of the joint stock company as it grew in size and influence.

In the USA, railway companies helped to develop and industrialise America, and because of the size of markets and geography this heralded in the growth of ever-larger corporations: Andrew Carnegie's steel plant in Pittsburgh; John Heinz's canned foods; Proctor and Gamble's soap works; George Eastman's camera company; Asa Chandler's drinks firm Coca-Cola, to name but a few. These companies became the corporations which moved from the US into world markets and, consequently, have become enduring multinational corporations. One of the biggest was Standard Oil which was formed by John D. Rockefeller in 1883 as a trust to control the oil fields in the USA. This firm grew very large and was broken up under anti-trust laws in the USA in 1911, so that each state had its own oil company, the largest of which was Standard Oil of New Jersey, now Exxon, previously Esso.[7]

In the UK, the original intention of Parliament was that the use of the joint-stock limited liability company would be confined to large-scale businesses requiring large amounts of capital, but once the privilege was granted it became difficult to prevent the small business from taking advantage of this concession.[8] This development was perhaps inevitable and so finally was recognised in the 1908 Companies Act with a clause that recognised the right to form small companies with a limited number of shareholders. These companies were termed 'private companies' and were even given certain privileges over the 'public companies' since they did not have to file their balance sheets for inspection but only a list of shareholders and their Memorandum and Articles of Association. However, the private company was not allowed more than 50 shareholders and was not entitled to appeal to the public for investment funds. The transfer of shares in a private company is a matter to be settled between the existing shareholders. This development, in turn, greatly encouraged the family business to register itself as a private company in order to help protect the business from secession problems when new members of the family needed to take over the business. The limitation of liability was also an attractive attribute for many small businessmen and many landowners also took advantage of this possibility.[9] Another consequence of the 1907 Act was that the opportunity to create 'subsidiary companies' was taken up by many firms wishing to branch out, enabling them to form a pyramid-like structure of companies with the shares held by the parent company. If the parent company was a public limited company and all the subsidiary companies were private then a company could virtually avoid the need to disclose to the public much real information about itself. This further effect of the company system allowed the large investor to exercise more control over a bigger spread of shareholder capital and for a minority shareholding to give effective control over a large multi-form company. The Companies (Consolidation) Act 1908 consolidated the 1862 Act with the various Acts amending it, and this was followed by the Companies Act 1929 which required that a balance sheet and profit and loss account be laid before the company every year.

In Britain a wave of mergers took place between 1888 and 1914, which reached a peak in 1899, making it the leading country of big business in Europe. By 1914, there were 63,000 registered companies and 77% of these were private companies indicating that family groupings still dominated in most of British business. In 1907, over 100 firms had a capital base of at least £2m; this was twice as many as in Germany, and four times more than in France. Large firms tended to be concentrated in heavy industries in Germany, but in the UK they were more diversified into textiles, food and drink, tobacco, chemicals and transport. Banks increasingly grew in size through a process of merger and amalgamation which reached its peak between 1890 and 1918. During this period, Lloyds, Midland and Barclays Banks were formed and London and Westminster, and London and County Banks merged in 1909. But as the result of their comparatively low share capital, British banks did not appear at the top of the list of the nations largest companies as measured by share capital. Lloyds Bank at £4m was only 14th in the list in 1907. The important position of finance in British industry did not depend upon the size of its banks but upon the role of the City of London which acted as the financial centre of the world prior to the first world war. The value of the securities quoted on the London Stock Exchange was larger than that of the New York and Paris Exchanges combined.[11] Consequently, some large investment companies existed in London with more than £2m in share capital, for example Debenture Corporation, Australian Mortgage and Land and Finance Company.

For most of the early part of the 20th century, large firms were dominant in heavy industry: coal, iron, steel, shipbuilding, machinery and armaments. In Britain, the leading firms in the heavy industry sector were diversified across the industry: Vickers, Armstrong Whitworth, and John Brown all employed more than 20,000 workers. Also large in employment terms were Harland and Wolff, Cammel-Laird, Workman Clark, Guest Keen and Nettlefolds, and Bolckow Vaughan. Britain also had large firms in brewing: Watney, Combe, and Reid with a share capital of more than £6m, Guinness with £4.5m, Bass with £2.7m, Whitbred with £2.3m. Big firms in the food industry were Cadbury, Fry and Rowntree; in tobacco, Imperial Tobacco had £15.5m share capital. W.D. and H.O. Wills became the dominant firm in the industry. In textiles, the Fine Cotton Spinners and Doublers' Association had 30,000 workers and £4.5m share capital; the Calico Printer's Association employed 20,000 workers and had £5m share capital; the Bleachers' Association founded in 1900 had capital of £4.5m and 11,000 workers; J. and P. Coats, thread manufacturers, had £10m capital and 13,000 workers.[12]

In many ways, big business had penetrated all industries in the early 20th century, and it had penetrated the service industries further than in the continent of Europe. For example, in shipping Britain owned 40% of the world's merchant tonnage in 1914, and vessels under the British flag carried over 50% of all international trade by volume in 1912. Through mergers and amalgamations, British shipping companies were consolidated into the so-called big five: Cunard, Furness Whithy, Ellerman Lines, Royal Mail Steam Packet, and P&O. Merchant houses also turned into large firms such as E.D. Sassoon and Co., Finlay and Co., Ralli Brothers, Butterfly and Swire. Firms in the retail trade also reached large sizes: Harrods, Whitley's, Thomas Lipton, Home and Colonial Stores. W.H. Smith had a workforce of 10,358 in 1911. Newspaper companies were also large firms in terms of capitalisation: The *Daily Mail, Daily Mirror, Observer*, and other papers were established during this period. Lord Nothcliffe's company, Associated Newspapers, was incorporated in 1906 with £1.6m capital. Many large companies in Britain operated abroad under the protection of the British Empire. Most prominent of these were Rio Tinto, De Beers Consolidated Mines, Consolidated Gold Fields of South Africa, and Anglo-American Telegraph, all with capitals of several million pounds.

A similar picture emerges in the USA.[13] The dispersal of shareholding began to spread in the early 20th century and family control of enterprises experienced a rapid decline in the 1930s when the management-controlled enterprise became much more prominent. By the 1950s the control by institutional shareholders of the majority of American companies was apparent, though family ownership has persisted in many sectors of the economy.

The first world war shattered the fortunes of many companies in Europe but greatly increased those in the USA. Britain, which had been the world's great power, now began to cede this position to the USA. After 1914 changes in the economy were affected by several factors: the growing importance of new industries, higher levels of business concentration and rationalisation, and the growth of state intervention in the economy. In the UK, the number of large companies rose significantly in the inter-war years, and again after the second world war.[14] In 1929, the number of companies with capital of more than £3m was 186; this was three times as high as in Germany (55) and well beyond that in France (2). If size of workforce is the measure, then again 40 British firms had over 10,000 employees in 1929 as against 27 in Germany, and 22 in France. By 1955, in the UK 65 firms had workforces over 10,000 compared with 20 in France, and 26 in Germany. In 1953, 150 British firms had capital of over £5m compared to 12 in France, and 67 in Germany. However, in Germany during this period some extremely large firms began to emerge each employing over 100,000 workers: Vereinigte Stalhwerke in iron and steel, Seimens in electrical engineering and IG Farben in chemicals. In Britain, the two largest employers in the mid-1930s were Unilever (60,000) and ICI (56,000). Two of these German firms, however, did not survive the second world war and were broken up leaving Seimens as the only employer of over 100,000 in 1950.

The rise of large firms in Britain during this period is mainly due to merger activity, starting with the banks in 1918 when the big five clearing banks were created, and then moving on into chemicals and electrical engineering motor cars, shipbuilding aerospace, oil and rubber.[15]   During this period 3,700 companies were involved in mergers and so the foundations were laid for the modern corporate economy. Large firms were less numerous in other industries, but post-second-world-war nationalisations created giant firms in the coal industry (NCB 700,000 workers), Post Office, and Railways. The big firms that came to dominate the British economy at this time were: Vickers in shipbuilding and armaments, Guest, Keen and Nettlefolds in engineering, United Steel Companies in steel, J. and P. Coats, and Coutaulds in textiles, Imperial Tobacco, Guinness, Watney, Distillers, J. Lyons and Co. in tobacco, drink and food, Marks and Spencer's in retail, P & O in shipping. Of the top two hundred firms in the 1930s at least 70% had family members on the boards of directors. This fell to about 30% in the 1950s as firms dominated by institutional shareholders and managers grew in the post-second-world- war period.

The next revision of significance to the Companies Acts was in 1948. This Act introduced the exempt private company which did not need to make its balance sheet and profit and loss account available to the public. (This provision was of benefit to the 'family' private company). The Act also made fundamental changes in the law relating to company accounts, and required that the auditor of a public or a private company had to have a professional accountancy qualification to sign the accounts. Holding companies were required to publish accounts covering themselves and their subsidiaries in the group. An accounting distinction was also made between 'reserves' and 'provisions' in published accounts which helped the investing public compare the share values and asset values. As there was no Capital Gains Tax levied before 1965, the shareholders were able to pocket all the proceeds from their market transactions.

In 1962, the Jenkins Report was issued after a full enquiry into the state of Britain's company law.[16] Only some of its recommendations were implemented in the 1967 Act, which abolished the status of the exempt company, and new provisions for the reporting of company accounts were introduced. The idea was to try to ensure that shareholders were kept informed of the company's activities. The Act also gave the Department of Trade and Industry wide powers to compel companies to produce books and papers for inspection. In order to take into account some of the implications of joining the EC, the Companies Act 1976 was introduced, which provided for the disqualification of persons involved in a company if they had not lodged documents with the Registrar. The regulations regarding auditors was also amended and the Act introduced new regulations regarding the registered office of a company and the approval of company names.

Florence's study of UK share ownership in the early 1950s is the best account of how the company form had changed up until this time.[17]   Florence discovered that wholly-owned subsidiaries comprised a large proportion of big companies at this time compared to the USA. Shareholding was less dispersed than in the USA but the process of dispersion had been under way much more markedly since the 1930s when the average percentage of shares held by principal shareholders in large firms fell from 30% to 19%. In 1936, he found that 21 of the largest 120 firms were majority or minority controlled by personal shareholders, and 16 firms were family controlled. By 1951 this had changed and 17 of the top 120 were majority or minority controlled, only nine were family controlled. The growth was in institutional shareholding and an increase in the number of firms controlled through constellation of interests. By the 1950s large firms were the dominant players in many sectors of British industry, several years ahead of large firms in both France and Germany.

Since the 1950s, a period of strong economic growth meant that large companies developed in size and scope, especially during the 1960s.[18] This trend has continued to manifest itself. In 1975, 39% of the top 250 firms in the UK had no holder of shares of more than 5% of the capital. About a third of the top firms were wholly owned by a majority or minority shareholder. There has been a massive increase in the number of shares held by financial institutions in the UK, as in the USA. Investment trusts, life insurance companies, pension funds and banks are now the major shareholders (1993: 61.2%); personal holders of shares although large in number own a relatively small proportion of shares (1993: 17.7%) on the stock exchange. The number of companies with over 10,000 workers grew in the UK to 160, in France to 62 and in Germany to 102. But in the period to 1990, the numbers have remained fairly static: 162 in UK, 81 in France, and 80 in Germany. During this period the giant firm employing over 100,000 workers became more prominent: in the 1970s there were 9 in UK (GEC 211,000, ICI 199,000, British Leyland 191,000), 8 in Germany (Siemens 301,000, Volkswagen 192,000), and 6 in France. By 1990, in Europe only three companies employed over 300,000 workers: Daimler-Benz 368,226, Siemens 365,000, Unilever 300,000; only three over 200,000: Volkswagen 250,616, BT 237,400, and Alcatel Alsthom 210,300. Most of these firms have downsized their workforces considerably in the late 1990s. The processes of rationalisation has been driven by competitive pressures to cut cost and improve efficiency , by the introduction of new technology and the spate of mergers and take-overs in this period. Large firms still dominate most industrial sectors in the UK, Germany and France, whilst the trend in each country has been towards greater convergence, cross-European mergers are, so far, rather few in number but may increase with the greater integration of EU markets. Big companies are in fact a small proportion in both the UK and USA of the total number of companies that are registered. Over one million companies were registered in 1992 but of these only 1% were public companies. Nevertheless, they are the dominant players in the UK economy.

Large firms came to prominence in the UK at the beginning of the century and became particularly concentrated in many sectors of the economy in the 1950s. France and Germany lagged behind but caught up in the post-war period. This is not to claim that this is necessarily good for the economy; performance and profitability are another matter. Often small and medium companies in certain industrial sectors are extremely profitable in the City of London, for example, or in the case of Germany its small and medium-sized enterprises in the engineering sector. Indeed Britain's relatively poor economic performance has often been attributed to the weakness of the small and medium enterprise sector.[19]

The Companies Act 1980 provided for the first time a major distinction between public and private companies, including a threshold financial requirement to obtain public company status. Issuing shares and the payment of dividends became the subject of statutory rules. The duties of directors were strengthened and the practice of 'insider dealing' became a criminal offence. Once again directives from Europe were the prompt for the 1981 Companies Act which brought in new rules on the format for company accounts and their public disclosure. New rules for company names, the purchase and redemption by a company of its own shares and the requirements for disclosing shareholding were tightened. To clarify and consolidate a now complicated situation in company law it was recommended in 1981 that a new consolidation act be passed by two law commissions which sat in England and Scotland.

The Companies Act 1985 has 747 sections, 25 schedules and three satellite Acts: Business Names Act 1985, Company Securities(Insider Dealing) Act 1985, Companies Consolidation (Consequential Provisions) Act 1985.[20] Whilst it did much to improve the legislation in this field, shortly after it came into force two more EC directives on company law were passed, and the Cork Committee recommendations on company insolvency were enacted in the Insolvency Act 1986 and Company Directors Disqualification Act 1986. The provisions of the 1986 Financial Services Act also repealed sections of the 1985 Act which controlled the public issue of shares on the stock exchange. We will be considering the present state of company law later in chapter 3, but it should be noted that, so far, no attempt has been made to codify company law. It remains a mixture of common law and statute that responds to pressure and the evolving nature of business practice.

In the late 1990s, there were an estimated 37,000 multi-national companies controlling about 170,000 affiliated companies in the world.[21] Of these, 24,000 (about 70%) were 'home ' based in the 14 major developed countries; 90% of company headquarters are in the developed world. These large companies control up to 80% of foreign trade and are responsible for massive amounts of foreign investment in the developing world. The income of many multi-national companies exceeds that of many countries in the world. In Europe, there are 8,500 companies which employ over 1,000 employees. In the UK, there are 332 companies employing 6.1m workers; in Germany 257 companies employ 3,4m; in France 117 employ 1.9m; and in Italy 32 companies employ 0.67m workers. Indeed, the emergence of a growing number of multi-national companies organised on a European scale and controlling large investment portfolios abroad, has major economic and political implications.

This means that those in charge of companies can make private choices that will have public consequences. And although company decision-makers do not do this in an unconstrained way (laws, regulations, trade unions, pressure groups, customers and competitors, all try to put constraints on the company), the degree of discretion for the company is often quite considerable. We live today in a corporate world and how this power is used can affect us all.

The power of the company

All companies, when they move beyond the one-person business, have the power of organisation, particularly over employees. After all, an employee has to obey all lawful and reasonable orders of his employer. Indeed, the authority relationship between employer and employee in the firm is unusual in that most people in a market economy are in a supposedly free and equal exchange relationship. The employer's right to discipline and ultimately dismiss the employee, particularly when the level of unemployment is high, represents a formidable set of powers which, even when trade unions are allowed to represent the employees' collective interests, is still decisive. However, when the company is of some size in terms of employees or capital, it begins to acquire the power of decision making or choice which can affect the lives of many people far and wide and also the natural environment.

Companies and the market

In economic theory, the firm in a competitive market is a price-taker and so has little power to exercise control over the forces of supply and demand in the market, beyond the decision to buy or sell. However, in many markets a small number of firms are able to influence prices in their favour or exercise control over the profits of supplier firms. An uncompetative market may exist for a long time, particularly if there are barriers to entry which deter the competition. The effect of these market imperfections is to allow discretion and some power of choice to the company. Moreover, the oligopolistic firm may even be able to escape the influence of consumer sovereignty. The theory of consumer sovereignty is that companies in a market are obliged to produce the goods and services consumers require at the lowest price in accordance with the quantity and quality desired. However, once again it is open to question whether consumers can influence the process of offering products and services in the market place. It would appear that the consumer may enjoy the power of veto over offerings that they do not like but they cannot necessarily call forward products or services that they would like. For example, many consumers would like to buy a machine that would iron their cloths but few machines are currently on the market that are affordable or acceptable to most consumers. The notion of the sovereign consumer is also open to question, in that modern consumers are often manipulated or influenced by the producers of goods and services through sophisticated advertising and marketing campaigns. It is true that these campaigns do not always work, but creating wants rather than simply satisfying consumer needs is a real possibility in contemporary society, once again giving companies more power and discretion over aspects of our lives.

Decisions over organisation

There are decisions in the management of companies beyond those of the products, services, quality and price type to be made by managers; these are over the organisation of the firm itself. The location of the company, the size and distribution of the plants, the nature of the technology used, the structure of the organisation, the culture and policy that will be pursued in the organisation, are all arenas affording some discretion and choice for those in charge of the company. Obviously they are not unconstrained in these choices: investment incentives, local loyalties, a sense of responsibility, traditional values, trade unions, and many other influences might be brought to bear upon such decisions. But the fact of the proactive power of management in most of these decisions up against the reactive power of its opponents is often decisive and of great import for society and the natural environment.

Influence in politics

Businesses are also very influential in the political process; they are an important interest group and seek to sway government decisions in their favour, often through the activity of lobbying. The decisions they make also have a big impact on government policies because of their social implications and consequences. For example, a factory closure can have a considerable impact upon the fortunes of a particular region, which in turn calls forth a government response in the face of discontent in the electorate in this region. Political parties and governments that do not enjoy the confidence of business often suffer a credibility gap when it comes to election polls and the implementation of their policies. Consequently, the courting of business support is very important for party politicians and government ministers in the major political parties.

In a democratic society, the control of power and its dispersion are very important concepts, if the rights of the people to govern themselves in independence are to be upheld. Private property is an important source of freedom but, if not distributed fairly, it can be a source of exploitation. Consequently, a justification for holding and controlling large amounts of private property needs to be put forward and the claims made accepted as legitimate in a democratic society. The philosophical defence of private property rights and the transfer of these rights into company law as another form of private property holding will now be briefly examined.

Private property and society

The nature and meaning of property is not fixed but is something which changes in the course of history and in the context of a particular society.[22] The ancient view of property saw ownership of land and arms as the condition of citizenship and was hostile to money making; the modern view of property sees it as an economic resource, which is supportive of money making and views the taxation of wealth by the state as a drain on this resource and a threat to its owner's liberty.

The Greeks thought of property as family property rather than individual property. Plato thought that property was a necessary nuisance for the philosopher king and that the best way to handle it was to make the powerful property-less and the propertied powerless by dividing up the classes such that the ruling class are in charge of the productive classes. Aristotle's view was that the point of property is the maintenance of the household and in this respect farming and landowning are necessary but making money for its own sake is distasteful and potentially corrupting. The citizen's task is to be sufficiently wealthy to be able to take an active interest in the affairs of the city state and this means that owning slaves who do the drudgery is acceptable. Moreover women might run the households of their husbands but were not allowed to own property or take part in the affairs of the polis. The Romans broke with these views by giving successful generals farms and land which helped to pay for the funding of its armies. However, this eventually had destructive consequences in that the wealthy generals began to build up power bases of their own with which they could challenge the existing political regime.

With the spread of Christianity, and towards the end of the Dark Ages, the creation of a feudal society gave rise to a social structure where tenants and landowners held land in return for military services to a king. The notion of property developed during this period was based on Christian scholarship, which made appeals to the principles of mutual obligations based on oaths of allegiance on the one side and coronation oaths on the other. Whilst the balance of feudal society was maintained for a long time, military success and empire building began to create more prosperity and enabled rich barons to appear, and then power struggles began to undermine the power base of the medieval kingdoms. Charles 1st was brought down by trying to levy unpopular taxes to support his armies and the English revolution began to provoke debate about the constitution of society and the role of property in the balance of power. David Hume was an astute commentator on this situation and recommended that Britain should adopt a 'mixed constitution' of democratic, aristocratic and monarchical elements, where private property allowed for representation in Parliament and balanced the powers of the monarch who had to finance a standing army through taxation against approval by Parliament.[23] Later on Bernard Mandeville in the Fable of the Bees provided support to the view that private property was conducive to the public good by showing that a freeholding citizenry exercised self-control and upheld liberty even when pursuing its own self-interest.[24] This idea, refined and developed by Adam Smith, became the political doctrine of laissez-faire where the invisible hand of the market worked in the interests of the common good when people were allowed to follow their own interests in the management of their own property.[25] This view grew and developed the law of property in the 18th and 19th centuries and these changes in society have been described by the great historian of law, Henry Maine, as the movement of society based upon status to one where contract was the basis of the social order.[26] As he saw it, the industrial revolution had created a society of independent individuals, encountering one another through contractual relationship. Property had been liberated from customary ties, and persons liberated from their positions in the social hierarchy and the traditional ways of life.

In the 19th century the ideology of laissez-faire was supplemented by the utilitarian justification of the existence of private property and the necessary freedom to use that property according to the best rights of the owner. A further defence of property rights was needed at this time because, although industrialism had brought about a great increase in wealth, the inequality of its distribution was beginning to put a considerable strain on the social order. A formidable critique of private property was also developed in this century by Karl Marx in his analysis of the capitalist system which is now best remembered in the radical's slogan 'all property is theft'.[27] We will examine this critique in more detail below but, first, the utilitarian case for private property will be examined.

Utilitarianism, as propounded by Jeremy Bentham and refined and developed by J. S. Mill, is the theory that moral and legal rules are acceptable if they promote the greatest happiness of the greatest number in society.[28] Ownership of property, which is a collection of rights to possess, use, manage, and transfer property along with certain obligations not to use to cause other harm or to possess without title, is considered by utilitarianism best assigned to a single person. This is because in a difficult world, where resources are scarce and human nature weak, we need to make the best use of these productive resources with the minimum expenditure of effort. Rules about ownership are important because people are limited in their generosity and some will try to use their force to deprive others of the fruits of their labour. Ownership rights are also useful to help in problems of cooperation and coordination because they give someone a decisive say and guide us as to the allocation of the share of benefits produced. Property gives its owner a sense of security and an incentive to preserve and protect the property, and a desire to work hard to increase it. Private property is justified upon the basis that this gives rise to a greater abundance of wealth and so fulfils the utilitarian requirement for the greatest happiness of the greatest number. In this respect, if communal property rights are more economically efficient in generating wealth then this would support public rather than private ownership of property. However, economic arguments for private property rights are usually supported by the proposition that private property is more economically efficient. The ecological disasters in the former Soviet Union and the failure of their economy might be taken as supporting the view that, in general, giving people property rights in any thing of value is the best way to ensure resources are used a efficiently as possible. Indeed, the problems of environmental pollution in capitalist countries often arise because the creators of externalities are not paying the full economic cost of the factors they are using or disposing of in their production process. The development described earlier in company law can be justified under this utilitarian theory as bringing about changes in the law which made the creation of companies a vehicle for improving the wealth-creation process and importantly allowed more investors as shareholders to be involved in the process. The greater wealth generated by companies provided more employment which, when unproductive labour was fully-employed, would in turn lead to the increase of wage rates and better incomes for the new working class. The generation of good profits was an encouragement for even more investment and so, by the invisible hand of the market mechanism, the general happiness of society would increase. However, despite the theory, the practice of business did not always deliver the increase in prosperity for everyone, particularly for a poor mass of urban working class in the new factories and cities of the industrialised countries.[29]

A number of objections to the utilitarian view of property rights can be made: that the proof of efficiency in the distribution of resources is more apparent than real in practice; that bad bargains are often struck between the rich and the poor which are more reflective of a power imbalance than freedom of contract; that efficiency is not always the best criteria to use when measuring the improvement in a system of property allocations; and that a better system of property ownership is to be found in a socialist society. This later view was put forward most forcefully by Marx, and the Fabian socialists in Britain.

Marx thought that property was both the object of human freedom and at the same time the external force which enslaved us. Capitalism meant that the wage labourer was dominated and exploited by the master of capital and that until they overcame the illusions of property they would remain in a condition of alienation. The more developed the forms of property and the more perfect the market, the less workers can decide what is to happen in the world, and the more it is decided by the impersonal forces of capitalism. So what is produced by labour only minimally reflects human needs, because its value is its exchange value rather than its value as a useful product or service. Labour itself is not an adequate expression of human creativity and imagination but is forced at a pace and in the direction of the organisational machine. It is because our social interaction is governed by the demands of our property, and not rationally organised for the benefit of all, that the movement towards a socialist society where property is held in common, once again, should be welcomed by everyone. However, it has to be noted that the only continuing experiments in the sort of property-less societies that Marxists have helped to bring about (Soviet Union, China, North Korea, Cuba) do not inspire much confidence in his predictions.

The Fabian critique of private property was influenced by John Stuart Mill and Henry George, who had both noted that the workers received very little of the fruits of their own labour because most of it was taken by the passive capital-owning classes.[30] The Fabian programme was to reorganise society by the emancipation of land and industrial capital from individual and class ownership, and vest them in the community for the general benefit. Workers employed by the municipal corporations would draw a salary and the surplus product would be reinvested for the benefit of the community. The Fabian Society policies of 'permeation' and 'inoculation' were both very successful and they ultimately encouraged the Labour Government into launching a nationalisation programme in 1945. However, since 1979, the policy of nationalisation of the commanding heights of the UK economy have largely been abandoned under the privatisation process set in train by the Thatcher Government, and now endorsed by New Labour.

The collective ownership of property and the property-less society are difficult concepts to realise in practice, and perhaps are expressions of a utopian vision of an alternative society. Property rights are indeed useful and can help to build a good society, after all we can only give to others if we have something to give. Moreover, it would seem that property, freedom and security are connected in intimate ways which gives people a sense of identity and belonging and the motivation to preserve and protect what is theirs. However, the use of the argument for private property rights to justify an absolute claim on the property of the company by the shareholders needs to be examined more closely.

Companies as private property

Two arguments underpin the logic of the private ownership of companies today. The first is based on the rights of entitlement and ownership; this justification of company power rests upon the belief that shareholders are the proprietors of the business. The second argument is that this pattern of ownership is the best arrangement, in the long-run, for the wealth creating and distributing process in society.

Whilst, in law, the shareholders are not the owners of the company, they are in substance treated as if this is the case because they contribute to its capital. The creation of the company as a separate legal personality makes the shareholder the near equivalent of a slave owner, if this argument is accepted. Consequently shareholders are supposed to be able to do what they like with their own property, even if they decide to pool their property and act as a corporate body. The state has no right to intervene in this activity except to ensure the law of the land is upheld and that others' rights to enjoy their own property are upheld. Under this justification there is no requirement that the firm operate to improve the public good or the interests of the state.

The main problem with this view, first identified by Berle and Means, is that the potential divorce of ownership and control in the large company means that a dispersed and fragmented shareholder group may only have weak powers to make a small but powerful management team accountable for its running of the company.[31] Another objection to this theory is that it is questionable whether property rights should be absolute in the company form. Should the owner of a property right be able to exercise that right regardless of its consequences for other people? This is, in effect, an attack on the notion of rights as fundamental human entitlements to be upheld before other considerations are brought into the picture. This is not a popular position to advocate in a dangerous world where rights are often important protections against the state and often are thought to be one of the distinctive features of democratic freedoms. However, it will be argued later that our view of company property rights is indeed changing and a new concept of property in this form is beginning to become apparent, in a form that is less absolute and more constrained. We ought to now make the distinction between personal property and company property as two completely different notions, and to be governed by separate system of the law. In the meantime, the other principal justification offered to legitimise the shareholders property in the form of a company is still based upon the general consequences for society of such a concession.

The staying power of the so-called invisible-hand argument offered by Adam Smith is quite remarkable and is applied in the same way to cover the company as just another form of private property.[32] The argument is then that the corporate economy is the most efficient system for generating wealth in society. By seeking to maximise company profitability a pattern of interactions is set in motion, almost like an 'invisible hand' which serves the common good by generating the maximum wealth for society. The distribution of this wealth by the companies will, if maximisation and principles of entitlement are followed, be widespread and beneficial even for the poor. However, this justification is dependent upon the working of a perfectly competitive market that is not prone to market failures and monopoly practices. In the imperfect and often problematic markets of a large corporate economy there are often periods when business companies do not seem to be serving the public interest but merely serving the interests of owners and managers in these large companies. There are periods when it is fitting to describe the situation as a legitimisation crisis. An institution claiming to serve the general good is in fact serving only selective interests. These would appear to happen periodically in capitalism and when they do the justification of business power and the existence of the company form are both called into question. When this happens the meaning and justification of shareholders absolute property rights come into question. It is at these points that the institutionalisation of companies is open to change and the nature of the company as private property is reappraised. Indeed, it will be the contention of this book that our notions of property, particularly those vested in the corporation under company law, are at present undergoing a profound, and in the longer run, fundamental change.

The assumptions that an economy made up of many buyers and sellers of traded goods in an open market combined with private property is the most efficient way to organise production and exchange may now be under question. The new informational economy contains many goods that are more like public goods; they can be used by many people at once without making anyone less well-off. This means that private property ownership in the form of companies may not be the most efficient way to organise the economy. Instead we will probably need more hybrid forms of ownership which combine public and private ownership rights and altogether more sophisticated corporate institutions. It is important to recognise that the concept and meaning of property as embedded in the company form has been undergoing a process of change since it was established under the first Companies Acts. This is a process that needs to be charted and understood because our notion of capitalism has itself changed: it has in fact moved a long way from the model of Adam Smith. As Berle and Means noted, the entrepreneur of Adam Smith was the owner-manager. He 'very emphatically repudiated the stock corporation as a business mechanism holding that dispersed ownership made efficient operations impossible.'[33] His concepts and justifications for the laissez-faire private enterprise are inappropriate to describe modern realities. A change in the meaning of property has been brought about and this change can be thought of as an evolutionary process. The concepts necessary to describe and understand this process are explained in the next section.

The insight of Schumpeter

That change in the company form that appeared to be brought about by kind of evolutionary process was noticed and commented upon by the liberal economist and critic of Marx, Joseph A. Schumpeter. He was of the view that property rights and entitlements do not remain fixed but change in relation to the social and cultural context of capitalism. Joseph A. Schumpeter (1883-1950) was born in Moravia, then part of the Austrian Empire, to a textile manufacturer who died when Joseph was four years old. He was, however, brought up in a very privileged setting because his mother remarried the commander of the Vienna garrison. Schumpeter attended the University of Vienna graduating in law and economics in 1906. He married in England but was divorced in 1920. In 1907 he went to manage the financial affairs of an Egyptian princess and published his first book on economic theory in 1908. He became a professor at the University of Czernowitz in 1909. After the first world war he was briefly a consultant to the Socialisation Commission in Berlin, and was then for a few months the socialist Minister of Finance in the first coalition government of the Austrian Republic. After this Government fell he was the president of a bank in Vienna and in 1925 accepted the appointment of a professorship at the University of Bonn. In 1932 he moved to Harvard University in the USA where he remained a professor of economics until his death in 1950. He published a number of original contributions to economic theory and history. However, he was very widely read and did not consider economic questions to be divorced from wider social analysis. Although in the post-world-war-two period his work was very influential, it tended to be neglected in economic circles until the 1980s when a renewed interest in the Austrian school of economists revived interest in his work and in recent years his foundations for the theory of economic growth have been very influential in contemporary developments. His great work, *Capitalism, Socialism and Democracy* is itself a wide-ranging synthesis of economics, sociology and politics, showing that he learnt as much from Marx and Weber as he did from the Austrian school of economists.[34]

For the purposes of this analysis we will be drawing upon some of the insights of Schumpeter, particularly those concerned with tendencies in the decomposition of capitalist societies. The general thesis of his study will be briefly outlined to provide a context for these concepts. Industrial society for Schumpeter is characterised by ceaseless motion and the dynamic process of creative destruction as new businesses come to replace old ones in the economy. The cycle of economic exchange is not a smooth flow of transactions but one where there are periods of intense activity and radical changes in the nature of goods and services exchanged and then periods of slackening progress and the gradual erosion of the volume of transactions until a recession or slump is at hand. In this process the work if the entrepreneur is vital. The entrepreneur is the person who takes upon themselves the burden of trying to improve the productivity of the present system of business either by improving the process of production or finding new products and markets for the product of this process. The entrepreneur is the person who attempts to find new profits from the development of new combinations in the way business is done. As such entrepreneurs are pioneers and innovators and often run the risk of social ostracism for breaking down traditional barriers and restrictions on the conduct of business in society. Their reward is successful extraordinary profits and these can, in the early instances of an innovation, be considerable. However, in the long run the tendency is for the innovation to be copied and other players to enter the same market and for extraordinary profits to decline to zero. Nevertheless, it is the work of revolutionising the nature of industry that leads to the development of the economy and general economic growth.

Schumpeter, in many ways, can be see as an early forerunner in the development of social capital theory. He was not just an economist in the narrow sense of the term but a considerable social theorist who tried to bridge the disciplinary divide between economics and sociology. He maintained a broad and historically informed view of society and its historical antecedents. This can be illustrated in his consideration of the roots of motivation for the business entrepreneur. In traditional economics it was taken for granted that all the root impulses to buy, sell, save, vote, learn and so on were contained in the individual himself. Seldom was the fact acknowledged that the relation between crucial economic motivations and the social groups in which individuals actually lived was the foundation of these motivations. As Schumpeter wrote,

> In order to realise what all this means for the efficiency of the capitalist engine of production we need only recall that the family and the family home used to be the mainspring of the typically bourgeois kind of profit motive. Economists have not always given due weight to this fact. When we look more closely at their idea of self-interest of entrepreneurs and capitalist we cannot fail to discover that the results it was supposed to produce are really not all what one would expect from the rational self-interest of the detached individual or the childless couple who no longer look at the world through the windows of a family home. Consciously or unconsciously, they analysed the behaviour of man whose motives are shaped by such a home and who means to work and save primarily for wife and children. As soon as these fade out from the moral vision of the business man, we have a different kind of *homo economicus* before us who cares for different things and acts in different ways.[35]

Indeed, it might be said that, had it not been for the incentives supplied by the family and the extended family as well as the support they provided in times of stress or failure, capitalism might never have survived as a system. The high rate of capital accumulation in the early years of capitalism was dependent partly upon a low wage structure that in turn was supported by an extended family that supported each other, even when this involved child labour in factories. Consequently, the point Schumpeter is making is that any change in the social circumstances of kinship and locality are bound in the long run to influence the psychology of industry and business. In other words, changes in social capital will affect capitalism itself.

The problem for capitalist society was not its failures but its success. Given that Schumpeter was writing in the catastrophic breakdown of economic life in the 1930s, this is an arresting thesis. Capitalism, in his view, would be extinguished in the long run and possibly superseded by socialism because it created the seeds of its own destruction by eroding its own ideological and social foundations. This was achieved by three processes. First, the entrepreneurial role is undermined by the institutionalisation of this role as the business corporation grows larger and technologically more sophisticated. This tends to make innovation and change a routine process and one that can be handled by experts in research and development. Moreover, as industry develops, the public gets used to new products and services being introduced and so becomes progressively more inclined to accept change. Second, the cultural and social supports for capitalism are gradually eroded as the older strata of aristocracy, farmers and small businessmen, are diminished and the notion of property ownership begins to change into a less materialistic one. And finally, in intellectual circles that tend to influence others a rational and critical attitude seems to develop which is turned against the system of capitalism itself. This creates social unrest, which in turn puts pressure on the government to take more and more control over industry until the forces of democracy overwhelm the system and a socialist system of central administration of the production process is brought into place.

He did not personally welcome this movement, and whilst he claims to have learnt a lot from Marx he was a fierce critic of his theory and disavowed the fact that there could be any thing like a scientific prophesy of social trends. He merely claimed to be observing tendencies and then discussing what the results should be if these were to work themselves out logically. In hindsight, he got some aspect of this thesis wrong. There has been a diminution in the role of the entrepreneur but there are still distinctive individual entrepreneurs about and they continue to be influential, the institutionalising of this role has therefore only been partly successful. Moreover the limits to the size and scope of the bureaucratically management firm would appear to have been reached and the use of the market once again found to be a better source of efficiency and profitability. The erosion of the protective strata had continued but the small Business class continues to exist and elements of the aristocracy still flourish in the UK and other countries, showing that there are limits to these rationalisations of social classes. The growth of the rational and critical elements in the intelligence has certainly taken place but this has not always been turned upon the nature of the capitalist system but often on the notion of rationality itself and at the experiments in socialism elsewhere in the world. So, on a number of counts he did not prove to have fully foreseen the trends in our society. However, as in many studies of this kind the attempt to understand the dynamics and processes at work in a complex social system can be built upon and important insights still rescued from the original analysis. In this respect the points Schumpeter made about the changing nature of property and the concept of ownership embedded in capitalism, remains an important observation and one that can be taken further in this analysis of the evolving company.

Schumpeter on private property

In the film *Gone with the Wind* the notion of property or rather land as the fundamental essence of identity and loyalty between generations that is more important than love and happiness is powerfully conveyed by the turning away from Rhett Butler by Scarlet O'Hara to remain on her family property on her own. Schumpeter considers this the essential problem that capitalism faces: those who share this fundamental and materialist view of property are gradually replaced by a system of corporations that are conceived as owned by shareholders and are managed by employee managers rather than capitalist owner employers. It is worth quoting him at length on this process of change in the notion of property in a capitalist society.

> The capitalist process, by substituting a mere parcel of shares for the walls of and the machines in a factory, takes the life out of the idea of property. It loosens the grip that once was so strong - the grip in the sense of the legal right and the actual ability to do as one pleases with one's own; the grip also in the sense that the holder of the title loses the will to fight, economically, physically, politically, for 'his' factory and his control over it, to die if necessary on its steps. And this evaporation of what we may term the material substance of property - its visible and touchable reality - affects not only the attitude of holders but also that of the workmen and of the public in general. Dematerialised, defunctionalised and absentee ownership does not impress and call forth moral allegiance as the vital form of property did. Eventually there will be nobody left who really cares to stand for it - nobody within and nobody without the precincts of the big concerns.[36]

What this means is that, over time, the old notion of possessive property that was initially embodied in the concept of the company will change and become less substantive and more abstract and impersonal. Schumpeter is not passing comment upon the personal notion of private property which has remained material and possessive and indeed may have been increased and made more important to the concept a person has of themselves as the result of the proliferation of the consumer society and increasing affluence. The notion of corporate property that the owners of a business will seek to protect and defend as their own property is perhaps still to be found in the small business but, for the management and workers in a large company, the advent of employee share ownership and the artificial notion of property involved has changed its meaning into something more abstract and less personal. This signifies that the nature of company property and the forms of ownership over this property may have evolved and the meaning shifted to one with more complexity and nuance.

This change in the company form would appear to follow an evolutionary path in the sense given to this expression in the social sciences by Schumpeter. 'The essential point to grasp is that in dealing with capitalism we are dealing with an evolutionary process.'[37] The insight has biological connotations but it is not to be taken as a literal interpretation of a Darwinian process at work in the manner of Herbert Spencer, rather it is to be used as a metaphor to explain a process of adaptation and change in the face of a different set of circumstances. This is a process of development that arises from change within the system and its context and one that moves forward in cycles of adaptation rather than continuous adaptation. The metaphor will be used in the manner of John Maynard Smith's model of evolutionary change which is 'lumpy' or punctuated rather than constant and incremental.[38] To fully explain this process, a theory of change in the company form as the result of a crisis in business legitimacy needs to be added to Schumpeter's fundamental insight into the dynamics of the capitalist system.

Most of the models of change in studies of business history are concerned with the changing administrative structures that facilitate the movement towards big business: from personal over sight to functional structures, and then into the multi-divisional organisations. This work has been stimulated by the seminal work of the American business historian Alfred Chandler.[39] Some attention has also been paid to the changing nature of share ownership and its implications for control, building upon the pioneering study of Berle and Means in 1932. However, not enough attention has been paid to the process of change in institutional form, since the creation of limited joint-stock companies in 1862.

A theory of evolutionary change in the company form

It is often assumed in discussions of the development of capitalist system that the pattern of change will follow a particular direction or route and that, by and large, all societies will eventually go down the same road, albeit that some start out on the road earlier than others. This idea (the convergence thesis) has its roots in the view that social science would be able to produce a transcendental and unitary theory of social development, and one that could be taken out of its manifestation in a particular national context and applied to other societies as a tool of analysis. In recent years, it has come to be recognised that a general theory of capitalism above and beyond the society in which it is grounded is going to be an unlikely outcome of social research. There is no one theory of social change, management, capitalism or for that matter the company form, but simply variations on practises embedded in different societies that share a family resemblance. This point is made most forcefully by John Gray in his recent book *False Dawn,* when he makes the claim that the Anglo-American view of the ingredients of liberal capitalism cannot, with success, be simply followed like a recipe in the newly-developing and post-communist counties.[40] If they are to emerge into capitalist market forms, then they need to formulate their own versions of a social contract around which markets can develop. They cannot simply transfer the institutions and practices of the Anglo-American model into their own social context, they have to make their own versions of capitalism. When we are analysing the development of the company form, therefore, we have to be mindful of the social context in which the companies exist, and cannot necessarily expect to generalise about the company form across all societies. There may be not single theory that will explain the evolution of the company form; there are different cultural factors to be accounted for which are not always applicable to the interpretation of other national patterns. For the purposes of this analysis, several distinctive patterns of company form can be identified: Anglo-American, German, Franco-Italian, Japanese, and Chinese. They are not the only forms of capitalism to be found in the world economy, but they do compose its   core. However, this study will be concentrating on the development of the company in the Anglo-American context and only making reference to other company forms for comparative purposes.

It is contented that the changes in company form are important points in our business history because there are times when, often after a period of legitimisation crisis, the voice of non-business interests, more generally, is heard by the politicians, and is taken into account in the legislative process. At such times, the contract between business and society is renegotiated and put on a new footing. In between these periods, the development of business can be said to run its course according to economic imperatives rather than socio-political ones. The explanation of these step changes in company form may provide an important corrective in our economic theory of the growth of the firm. The process that unfolds can be generalised as follows: during a successful period of capitalist growth the development of the company is substantially determined by economic factors. However, the capitalist process is essentially a movement of creation and destruction where change rather than stability is the only constant. This has a destabilising impact upon the different interest groups in society, and in particular the non-business owners tend to fall constantly behind in not having their interests adequately served by the growth and development of the economy. In the absence of suitable redistribution mechanisms, over the course of time, discontent and resentment grow, leading to a general disenchantment with the capitalist system and its representative business institutions. These tensions are likely to grow to crisis proportions when economic fortunes generally are depressed or in the face of other cataclysmic events. This period might be described as a business legitimisation crisis, as stress is heightened in the relationship between the business and non-business interests. At this point the non-business interests have a much greater chance of having their concerns put onto the political agenda.

In a normal period, the power of business in a democracy is usually so considerable that it can effectively ignore or defeat opposition interests and their representatives fairly comfortably and diffuse any political pressure for change. However, during a crisis period, the interests of business are more vulnerable and they may, on occasion, lose out or become overwhelmed by the forces of non-business interests, particularly when these are channelled into left-leaning political parties. The reason why business can lose on these occasions is that socio-political forces override economic forces: social justice arguments are expressed in forceful opposition to liberty arguments, and some times these arguments have a direct influence on the legislative framework protecting property interests. It is difficult to predict the cycle of these events with any certainty and the determination of normal periods against crisis periods cannot be measured with any precision. However, history shows that, in retrospect, crisis periods have occurred from time to time, and that the general level of tension increases, with discontent finding its outlet in a variety of channels and movements.

In the next chapter, a more detailed examination of some of these crisis periods will be attempted and an assessment made of the temperature of the present situation as we move into the new millennium. One aspect of the theory that should be described in a little more detail is the nature of the circumstances in which business power is likely to be overcome by social power.

Work by Lindblom and latterly by Mitchell is drawn upon for this aspect of the explanation.[41] Lindblom in his study of polyarchy and markets asks why, in a democracy, the citizens do not exercise more control over markets. 'Why do we not see more frequent electoral demands for, say, corporate reform, curbs on monopoly, income redistribution, or even central planning?'[42] The answer he gives is that the business interests are able to exercise control over the democratic process. Business interest is privileged because it is able to influence the control of the economy and use its resources to bring ideological pressure to bear on politicians by engaging in lobbying. Business, therefore, enjoys a beneficial climate of opinion in normal times because this is partly of its own making. Second, good economic performance matters to government officials, and consequently government acts more deferentially to business than to other interests. Third, business interests devote more resources to the party and interest group competition than do rival organisations. These factors enable business to win a disproportionate number of power struggles in politics.

Business power may even go further and actively indoctrinate the citizens of a democracy to accept its privileged position and that the government should put business interests ahead of the citizens interests. In this case, no great struggles have to be fought and conflict does not arise very often. However, this circularity is never complete and the constraint of volition is never total. As Lindblom noted, the fundamentals of the economic system can, over time, become eroded by debate.

> Political reform on secondary issues implicitly raises aspects of grand issues for discussion. Corporations are increasingly regulated - more than in 1890, or 1932, or 1946. They are now being pushed again by demands for new restrictions arising out of ecological concerns. Income distribution is being altered, we shall see, even if at a glacial pace. Corporate advantage in manipulation of volition's does not make popular control wholly circular.[43]

In fact, there are occasions when business become the loser and politicians are prepared to undermine business interests. These situations have been analysed in a recent study by Mitchell, where he examines a number of cases when business lost the political debate. His conclusions are that business can lose the debate when: there are divisions among business interests; there is oligopoly or monopoly and business is perceived to have power and responsibility; there are foreign business ownership interests; there are vocal and highly organised anti-business groups; there are business practices that are inconsistent with widely held social values; there are restrictions on business access to elected and appointed government officials; there is the election of social democratic party government; there are civil servants insulated from external incentives; it is, early in the electoral term, giving the politicians time to recoup if they miscalculate public support for an issue. When a number of these risk factors occur at the same time (the more, the better) then a legitimacy crisis is likely and the tide of business interests can be turned back on some issues. Company law may be redrafted and the regulation of business practice tightened up. A new institutionalisation of the company form can emerge and although it may be accepted rather grudgingly by the business community it must do so, until it has the chance of turning the tide of events once again and can restore its privileges. However, a complete return to the status quo is unlikely, but perhaps not impossible. A fuller exploration of the concept of a legitimisation crisis and the circumstances in which it might occur will be the subject of the next chapter.

References

[1] Wells, H. G., (1967), *A Short History of the World*, Harmondsworth, Penguin, p 268.

[2] Alborn, T. L., (1998), *Conceiving Companies*: *Joint-Stock Politics in Victorian England,* London, Routledge.

[3] Cole, G.D.H., (1938), *Socialism in Evolution*, Harmondsworth, Penguin, pp 97 132.

[4] Hobson, J.A., (1987), *Imperialism: a Study*, London, Unwin Hyman.

[5] Cassis, Y., (1997), *Big Business: the European Experience in the Twentieth Century*, Oxford, Oxford University Press.

[6] Cole, op cit. p 99.

[7] Sampson, A., (1995), *Company Man: the Rise and Fall of Corporate Life*, London, Harper Collins.

[8] Alborn, op cit.

[9] Cole, op cit.

[10] Jeremy, D.J., (1998), *A Business History of Britain*: 1900-1990s, Oxford, Oxford University Press.

[11] Cassis, op cit.

[12] Ibid.

[13] Berle, A.A. and Means, G.C., (1968), *The Modern Corporation and Private Property*, New York,Harcourt Brace.

[14] Cassis, op cit.

[15] Jeremy, op cit.

[16] Morse, G., (1987), *Charlesworth's Company Law*, 13th Edition, London, Stevens andSons.

[17] Florence, P. S., (1953), *The Logic of British and American Industry*, London, Routledge.

[18] Cassis, op cit.

[19] Jeremy, op cit.

[20] Morse, op cit.

[21] Cassis, op cit.

[22] Ryan, A., (1984), *Property and Political Theory*, Oxford, Blackwell.

[23] Hume, D., (1963), *Essays, Moral, Political and Literary*, Oxford, Oxford University Press.

[24] Mandeville, B., (1970), *The Fable of the Bees*, Harmondsworth, Penguin.

[25] Smith, A., (1976), *An Inquiry into the Nature and Causes of the Wealth of Nations*, Oxford, Clarendon Press.

[26] Maine, H., (1903), *Ancient Law*, London, John Murray.

[27] Marx, K., (1974), *Capital*, Harmondsworth, Penguin.

[28] Mill, J.S., (1914), *Utilitarianism, Liberty and Representative Governement*, London, Dent.

[29] George, H., (1880), *Progress and Poverty*, London, Bell.

[30] Shaw, G.B., et al., (1890), *Essays in Fabian Socialism*, London, Fabian Society.

[31] Berle and Means, op cit.

[32] Smith, op cit.

[33] Berle and Means, op cit, p 303-304.

[34] Schumpeter, J., (1987), *Capitalism, Socialism and Democracy*, London, Counterpoint.

[35] Ibid, p 160.

[36] Ibid, p 142.

[37] Ibid, p 82.

[38] Maynard-Smith, J., (1993), *The Theory of Evolution*, Cambridge, Cambridge University Press.

[39] Chandler, A.D., (1962), *Strategy and Structure*, Cambridge Mass. MIT Press.

[40] Gray, J., (1998), *False Dawn*, London, Granta.

[41] Lindblom, C.E., (1977), *Politics and Markets*, New York, Basic Books. Mitchell, N.J., (1997), *The Conspicuous Corporation*, Ann Arbor, University of Michigan Press.

[42] Lindblom, op cit. p 192.

[43] Ibid, p 213.

chapter two

The Legitimacy of Companies

'An industrial society based on the corporation can only function if the corporation contributes to social stability and to the achievement of the social aims independent of the good will or the social consciousness of individual corporation managements.'[1]

Introduction

The relationship between business and society is a significant and important one. There are many aspects to this relationship besides the economic one that is the centre of attention in most studies of the firm. The social, political and environmental aspects are also important, as studies of the contribution that social capital makes to economic prosperity have recently shown.[2] This chapter will focus upon an aspect of this relationship to do with the power of business over large areas of our life in society and what makes this power relationship acceptable. It has been hypothesized in the theory of the evolution of company form outlined in chapter 1 that the relationship between business and society changes over time and periodically a legitimization crisis can be seen to arise.

Legitimization is a term used to analyze the relationship of power that exists between an institution and society. In society, a legitimization crisis arises when the power of an institution is challenged or where it comes into conflict with other groups who ask questions about the authority and scope of the institution. For an institution to function, its activities have to be generally accepted and the decisions of its leaders complied with both inside and outside the institution. Consequently, an institution needs a certain amount of authority if it is to pursue its purpose in society. Authority can be defined as a rightful claim to deference or obedience. As such, institutional authority rests upon a kind of power, the need to gain assent or deference on the basis of a claim recognized as of right by those both inside and outside the institution. So a claim to authority must be accepted as right and proper by the relevant groups of people in society, but not necessarily from all those who are expected to obey that authority. For example, criminals may not respect the authority of police officers, but the civil population generally does and so do most police officers inside the hierarchy of the police force. A claim to authority may rest upon a broad or narrow base of consent, and is often deeply rooted in law, custom or institutional practice. Authority can be swiftly eroded when this assent disappears and, at times, this can happen very quickly. For example, the authority of the communist governments in the eastern European countries in 1989.

The major institution of business in society today takes the form of the company or corporation, either private or public, under company statutes. But the moral character of a company is largely determined by the kind of authority its executive sustains and how that authority is used inside and outside the company. If a company's authority presumes consent then, when this consent is called into question and the claim to authority needs to be justified, legitimacy questions are asked. When a legitimization crisis occurs, and it might be a long time before this is recognized and acknowledged, then a new basis for company legitimization may be in need of negotiation, so that a new consensus can be built or formed in society. The term 'legitimization' is indicative of this fact, in that it implies legality or acceptance of a state of affairs, that power is held 'rightly' in the view of the community, and that the institutions of business are legitimized because they are granted by the consent of the governed.

This chapter will explore the concepts and issues that arise from the study of the conditions and maintenance of company legitimacy. In this respect the question of legitimacy is not discernible without a discussion of the social context of business in society at a particular point in its history. Consequently, we need to ask some important questions about company legitimacy. Why is company legitimacy important? Why do legitimacy crises occur? What have been the causes of legitimacy crises in the past and how were they resolved? Will crises recur in the future? Finally, are we in a crisis at the moment, and if so how can it be solved ?

Why is company legitimacy important?

It is often not enough for someone or for an organization to be powerful and to be able to get others to comply. They want the respect of those they wield power over and they want them to accept this bidding as being right and proper. As the great commentator on legitimacy, Max Weber, observed, 'the generally observable need of any power, or even of any advantage of life, (is) to justify itself.'[3] Weber, in his study of rationalization in society, distinguished three kinds of legitimate authority: traditional, charismatic and rational. In the first, obedience is a matter of personal loyalty to some one in society with a traditional institutional role, perhaps a teacher or a priest. In the second, authority is claimed by the prophet or hero of a charismatic nature in order to reaffirm or reconstruct the values of a community. The leader's authority is derived from personal qualities and achievements not from social position. The third kind of obedience is based upon rational authority embodied in rules and commands in an impersonal order. Faith in a legal order is important for the legitimacy of this form of authority. It is important that the legal system is perceived to be consistent and faithful to abstract principles to retain the consent of those governed by this order. For example, people in Italy are often suspicious of the tax authorities because they presuppose that everyone cheats on their tax returns and they are skeptical about where the revenues are spent.[4]

Company legitimacy is important because great power in terms of resources and life chances are now wielded by modern companies in the global market place. This power is often transnational and weakly regulated by the nation state, and although companies are nominally accountable to the shareholders, decision making is firmly in the hands of a professional management elite. Transnational companies are also subject to varying expectations regarding the social norms and methods of operation they are expected to adopt when doing business in different parts of the world. The legitimacy of companies is under scrutiny when there is a perceived inconsistency between the way companies do business and the changing goals and priorities of people in various societies. A company is legitimate if, and only if, the way it does business is consistent with the norms of society it does business in. Free market economists such as Hayek and Friedman have argued that business should only be accountable to shareholders and the law, and that as instrumental organizations little else can be expected of them, nor should we expect more of them.[5] Notions of stakeholder accountability or corporate social responsibility are dangerous notions that are damaging to the wealth creation process and represent the thin edge of the wedge that opens the door to totalitarian socialism. However, from time to time this justification of the limited responsibility of business wears thin and evidence of the social costs of moral indifference begins to mount in terms of market failures, environmental degradation, distorted priorities, defrauded consumers, etc. The demand begins to mount for greater corporate responsibility and accountability through greater regulation and a greater sense of company responsibility. To maintain its legitimacy, a corporate response on these two fronts is then required to defuse the crisis of confidence in the institutionalization of productive private property.

Our discussion of company legitimacy involves issues of internal organization and management, and that attention be paid to external expectations and criteria in society. Hence company legitimacy is about corporate governance and accountability and how this is related to shareholders and stakeholders. Company legitimacy requires that management pay attention to external constraints and internal consistency of policy. General standards to which a company must adhere need to be developed against which companies can be held accountable by legislatures and courts. Principles of corporate governance defining the mission, policy and responsibilities of the directors also need to be developed and refined. Within this framework the company makes its own decisions regarding specific objectives, internal organization and the allocation of resources. However, it is important that the company exercise restraint and show responsibility within these constraints and establish a moral order within the company. Legitimate companies build moral competence into the structure of the organization. To be a responsible company requires more than conformity with an external standard; it also requires an inner commitment to moral restraint and an aspiration to be responsible.

Why do legitimacy crises occur?

There are several theories about why legitimization crises arise and what causes them. Marx and Engels were among the first to point out tendencies towards endemic crises in capitalist societies.[6] Building upon this analysis, the noted German social philosopher, Jurgen Habermas attributes them to the structural contradictions of capitalism.[7] The conflict between the owners of capital and the workers for capital is endemic to the economic institutions of society and when a crisis of over production occurs then this economic crisis sets off a crisis in the political sphere because the inequalities of capitalism are then exposed to scrutiny. As he notes: 'Because the reproduction of class societies is based on the privileged appropriation of socially produced wealth, all such societies must resolve the problem of distributing the surplus social product inequitably and yet legitimately.'[8]

We may note from this that legitimization crises are more likely to occur when there is an economic crisis, but that this may not be the only trigger to cause a crisis. Business cycles and periodic slumps seem to be an endemic feature of capitalism despite the attempts of economists such as J. M. Keynes to show governments how they can be managed and smoothed over. Economists speculate about why they occur and a variety of theories have been put forward to try to explain them, but it has to be said that we still do not understand them fully. As a leading US economist, Paul Krugman notes:

There are many economic puzzles, but there are only two really great mysteries...One of these mysteries is why economic growth takes place at different rates over time and across countries... The other mystery is the reason why there is a business cycle - the irregular rhythm of recessions and recoveries that prevents economic growth from being a smooth trend.[9]

The proposition that legitimization crises occur only when there is an economic crisis is open to challenge, however, because in recent decades the legitimacy of business has been questioned by other interest groups who are focusing upon social and environmental concerns. Whilst these factors are not sufficient in themselves to trigger off a legitimacy crisis, when they arise in conjunction with an economic down turn they tend to broaden and deepen the crisis that companies then face. The factor which is putting considerable pressure on the legitimacy of the company today is its environmental impact. Concern with this issue is not new, but it is beginning to grow in terms of its importance and influence on whether company strategies can meet the demands of the environmental movement. Business has always had a detrimental impact upon the environment, but the scale and scope of this impact, and the concern with which it is viewed by scientists and others, is now considerable.[10] It is questioned whether business can be run in a way that will not destroy the planet in the future, and whether it can be organized so that sustainable development can replace unsustainable development that degrades and denudes the natural environment. Increasingly, large multinational companies are being brought to book on environmental concerns by green pressure groups and media attention. Greenpeace and other consumer organizations are looking to impose new social and environmental disciplines on the market. Green pressure groups are developing networks of intelligence and leverage, to help by-pass national governments and to put pressure on companies directly. As public pressure mounts over green concerns and the impact business has on these matters, the legitimacy of companies as tools of accumulation comes increasingly into question. When these concerns arise at the same time as economic and other social concerns, then the challenge to business institutions is both magnified and deepened.

Past crises and their resolution

The recognition of the existence of a legitimacy crisis is not just an event that is measured by social consequences, it is also signified in the history of ideas by a stream of literature and debate on the nature and extent of the crisis and a variety of proposals regarding its solution. The legitimacy crisis is therefore reflected in a quickening of the pace of debate and by the arrival of new and influential books putting forward suggestions for resolution of the problem. Often it is possible to single out a debate or a text which is the definitive statement of the nature of the legitimacy crisis of the period, and then chart the resolution of the crisis by the way these ideas work their way into policy debates and changes in the institutional framework. In our analysis of company legitimacy we will be identifying some of these texts and the debates which they helped to foster, and then the changes that they helped to bring about in the relationship between business and society.

Legitimization crises tend to occur in times of change or when the power of firms comes into question for some reason. In the past we can note several legitimization crises that were sparked off by different factors and were resolved by different processes of negotiation and compromise each time. Let us consider three such cases.

The factories or not debate in America

The creation of joint-stock companies, and the move away from direct entrepreneurial control and responsibility in business created an early legitimacy crisis about the role of business in society. This can be illustrated by the interesting case of the debate in America on whether, in the newly established republic, factories should be allowed. The question of whether factories and industry are legitimate activities and good for people is not often asked in contemporary society. But, historically, in the development of new societies such radical questions have been asked and the issues openly debated.

Michael Sandel in his book, *Democracy's Discontents*, uncovers the intriguing debate that took place in America in the 18th century.[11] The question posed by the founding fathers of the constitution was whether America should become a manufacturing nation or not. Thomas Jefferson argued that America should remain an agricultural nation and avoid factories and industry on the grounds that this would impoverish the moral and civil life of the citizens of the republic and diminish their self-governing capabilities. His fear was that manufacturing on a large scale would create an urban property-less class of impoverished workers who would be incapable of exercising the independent political judgment that democracy required. Jefferson wrote in *Notes on the State of Virginia*, 'Dependence begets subservience and venality, suffocates the germ of virtue, and prepares fit tools for the designs of ambition.'[12]   The argument against Jefferson's position was that foreign trade was the greatest source of corruption and could lead to dependence and luxury. To rely on overseas commerce for its manufactured goods would impoverish American republican virtues by making it dependent upon trade with a foreign power. An influx of luxury goods and finery would erode the moral character of its citizens who were fiercely independent and self-reliant. The case for engaging in domestic manufacturing was advocated by Alexander Hamilton in his *Report on Manufactures*, presented to Congress in 1791. His argument was that, in the interests of national prosperity and independence, America needed to develop an industrial economy which could export goods overseas as well as satisfy domestic demand. In order to get this industry off the ground, a system of state bounties and subsidies would need to be raised by public borrowing and finances. In the event, Hamilton's report was never adopted because demand for agricultural exports in Europe was still very strong. However, his arguments did prevail over the anti-manufacturing lobby because of the restrictions on American commerce put in place by European nations. The American Society for the Encouragement of Domestic Manufactures issued a pamphlet in 1817 arguing that contrary to popular belief manufacturing would indeed elevate rather than erode the moral character of the people. Factories in America would not be located in crowded, dirty urban areas 'but rather on chosen sites, by the fall of waters and the running stream, the seats of health and cheerfulness, where good instruction will secure the morals of the young, and good regulations will promote, in all, order, cleanliness and the exercise of the civil duties.'[13] In the end, America embraced manufacturing and developed an industrial economy because the argument that the nation needed to be free from excessive dependence on imported goods was accepted by its elected politicians and after the economic advantages of cities were realized for the development of large factories.

How to respond to the concern about the consequences of factory life on the moral character of the American citizen was to remain a recurring theme in democratic debate throughout the industrialization period. This concern with civil conduct is evident on the early designs of the first factory towns produced by some of its leading entrepreneurs. Francis Lowell's textile factory at Lowell, Massachusetts was designed to run on water power rather than steam so that it could be located in the country rather than in the city. Its labour force was to be made up of unmarried women who would lodge in company boarding houses supervised by matrons under a strict code of conduct; factory work would only be a short experience for them prior to marriage and a return to the home. Of course, the concern for the moral character of its workforce was a commercially enlightened decision as well. The parents of the factory girls were willing to allow their daughters to work in this environment, and the strict code of conduct helped enforce and instill the discipline required to make the new factory system work. In fact, the commercial success of the Lowell factory reassured republican doubters that factories would not breed poverty and vice as they had done in European cities. But although the Lowell factory town was used as a model for others, it began to break down in the face of an economic downturn in the 1830s when wages were cut and strikes occurred. As working conditions deteriorated, the young women of unmarried rural backgrounds were replaced by the large number of Irish immigrants who flocked to America in the 1840s. Soon after this, a dependent, poor and proletarianised workforce was created with few of the virtues of the independent republican citizen and many of the vices of an urban mass population. This heralded the rise of larger factories in urban settings and the abandonment of the factory owners of a sense of moral responsibility for the character development of its workforce. A society based upon widespread political participation and the ideal of an independent and self- reliant citizenry also faded from view. Instead, the democratic aspirations of American society had to be satisfied by representative democracy and what Sandel has called 'procedural liberalism' which assumes little about the moral character of the citizen and the requirements needed to bring about the good society. In his critique of modern libertarian tendencies in American politics, Sandel proposes that all social institutions, including business, should explicitly affirm a certain way of life and help to cultivate a certain kind of citizen. The failure of businesses and other institutions to do this is, in his view, indicative of the disenchantment with democracy and the decay of civil society that plagues the USA today.

The ownership and control debate

The divorce of ownership from control in companies, and the creation of the giant corporation in the 1930s-1950s caused a legitimization crisis on both sides of the Atlantic. As the USA was the seedbed of large-scale industry it is perhaps appropriate that American writers were amongst the most concerned about the problem of the power of business in society. Although industrial concentration is an imperfect indicator of the power of business in society, it is, at least, a starting point for analysis. Industrial concentration grew markedly in the USA before the first world war but remained fairly constant between 1914 and the late 1940s, and then it began to increase in the 1950s until the present day. In the UK, there was some concentration increase in the mid 1930s, then little change to the 1950s and growing concentration until the 1980s.[14]   Consequently, in the 1930s, more attention began to accrue to the impact of large firms on society, particularly in the USA where they appeared to pose a threat to its political culture. Concern over the power of business and its legitimacy had been focused mainly on the economic impact of company activity regarding investment decisions, pricing policies, location and product issues, and the influence of business upon social and political life. Yet the central question posed in this period of depression was that of Berle and Means who asked if shareholders were becoming less influential in the conduct of corporate affairs, and whether the control function of ownership was now being superseded by that of management. They had noted in their study of these issues, *The Modern Corporation and Private Property*, that as companies grew larger the proportion of shares held by the largest shareholders decreased so that the company was increasingly becoming 'managerially controlled'.[15] Indeed, they estimated that in the USA in 1932, 65% of the top 200 largest non-financial corporations were managerially controlled (defined as individuals controlling less than 5% of the voting stock). The implications of a growing divorce of ownership from control were they argued considerable. For example, if it could no longer be assumed that managers were effectively being made accountable to shareholders, then to whom were they accountable, and to whom should they be accountable? On what criteria should managers be selected for office, and what objectives would they and should they be pursuing? Interestingly, Berle and Mean assumed that because management were not significant shareholders, they would be guided in their behavior by a sense of responsibility to society, and there would be a softening in the aggressiveness of capitalism and the beginnings of a managerial revolution in the operation of a 'people's capitalism'. This would require changes in corporate law to reflect the new contract between business and society.

> When a convincing system of community relations is worked out and is generally accepted, in that moment the passive property right of today must yield before the larger interests of society. Should the corporate leaders, for example, set forth a program comprising fair wages, security to employees, reasonable service to their public, and stabilization of business, all of which would divert a portion of profits from the owners of passive property, and should the community generally accept such a scheme as a logical and human solution of industrial difficulties, the interests of passive property owners would have to give way. Courts would almost of necessity be forced to recognize the result, justify it by whatever of the many legal theories they might choose. It is conceivable - indeed it seems almost essential if the corporate system is to survive - that the 'control' of the great corporations should develop into a purely neutral technocracy, balancing a variety of claims by various groups in the community and assigning to each a portion of the income stream on the basis of public policy rather than private cupidity.[16]

In essence, what Berle and Mean were suggesting is that stakeholder management would replace shareholder joint stock companies. Instead of managers being accountable only to the shareholders under the law, two new types of accountability would supplement this check on mis-management. The development of a 'corporate conscience' which would restrain management from acting in their own self-interest, or in a socially irresponsible manner, and then the requirement to be answerable to the 'public consensus' or public opinion. Clearly, this would imply the development of a professional management that conformed to a professional code of conduct and were in touch with and were prepared to justify their actions before the court of public opinion. Interestingly, there are clear resonances here with today's calls for codes of business ethics, a stakeholder approach to corporate governance, and the practices of corporate dialogue and two-way semetrical public relations.

Berle and Means were writing in the 1930s at the time of the Great Depression. Economic prosperity was eventually rekindled in the US, Europe and Japan after the war, partly upon the back of large US corporations who had grown in size and scale during the war effort. In the UK many firms had lost ground in international trade to US competitors and those that survived and prospered did so by processes of mergers and takeovers. These large companies also fell into line with government efforts to create a welfare state 'fit for the war heroes', and recognized trade unions as legitimate participants in the company that either had to be bargained with, or kept at bay, by generous company provision of conditions and benefits for employees. Consequently, the welfare provisions of the interventionist state and the provision of company welfare helped to restore company legitimacy in the early post-war period.

The corporatist economy debate

The crisis in the relationship between the interventionist state and the company in the planned economies of the 1960s and 1970s is the third legitimization crises we will consider. In the UK, in the early 1970s, the change to a Conservative Government saw the abandonment of a consensus approach to economic expansion in favor of a dash for economic growth. However, recurring balance of payments difficulties, and the emergence of rapid inflation combined with unemployment at very high post-war levels, forced a reconsideration of these more liberal economic policies, to such an extent that government was forced to intervene in private industry and take into state ownership firms in the aviation and electronics industries. Plans for strengthening competition policy were postponed and attempts were made to steer the economy by striking up a consensus between the peak organizations of Labour and the employers. However, the failure of this economic policy in 1972 forced the Government to take extensive powers to control prices and incomes in the economy.

The increase in the rate of inflation in the UK during this period was to a large extent caused by international events and many other governments found themselves in the position of having to abandon free market principles in order to bring inflationary pressures under control. Consequently, business conduct began to be more closely regulated than at any time except in war or in the immediate post-war period. The control of prices in anti-inflation economic policies involved the regulation of profits, which, in turn, meant that the role of competition in the regulation of profits was displaced. Avoidance of monopoly and the promotion of fair competition were difficult criteria to use as the arbiters of the public interest in industrial policy. The formulation of business strategy was more likely to become subordinate to government policy and come under the influence of political criteria. Increases in profits and changes in business strategy were only allowed with government overt or covert approval. Increasingly, the government was thought to have become over-loaded with functions in managing the UK economy. The role of the state had become vital not only to ensuring that the welfare services were maintained and extended, but also crucial in trying to create the conditions of full employment and stable prices needed for economic growth. The questions asked by many commentators were: is business to be subservient to government policy, and should business consider its contribution to the social agenda along side the making of profits? Consequently, the issue of corporate social responsibility began to be debated with renewed interest during this period.

One of the seminal books that shaped the debate at this time was J.K. Galbraith's *The New Industrial State*, which discussed the conduct of large companies in a democracy.[17] This built upon the notion of James Burnham, that management had formed a new power elite that was so entrenched in large firms that they could not be challenged or overthrown, because shareholders' power was so dispersed and difficult to coordinate.[18] Galbraith thought that management could thus perpetuate its own power, so that market forces would not be the determinant of survival but giant corporations would, themselves, control the market and perpetuate themselves indefinitely. As long as shareholders got a reasonable return on investment they were unlikely to sell their shares, giving management considerable leeway to pursue other aims than just profit maximization. Other objectives of a social or political nature could be pursued alongside those of profits. Large firms would then be characterized by high costs and low profits, as many markets were dominated by a few firms, which were run in a similar way by professional managements. Free competition between these firms, in an oligopolistic situation, would be limited and prices would be set by markups on unit costs. Investment could then be determined on a long-term basis, and secured by long-term profitability that would ensure that demand for the firms products was maintained, and that other firms would be reluctant to enter the market due to the degree of investment involved. Capital markets would decline in importance as the allocator of new finance because the large corporations would be funding most of their investments through retained profits, and their dominance of many markets would reduce the competition from new firms. On this reading of the trends, the industries of most countries would be dominated by the giant corporations, and this would place considerable power in the hands of its management. As the income of some of these firms rivaled that of the nation state, then this was considerable power indeed. The big question was whether this power would be subsumed by governments in democracies where the state had taken upon itself the control and steering of the economy, or whether the power of a managerial elite constituted a threat to democracy and a source of illegitimate and unaccountable power that needed to be brought to heel.

Galbraith thought that industrial concentration would continue to increase indefinitely, but, in fact, it reached its high water mark in the 1970s in both the USA and the UK. Moreover, many big firms were overtaken by small firms in some markets and the economics of scale looked to be less attractive in some fields. Also, whilst the stockexchange has been criticized, it has remained a competitive market for company shares and a fairly good indicator of competitive performance. It has even been argued by some commentators that mergers and takeover bids have acted as an important mechanism for maintaining control over managements that grow too complacent or socially conscious in the objectives they set for their companies. Commentators asked questions once again about corporate legitimacy in this period but few changes in company structures or corporate governance were forthcoming. Many argued that, although shareholder control of firms has diminished, the firm's management was still held accountable by the institutional investors who acted on behalf of pension and insurance funds and wanted above all else high returns on their investment portfolios. In fact, the point began to be made that this was putting undue short-term pressure on managers to deliver higher dividends than was good for the long-term growth of the company, and its need to invest in new technologies and products. Moreover, the evidence indicates that the amount of company giving during the 1970s was very modest, indicating that little movement in the direction of corporate social responsibility was taking place.[19]   Although in France and Germany company law was reformed to allow experiments in more industrial democracy and participation in this period , little changed in the UK. George Goyder suggested in *The Responsible Company*, that every company should be required by statute to add to its memorandum of association a general purpose clause expressing its purpose in terms of its obligations towards shareholders, customers, workers and the community, and that trustees should be appointed to whom appeal could be made if management were violating these objectives.[20]   He also proposed that social audits should be conducted and published alongside the financial accounts of the firm.

In 1973, the government took some tentative steps to change company law to make companies provide a more extensive disclosure in their reports to shareholders on matters of health and safety at work, the conduct of industrial relations, the directors' shareholding transactions and emoluments, and the number of consumer complaints dealt with. But the government shied away from putting a more general social responsibility clause in into the Companies Acts. The attempt to gain greater democratic control of companies was pursued more on an intergovernmental and international basis, most notably in the formation and development of the European Economic Community. In the Treaty of Rome 1957, article 86 was designed to control the rise of monopoly firms created through cross-border mergers. At this time there were also attempts made to begin to harmonize the company law of member states, a task that has today still to be completed, although some progress has been made.

However, the difficulties of returning to economic growth and   full employment put a heavy strain on the relationship between government and trade unions and employers. When cooperation with trade unions was forthcoming and concessions were made in their direction on wages and supports for the extension of collective bargaining and employee rights, then the necessary cooperation of business and investors was often lacking. Likewise, when harsh measures were taken to reduce inflation and wages then conflict with the trade unions ensued such that investors and business were scared off, and the government again failed in its objectives of providing full employment and a high level of public services. Consequently, the attempt at a corporatist approach towards the economy, and the call for a more socially responsible business sector was put on hold when the government changed in 1979 and the Thatcherite campaign to free business from the shackles of regulation and the trade unions took hold. Issues of corporate responsibility and the relationship of business to government were dampened down for a while, by a return to the competitive outlook and the rolling back of government in the field of industrial policy and ownership of industry.

Predicting the next crisis

Whilst there is little precision to the theory about the causes of a legitimacy crisis such that they can be predicted with any certainty, there are some interesting speculations about when they are likely to arise. As was outlined in chapter 1, a legitimization crisis tends to occur if there is a widespread perception that power is being exercised without foundation. However, if the perception of the public is distorted or is deficient then a crisis of legitimacy might not occur, even in a situation of economic recession. This possibility has been analyzed by Jurgen Habermas in terms of the problem of cultural impoverishment.[21] As advanced capitalism develops, expert systems and discourses grow and become insulated from the ordinary citizen. Consequently, the capacity of the average individual to make sense of and understand the society they live in diminishes. As Habermas expresses it, 'Everyday consciousness is robbed of its synthesizing power and becomes fragmented.'[22] Although the citizens of a modern society are bombarded with large quantities of information they are unable to make much use of it to be able to criticize or understand the direction things are going in. The problem is not so much one of false consciousness of what their interests are but one of fragmented consciousness which does not enable them to gain a clear picture of what interests are in the first place. Consequently, legitimization problems may be stalled. Instead of a growing crisis between a capitalist class and the democratic values of the general population leading towards a breakdown in order, this critical consciousness amongst the broader population may be more problematic. Habermas has become convinced that the development of critical consciousness is seriously and systematically impeded by the splitting off of expert cultures and the resulting fragmentation of everyday thought. Ordinary people are then much more subject to the processes of alienation, the disintegration of collective identity and cultural impoverishment or loss of meaning. This in turn means that the state is relieved of some of the pressures it is under to legitimate its actions and reform the power structures of business. Also, the sort of solidarity necessary for opposition movements is impeded by the growing experience of alienation and isolation, and the possibility of challenge to business on the basis of other interpretations of events is undermined by the fragmentation of consciousness. Societies tolerance for motivations based upon instrumental attitudes, indifference and cynicism is expanded. An inclination for personal greed and accumulation of material wealth is combined with a growing indifference to the plight of the poor in society and the commitment to democratic and universalistic values is weakened. People with such values are less likely to be concerned when the state uses more repressive measures to manipulate and control this new underclass. There is more cynicism about the role of the state as a regulator of opportunities or protector against market failure. Consequently, there is growth in tax evasion and the underground economy. Such activities rather than being in opposition to the working of the state encourage people to keep a low profile and avoid taking on any radical political orientations.

The opposition or social movements that are resisting the encroachments of the market in advanced capitalism are different from the class-based collective associations which opposed earlier capitalism, for example trade unions and political parties. New social movements are typically feminist groups, green activists, peace protesters, gays, new age life-style groups. These groups are characterized by a narrow range of concern and a distinctive concern with questions of personal and group identity. From Habermas's perspective these groups are reacting against the intrusion of business and markets into many areas of life and the denigration of the natural environment in which different forms of life can exist. But they are defensive reactions to these encroachments and are unlikely to be able to challenge the totalising ideology of the institutions of capitalism because they are self-limiting in outlook and in their objectives. So, whilst they are unlikely to change the shape of society fundamentally, they will keep the state and business companies on their toes by challenging certain aspects of capitalism and by engaging in numerous border conflicts between markets and life styles. It is more likely that these new social movements will exercise influence on the economic and political system indirectly, through mass public opinion, for example, when green protesters use civil disobedience that creates symbolically important dissent that is projected to the public or the mass media. Public opinion will then become an important influence upon business and markets and, if not responded to, will affect the success or legitimacy of companies and create pressure for change from the state.

Are we in a crisis at the moment?

From a number of points of view we would appear to be moving towards another crisis in company legitimacy in the late 1990s and for a variety of reasons. After the initial successes of the Thatcher years, came the disappointment of Black Monday, the deflation of the economy, and the eventual collapse of the housing boom. Despite a small recovery of confidence in the early 1990s, the UK's ejection from the ERM plunged the economy once again into another period of recession. Many small businesses went bankrupt, unemployment began to rise again, and newly-purchased houses were repossessed. A generalized malaise took hold of the population signifying that the market mechanism was not working for the common good as they had been lead to believe that it would. The social contract between business and society is perhaps under pressure again. One of the signs that this might be so, is the emergence of a literature discussing the nature of this malaise, which has had an impact on the wider political debate. One book that became a publishing sensation was Will Hutton's *The State We're In* published in 1995.[23] This book catalogues a list of causes of the present crisis in the business and society relationship. Hutton tends to stress the contribution of structural factors such as the short termism of financial markets and the absence of participative management in industry in his analysis of the discontent; but he also puts the blame on changes in values and attitudes during the Thatcher years. Hutton offers a comprehensive diagnosis of the problems, and a questionable prognosis regarding their solution.

In the meantime, we need to explore in more detail the reasons that may be giving rise to a crisis of legitimacy in the institutions of business at the present time: the changes in industry in the face of global competitive pressures; growing job insecurity and increasing income inequality; problems in corporate governance structures; a failure of companies to deliver equal opportunities; and the detrimental impact of business on the environment and human rights.

Companies face up to the competition

In order to maintain their positions in global markets many companies undertook drastic changes and restructuring during the 1990s. Unemployment had remained high throughout the 1980s, but had started to move downwards in the early 1990s. However, it began to rise again in 1992, and whilst in the past the welfare state had provided a reasonable safety net, this had been much diminished in the 1980s, so that those who found themselves unemployed were now much worse off. Nearly 40% of those who became unemployed in this period took some form of early retirement or withdrew from being active in the labour market.[24]   Those who managed to return to work often could not find secure employment in full-time positions, so had to take lower-paid and part-time work. This represented an increase in flexibility of the labour market or, to use an older expression, a return to the casualisation of employment. The dual labour market talked about in the 1980s became an actuality in the 1990s as an increasingly periphery labour market developed for part-time and self-employed workers. Trade union membership wilted in the face of this trend, wage bargaining arrangements collapsed in some industries and, slowly, wage demands for existing employees were moderated, and strikes were reduced in number and significance.[25]   A large amount of employment was lost in manufacturing industry, but was to some extent replaced in the service industries. Some of the service industry employment created was in high-quality value-added occupations, but other area of low-paid personal service work also grew markedly and only offered limited job security, low pay and little prospect of training or promotion. There was also a shift in the employability prospects of men and women. Many young men found it increasingly difficult to find entry into employment and consequently became poor prospects as bread winners for young women. This has had a detrimental effect upon family structures as young women have found it easier to get a job and manage a family on their own without the assistance of a typically unemployed young male. Some commentators are concerned that this is giving rise to the creation of an 'underclass', which is below a working class, because they are unable to find and hold down a job and so become permanently dependent upon the welfare state and/or criminal activity for their survival.[26]

The middle classes have also had their sense of security shaken in the 1990s, not just by a pervasive sense of increased crime and lawlessness in society. Many white-collar workers in the public sector in the 1980s began to feel the effects of privatization on their terms and conditions of work in the 1990s. The assumption that they would enjoy the benefits of long and prosperous careers began to be undermined by the changes brought about in both the public services and in the privatized utilities. Security of employment was almost removed overnight, as executive agencies were created in the civil service, trust hospitals in the NHS and schools were released from local authority control to become self-governing bodies. Large-scale redundancies and job restructuring programs took place in many of the privatized corporations, for example BT, British Gas, British Railways, and water companies. Even local authorities and state owned enterprises like the Post Office and the BBC all underwent reorganization and the introduction of more market-based approaches to resource allocation and management. As an example of the growth in managerialism, the introduction of performance-related pay has almost been universal in both private and public sectors of employment in the 1990s, despite the research evidence on its limited effectiveness as a motivator for improving employee performance and team working.[27]

In the private sector, the restructuring operations that many companies had instigated in the 1980s were continued and increased in the 1990s and new management ideas about quality and continuous improvement were implemented. These programs had consequences for employees' job security and challenged their faith in the notion of a career ladder within the firm. Their career ladders may have been attenuated or broken by the changes of the 1980s, but now it seemed that they had been kicked away altogether for many middle-strata managers in large companies such as in banking and insurance.[28] The insecurity felt by blue-collar workers in the 1980s was now matched by that felt by white-collar workers in the 1990s.

Increasing inequality

These trends of insecurity and loss of confidence in the ability of companies to further their interests felt by the lower and middle classes are in stark contrast to the sense of opportunity and prosperity felt by these at the top of the corporate pyramid or at least those who can master the dragon of enterprise. The reduction of the higher rates of income tax to just 40% is largely responsible for the rich getting richer; added to the fact that wages for executives in the 1980s and 90s continued to increase well above the rate of inflation and the increase in industrial productivity.[29]   Senior executives have allowed their own levels of remuneration to become another contributory factor in the legitimization problem of companies. This has created a new climate of inequality that is only surpassed by that in the USA. This is in stark contrast to other European countries where income inequality is less marked and unemployment is still cushioned by a generous welfare state.[30]

The explanation of why income inequality is rising so fast is not clear. As Paul Krugman has noted, 'The bottom line of all this is that while we can make some interesting speculations, we really don't know very well why inequality has increased.'[31]   There are a range of answers offered, but the evidence supporting any of them is not decisive. The most popular explanation is that of globalisation of the UK economy. As the UK has increasingly become part of the global economy and more trade is with foreign countries, the competitiveness of the labour of unskilled workers compared to that of skilled or knowledge workers has begun to decline. In the global economy, unskilled labour from the developing world is abundant and highly-educated labour relatively scarce; this leads to decreasing wage rates for the unskilled and increasing rates for the skilled. This has given rise to the view that the wealth of the nation can only be increased if the education of the workforce is improved so that more trade can be in the high-value-added industries. Consequently, the outlook in terms of income for the unskilled or poorly educated is bleak; they will either be in competition with very low wage workers in the developing nations, or will have to take lower wages in the personal service industries designed to satisfy the needs of the well-educated. However, upon closer examination of the evidence, this argument is much weaker than is often thought.[32]   For instance the growth in global trade does not match up to the changing patterns of income distribution. The UK had a fairly constant or even narrowing distribution of income until the 1980s after which inequality began rising at a rapid rate. This was not because there had been a large increase in foreign trade; this had already started in the 1970s when incomes were much more equal. Moreover, the multiplier effect of increased trade is not large enough to explain the differences in income inequality that took place during this period. And, whilst the UK does trade with low wage developing countries, most of its trade is with the countries who have better paid unskilled workers than the UK. We also have to bear in mind that the inequality in not just between occupational groups but within occupations; the best-paid directors are paid at a much higher rate than low-paid directors even when they have a comparable education and skill profile.

If globalisation is a weak explanation then another one that is often used is the influence of technology on different rates of productivity. The argument here is that rising income inequality is due to the use of   increasingly sophisticated technology by some people who get a large share of the productivity increase due to this technology. Yet the point remains that those occupations where gains in income do not appear to be due to technology are often well represented in the high pay leagues. For example, lawyers, doctors, and sales executives are often paid a lot more than software writers, engineers and architects.

Another explanation is that of the 'star-player' model where the analogy is with the entertainment or sports field where high wages for a few stars coexist alongside many other performers who only make a modest living at best. The reason for the disparity is largely due to the media focus upon a few star-players or performers which can be broadcast to huge audiences, and so enables them to ask for and obtain huge fees. Likewise in business, where modern technology can increase the information available to and the span of control of senior executives across the world, allowing them to claim the lion's share of the rewards.[33] Remuneration in industry then becomes a winner takes all, or very nearly all, game to the obvious detriment to the other players in the system. Whichever explanation is correct, the political implications of this trend are clear: income inequality poses a threat to the unity of the nation, and if nothing is done about it, then the results of social friction will be to the detriment of rich and poor alike.

The perennial problem of capitalism is that the distribution of wealth becomes very unequal. This means that new mechanisms are needed periodically to redistribute this wealth and introduce more equality into the system. Although many societies have existed with large inequalities of wealth, most of them were controlled by elites that were not responsible to democratic institutions or at least not institutions the excluded could use to put pressure on the rulers for change. Rising economic inequality sits very uncomfortably with demands for political equality. After all, if the poor become a majority they have it within their power to vote away the wealth of the minority who are prosperous. Consequently, the inequalities that exist in democratic societies need to be justified and widely accepted as fair and necessary. The main defense offered to justify inequality in capitalist societies is that people are entitled to keep the wealth they themselves have created, and if it is acquired justly then others are not entitled to deprive them of it.[34] However, as all people do not start in an equal position, the differences that can be allowed to exist must be such that they will in the long run result in the best outcome for everyone.[35] In other words, those with wealth will invest it in the production of more wealth that will create jobs for others and help to raise the income of others as well as their own. When there are widespread market failures and unemployment results, or real incomes of workers start to decline, the legitimacy of capitalism begins to be questioned. People start to look for new principles of wealth distribution and entitlements and may use democratic mechanisms to bring them into existence.

Of course the wealthy can try to drive the poor to the wall or use force to keep them down, but when the poor become very numerous, it is unlikely in a democratic country that this strategy can succeed, although it may do so in an authoritarian regime. Oppressed peoples in authoritarian regimes may then see no other way to change the system than by revolution, or war if needs be. However, the popular response in advanced democracies has been to create the welfare state to help alleviate the problems of inequality and market failure. The wealthy are also very sophisticated in converting their money into political and media representation that can keep the problems of the poor and discontented at bay. The media and certain political ideologies can be used to pour scorn on the welfare state and undermine public confidence in its fairness and effectiveness by highlighting fraud and abuse by its claimants. People then become reluctant to pay taxes to support the welfare state, and vote for more of these services to be provided by the market, or for their abolition, so that everyone has to take more responsibility for themselves and become more enterprising. The poor are inclined to become despondent. As they become excluded from entitlements, alienation becomes more acute, which then further undermines society leading to an increase in criminal activity, and to a reduced commitment to political activity that will lead to change. Political representation of the underclass, or insecure working class, is difficult to organize, and can help to create fatalistic and unrealistic attitudes that are quenched by escapist behavior of drugs and lotteries, or are manipulated by fascist movements to blame others for causing the problem. In most of the EU where the poorer members of society are organized into voting for political parties, governments have maintained the provisions and entitlements of the welfare state in a much more generous form than in the UK or USA. There is also progressive taxation to ensure that income inequalities at the top do not become too pronounced. However, these EU social welfare provisions are coming under threat as business is calling for social costs to be reduced so that it can compete against lower cost competition in the developing world.

In the USA, and to a lesser extent in the UK, economic inequality has risen dramatically and many of the poor seem to be getting poorer even when they are in work.[36] But the progressive parties of the left have only modest measures for improving the lot of these constituencies. Most of them revolve around improving the education system and the employability of people in new higher value added industries. However, both parties are reluctant to raise taxes to pay for these changes, so the measures are unlikely to deliver the changes in the distribution of wealth that are needed. Consequently, a new road to social inclusion and the redistribution of income is needed in society. Neither state intervention in industry, nor the welfare state seem to be the answer to the present problems. These solutions were tried in previous legitimacy crises but are now largely discredited. New thinking is required on how the social contract between rich and poor can be established in society and inclusion and stability be rebuilt. A new conception of how wealth can be generated and yet be made democratically accountable to a diverse electorate needs to be formulated. An ideology of individual self-seeking, or propositions that society will take care of itself, will not be sufficient to maintain the legitimacy of the institutions of business. We will be considering some of the new conceptions that might reestablish the social contract between business and society in later chapters.

Trust and accountability

Rising inequality in industry makes it difficult to create and sustain trust relationships between management and the employees. Francis Fukuyama is right to insist in this book *Trust*, that a nation's sense of well-being is heavily conditioned by the level of trust within a society and in the workplace.[37] In many countries, company managements, instead of thinking of themselves as a separate class of people, usually have the same technical skills as the workers and gain the respect of workers through their leadership skills. Moreover well trained workers in these countries are more flexible and productive leading to much narrower wage differentials on the shopfloor and less of a disparity between management and workers in pay terms. When these ideas have been brought to the UK by foreign companies a miraculous improvement in productivity from a UK workforce usually results. In 1992, foreign companies employed 17.9% of the workforce in manufacturing industry in Britain, but they produced 40% higher value added per employee than comparable UK owned manufacturers, and made 31.6% of all capital investment.[38] Very often British company employees rate their managements much less favorably than those of any other European country. International Survey Research found in 1995 that UK employees were particularly critical of the training and information they received from their management.[39] Motivation in many firms was now lower than even in the turbulent times of the 1970s. The survey also suggests that that there is a great divide between an aggressive and competitive management culture at the top of many UK companies, and a down-trodden and insecure workforce beneath them.

This raises an important question about the sustainability of recent productivity gains which have made use of management techniques learnt from abroad such as TQM, JIT, and re-engineering. These depend upon processes of empowerment and teamworking right down the organization, and can only be sustained on the basis of trust and understanding between workers and management. In many of the countries where these ideas have been successful there are structures of employee security, investment and training in workforce skills and much lower pay differentials. Research on the use of these participatory management techniques indicates that long run performance is improved and workers suffer less stress when moved to another job, when the workers' skills are highly developed and they enjoy security of tenure.[40] Part of the legitimacy problem of many UK companies is that they do not encourage the development of self-respect and pride in their workforces. Downsizing and redundancy are a common terms in the vocabulary of management as they seek profitability by cost reduction through labour shedding and contraction of capacity, rather than by making the business grow, and trying to engage the workforce in a cooperative effort to fulfill joint aspirations for profitability. UK managers are often reluctant to pass information to their employees and have few formal structures of participation and involvement in their companies.[41] The short-term financial interests of shareholders are held to be pre-eminent, and managers have to keep a constant eye on the company's stock exchange price for fear that it should fall and gain the attention of the takeover specialists, or incur the wrath of investment institutions who are reluctant to see their dividends fall in any way.

Unaccountable financial institutions

Institutional shareholding and influence upon companies is, itself, one of the factors contributing to the new legitimacy problem. Share ownership in the 1930s was highly dispersed amongst mainly private individuals but, by the 1960s, individual share ownership had fallen to around 50%, and by the mid-1990s it was down to 20%.[42] Today, financial institutions own over 60% of shareholdings; in the main these are the pension funds and insurance companies that we all have a stake in. Ownership today, is, in fact, concentrated rather than fragmented. A great deal of power is conferred upon a small number of institutions which mange our collective savings. The representation of these institutions in the corporate governance of UK companies is one of the major determinants of the way these companies operate. But these institutions are not active investors, they are inactive, and tend to confine their role to buying and selling shares to make sure their portfolio of investments deliver a good return. Consequently, should a company run into trouble, the institutional investors are often the first to walk away and disinvest; they are not committed to the prosperity or welfare of the firms they invest in. This is at odds with investors in Germany who are often banks who take a pro-active stance towards their investments, or for that matter in the USA, where the world's most successful investor, Warren Buffett, takes a significant and pro-active interest in the companies his investment trust owns shares in.

Most UK institutional investors exercise weak or non-existent control over the companies they invest in. They play little or no part in the nomination of directors, or the appointment and remuneration of the auditors, and they take little part in the formulation of company strategy. Perhaps their only sanction is to seek to replace an underperforming management but this power is exercised rarely and only *in extremis* in practice. The reality, in corporate governance terms, is that the company's board of directors retains most of the powers of control that are usually associated with ownership and few questions are asked about their stewardship of the company as long as dividends and share values are maintained.

The record of institutional investors holding companies to account is a very poor one and this has been admirably demonstrated in the 1990s in the case of directors' remuneration packages. These have constantly outstripped the growth of company productivity increases or profitability growth, and often have born little relationship to the pay increases of other employees.[43] Consequently, this has been a source of resentment and a demonstration of unaccountable power that has weakened the legitimacy of the companies in the eyes of employees and the public. The slack practices of institutional fund managers means that, when a company is underperforming, the solution proposed is often that of a takeover bid, which will either put the assets into new hands, or spur the existing company's management into improving their performance. This can lead to a situation where, to regain the money spent on the takeover, the company is broken up and parts of it are sold, or a drastic rationalization means that many employees lose their jobs. Instead of change and adjustment to new markets and business conditions being managed in a slow and incremental fashion that will allow for job continuity and employee adjustment, in the UK, companies tend to change in fits and starts, which destroys trust between the management and the workforce and means that the change process is often stressful and painful for all concerned. Ultimately, business prosperity is put at risk, and innovation and continuous improvement are lost. This generates a culture of predatory and speculative capitalism rather than one which works for the prosperity of all, based upon rewarding investments that satisfy market demands with imagination and over a long period of time. Institutional democracy in our financial institutions is weak or indeed weaker than in our companies, once again exposing the problem of corporate governance. We all have a stake in these institutions, but have no say in the way they are managed, nor in the way they mange funds on our behalf in the companies invested in.

Another source of the weakening in legitimacy of business institutions is the behavior of the privatized companies in the 1990s. Whilst many people have made handsome profits from the privatization of the utilities and other state-owned enterprises, not least the senior managers who inflated their own salaries beyond compare, for many ordinary citizens the outcome of this process has been less attractive. Prices and customer service in many of these industries has not visibly improved, as in the case of water, gas, and electricity. Many employees have lost their jobs, and pay and conditions for many remaining employees have deteriorated. Some companies have changed hands and little of the wealth created has found its way into customers' hands or the local communities where the wealth was generated. Despite the windfall tax charges and the efficiency gains from the introduction of market disciplines in these industries, the rewards and benefits have often been shared disproportionately with shareholders and senior executives, to the detriment of customers.[44] This was partly because the process of selling state assets was intensely political; often the desire to merely get the assets into private ownership overode the need to restructure the industries to ensure that monopoly control was prevented and that greater competition would deliver better results for consumers. This was particularly true in the electricity, gas, water and telecommunications privitisations. Wider share ownership has been a byproduct of privatization but in terms of popular capitalism it has made many people discontented with the efficiency of these companies and resentful of the insecurity they now have to live with.

Not delivering on equal opportunities

On the wider social front, in recent years it has been widely acknowledged that three groups of people face special problems in realizing their true potential in companies: women, ethnic minorities and the disabled. The failure of companies to reflect the talents and abilities of these groups at all levels in the firm for a variety of reasons has called into question whether companies are really serving their communities in a just and impartial way. Some women writers on management have actually started to question whether the decline of large company organizations is not in its own way a big step in the right direction for women's career opportunities.[45]   This is because they have experienced unfairness and unnecessary impediments in their attempts to rise up the company career ladder. Research into the nature of female employment experiences has highlighted the fact that women are concentrated within a narrow range of industries and within specific occupational groupings.[46] They are also more likely to be employed on part-time contracts, enjoy less job security, access to training and other occupational benefits, and spend longer periods unemployed. Moreover, their pay rates are roughly 70% of those of men working in the same job groups. Women tend to hold low-paid, unskilled positions in many companies, and the number rising up into managerial positions has only been increasing slowly despite the rapid rise in women's educational attainments.   The proportion of women in senior managerial positions remains in single figures and is said to show there is a 'glass ceiling' in most company hierarchies.

Ethnic minorities face similar problem of under-representation in company hierarchies, and they tend once again to be concentrated in the secondary labour market and in low-paid, low-skill jobs, with restricted opportunities for training and promotion.[47] There are complex variations between the fortunes of different ethnic groups depending upon such factors as regional variations, country of origin, family structure, and cultural differences. Suggestions that companies with diverse workforces are in a position to take advantage of market diversity in the patterns of world trade made by some recent management writers, clearly have a very long way to go before they become a reality in many UK firms.[48]

Perhaps the group with the lowest profile in terms of unfair treatment inside the company is the disabled. One of the reasons for this is that they are often poorly represented by collective pressure groups and tend to suffer their deprivations and disappointments as isolated individuals. On the whole, disabled people suffer from limited career opportunities, their employment prospects are poor, and special facilities and assistance are under-resourced.[49] Once again rates of pay are low and training and development opportunities are restricted. The disabled experience very high levels of unemployment and great difficulty in finding new jobs with sympathetic employers. For many years the legal provisions on disabled workers were honored more in the breach than in their enforcement, until they were abolished and new disabled person rights enacted in their place but without much statutory regulation to back them up.

Although there is legislation and administrative support for the implementation of equal opportunities in society, the general record in their impact on companies is not impressive. Some employers have exemplary records but very many fall short of what is needed to show society that they do practice equal opportunities and are reflective of society's constituents. For companies to enjoy legitimacy in this aspect of their operations they must be seen to practice what their managements often preach on the topic of equal opportunities.

Environmental and human rights concerns

Another factor that is growing in importance in terms of its impact on the legitimacy of companies in society is their relationship to the natural environment. Concern is now widely expressed by pressure groups and increasingly by the public about the detrimental impacts companies are having upon the natural environment. Although in theory the price mechanism of the market should help us conserve the natural environment by making polluters pay for damage to the property of others, and by price-rationing scarce natural resources. In practice, companies seem to operate as a sort of perpetual motion machine for generating growth regardless of the cost to the environment. Market failures abound in this area. For example, global warming is an archetypal case of a tragedy of the commons, in that billions of separate acts, each individually innocuous, help to take us over the threshold of pollution of the atmosphere. The market pricing of these acts will not prevent the summation of them from producing global warming. Only government regulatory action can help or try to alleviate the problem. Another example is that it is virtually impossible to extend the notion of property rights to cover the land, sea and air to a sufficient extent that users and polluters of these resources are made to pay the owners for the use and damage done to them. If a forest belongs to no-one, then no-one will have an interest in planting the next generation of trees, or in developing logging techniques that leave saplings standing. Since no-one stands to benefit from such foresight, no-one will exercise it. The same could be said of fish stocks, which if left to open fishing would be harvested to extinction in no time at all by individual fishing boats. Consequently, there is mounting pressure for companies and market institutions to be constrained and supplemented by governmental and international regulation and enforcement procedures. In the eyes of green pressure groups, companies are predicated upon an ecological impossibility, and so they are doomed to bring about catastrophe and extinction in the long run. If this fate is to be avoided then business institutions have to embrace the notion of sustainable development if they are to gain the support of an increasingly concerned public who are becoming increasingly aware of environmental degradation.[50] This means paying attention to the impact their goods and services make upon the environment and embracing changes in products and processes to make this impact one that can be sustained in the future or at least to within what is acceptable to an increasingly sophisticated green public at home and abroad. But there is no handy policy tool-kit for companies to make the transition to sustainable development, as Shell Oil found out when it had to abandon plans to dispose of the Brent Spar platform by towing it into the Atlantic and sinking it, in the face of formidable opposition across Europe, when public identification with the campaign was threatening to have a runaway impact on its competitive position on petrol forecourts.

Then, hard upon the heals of the Brent Spar fiasco, came the difficulties of defending Shell's involvement in Nigeria in the wake of the execution of the dissident Ken Sarawiwa. Soon after this, a group of shareholders placed a resolution on the company's agenda at the annual general meeting in London about Shell's need to respect environmental and human rights in its world-wide operation. It is increasingly apparent that the issue of the company's respect for and support of human rights is also becoming an important issue for transnational companies in the 1990s. The roots of this concern are in the student boycott of Barclay's Bank over its investments in South Africa. Consumers more generally are now increasingly prepared to voice their concerns about what they perceive to be the negative effects of globalisation on the enjoyment of human rights and they are prepared to act to defend these rights on behalf of themselves and others. For example Nike, the sports shoe company in the USA, found that its profitability was substantially affected by allegations made in the Washington Post that it was mistreating its overseas factory workers and this had resulted in consumer resistance to the brand. Del Monte, the fruit canning company, in 1997 had a ton of banana skins dumped in front of its offices in Kent by the World Development Movement in protest at the company's alleged treatment of banana workers in Costa Rica. This protest group lobbies for human rights improvements and is trying to pursuade Del Monte, through its publicity campaign aimed at consumers, to give its workers better pay and conditions and better protections from pesticide sprays when working on its banana plantations. British supermarkets have recently been accused by Christian Aid, the international charity, of selling food produced by farmers in developing countries who are working for unacceptably low wages in dangerous and degrading conditions. The charity has proposed that the government should set up an independent monitoring body to oversee all supermarkets. The supermarkets themselves have responded by devising policies to ensure that the sourcing of their produce is done in accordance with a voluntary code of practice. Many companies are coming to share an interest in these human right concerns as, world-wide, individuals and groups are watching what they do and are expecting companies to act responsibly. Internal codes of conduct have been pioneered by Levi Strauss and Co. and other companies to prevent infringements of basic human rights in overseas operations, but groups like Amnesty International are pressing companies to go further and sign up to the Social Accountability 8000 Standard on human rights protection, which is like ISO 9000 and ISO 14000 for environmental management systems. ISO 8000 covers nine essential requirements which companies must comply with regarding: child labour; health and safety; freedom of association; anti-discrimination; disciplinary practice; work hours; and pay and management practices. Auditors are required to police these standards and a complaints and appeals procedure for workers, campaign groups and other interested parties has to be maintained by the company. These developments and other initiatives have been rippling out into the boardrooms of many companies as a sign of the mounting importance of public opinion for emerging concerns about corporate social responsibility.

Conclusions

The movement towards a legitimacy crisis for business institutions in recent years can be seen to derive from a diverse combination of factors. Some are new and circumstantial, others are the legacy of a prolonged period of political change designed to make the country a more enterprising and market-based society. The preoccupation with the state ownership of productive assets has been superseded by that of the private holding of such assets. Both viewpoints have exaggerated the benefits of what such systems of ownership could deliver by way of prosperity and wellbeing for the whole of society. The system has, perhaps, once again, become unbalanced. The legitimacy of companies as creators and distributors of wealth is beginning to be questioned. The employees sense of security which comes from working in a company is not as inclusive as it needs to be if legitimacy is to be reestablished. Many workers have a diminished stake in the system of capitalism, it offers them neither job security nor sources of income on which to live, nor an environment that is sustainable. With the state struggling to cushion the blow of uncertainty, an increasingly divided and unequal society is likely to grow. In fact, the social fabric of society could wear very thin if the base of social capital upon which capital accumulation depends is not rewoven in the near future. Increasingly, workers are being asked to shoulder the risks of a capitalist society without gaining a sufficient share of the rewards of company profitability. It follows that if something is not done to re-legitimize the operations of companies then there will be trouble. There could be a further deterioration in the moral and social order of society and a growth in property-related crime, and there could be the growth of political pressure for more regulation of industry and the protection of trade and companies that will serve the interests of the home market. These pressures do not bode well for the creation of an open and tolerant society that is able to shoulder its share of international burdens in the turbulent world of the twenty-first century. To see what responses companies have called forward and put in place to forestall this impending crisis will be the subject of examination in chapters 3, 4 and 5.

References

[1] Drucker, P. (1964), *The Concept of the Corporation*, New York, Mentor Books, p27.

[2] Fukuyama, F. (1995), *Trust: the social virtues and the creation of prosperity*, London, Hamish Hamilton.

[3] Weber, M. (1968), *Economy and Society Vol 3*, London, Routledge, p 953.

[4] Putnam, R. D. (1993) *Making Democracy Work: Civic Traditions in Modern Italy*, Princeton N J, Princeton University Press.

[5] Hayek, F. A. (1969) 'The Corporation in a Democratic Society: in whose interest ought it and will it be run?' in Ansoff, H. I. (ed.), *Business Strategy*, Harmondsworth, Penguin. Freidman, M. (1988) 'The Social Responsibility of Business is to Increase its Profits' in Beauchamp, T. and Bowie, N. *Ethical Theory and Business*, Englewood Cliffs NJ: Prentice Hall.

[6] Marx, K. (1865), *Capital III*, London, Lawrence and Wishart, 1959.

[7] Habermas, J. (1973), *Legitimation Crisis*, London, Hutchinson.

[8] Ibid, p. 51.

[9] Krugman, P. (1994), *Peddling Prosperity*, London, W.W. Norton, p 24.

[10] Kennedy, P. (1993), *Preparing for the Twenty-First Century*, New York. Random House. (For a good summary of these concerns see chapter 6).

[11] Sandel, M. J. (1996), *Democracy's Discontent*, Cambridge MS, Harvard University Press.

[12] Quoted in Sandel p 144.

[13] Ibid, p 148-9.

[14] Scott, J. (1997), *Corporate Business and Capitalist Classes*, Oxford, Oxford University Press.

[15] Berle, A. A. and Means, G. C. (1932), *The Modern Corporation and Private Property*, New York, Macmillan, 1947.

[16] Ibid, p 356.

[17] Galbraith, J. K. (1967), *The New Industrial State*, London, Hamish Hamilton.

[18] Burnham, J. (1941), *The Managerial Revolution*, Harmondsworth, Penguin.

[19] Kempner, T., Macmillan, K., and Hawkins, K. (1974), *Business and Society*, Harmondsworth, Penguin.

[20] Goyder, G. (1963), *The Responsible Company*, Oxford, Blackwell.

21   Habermas, J. (1987), *Theory of Communicative Action*, Vol. II, London, Heinemann.

22   Ibid, p 522.

23   Hutton, W. (1995), *The State We're In*, London, Jonathan Cape.

24   Gregg, P. and Wadsworth, J. (1995), 'A Short History of Labour Turnover, Job Tenure and Job Security, 1973-93' *Oxford Review of Economic Policy*, 11:1.

25   Burchill, F. (1997), *Labour Relations*, London, Macmillan.

26   Murray, C. (1994), *Underclass: the crisis deepens*, London, IEA.

27   Marsden, D. and Richardson, R. (1994), 'Performing for Pay? The effects of merit pay on motivation in a public service', *British Journal of Industrial Relations*, 32:2. pp 243-261.

28   Guest, D. and Mackenzie, K (1996), 'Don't write off the Traditional Career', *People Management*, February, pp 22-5.

29   Institute for Fiscal Studies, (1994), *Update: the changing face of inequality*, London, IFS, Autumn/Winter.

30   Glyn, A. and Milliband, D. (1994), *Paying for Inequality*, London, Institute for Public Policy Research.

31   Krugman, op cit. p 150.

32   Hirst, P. and Thompson, G. (1996), *Globalisation in Question*, London, Polity Press.

33   Williams, A. P. (1994), *Just Reward? the truth about executive pay*, London, Kogan Page.

34   Nozick, R. (1977), *Anarchy, State, and Utopia*, New York, Basic Books.

35   Rawls, J. (1971), *A Theory of Justice*, Oxford, Oxford University Press.

36   Reich, R. (1991), *The Work of Nations*, London, Simon and Schuster. Chapter 17.

37   Fukuyama, op cit.

38   Plender, J. (1997), *A Stake in the Future*, London, Nicholas Brealey.

39   International Survey Research, (1997), *Tracking Trends: Employee satisfaction in Europe in the 90's*, London, ISR Ltd. pp 1-12.

40   Cappelli, P. et al. (1997), *Change at Work*, Oxford, Oxford University Press.

41   Millward, N. (1994), *The New Industrial Relations?*, London, Policy Studies Institute.

42   Plender, op cit.

[43] Gregg, P., Machin, S. and Szymanski, S. (1993), 'The Disappearing Relationship Between Directors' Pay and Corporate Performance', *British Journal of Industrial Relations*, 31:1.

[44] Plender op cit. chapter 9.

[45] Kanter, R. M. (1993), *Men and Women of the Corporation*, 2nd Edition, New York, Basic Books.

[46] West, J. (1982), *Work, Women and the Labour Market*, London, Routledge.

[47] Collinson, D. L. et al. (1990), *Managing to Discriminate*, London, Routledge.

[48] Herriot, P. and Pemberton, C. (1995), *Competitive Advantage Through Diversity*, London: Sage.

[49] Barnes, C. (1992), *Disabled People in Britain and Discrimination*, London, Hurst and Company.

[50] Welford, R. (1995), *Environmental Strategy and Sustainable Development*, London Routledge.

3

chapter three

Changing Corporate Governance

'Sometimes to the company's detriment, but usually to its advantage, managers came to assume that shareholders and customers alike were incapable of participating directly in their firms administration.'[1]

Introduction

The term 'corporate governance' has gained ground in recent years as the debate over the legitimacy of the ownership of business and its social responsibility has grown once more. Today, there are many books and journals devoted to the modalities and repercussions of changing ideas about corporate governance. The report on Financial Aspects of Corporate Governance (Cadbury Committee) defined this term as 'the system by which companies are directed and controlled'.[2] The term includes two aspect of governance: to rule and to control; they are not synonymous but often are treated as such in many of the discussions of the subject. Both aspects will be addressed in this chapter, which aims initially to give a brief outline of the system of corporate governance in Britain, and briefly in other developed countries. In the next section, an assessment will be made of its effectiveness and some of the major criticisms level against it will be highlighted. The chapter will also give an account of some of the changes to this system in recent years, and review the debate about the role of shareholders and stakeholders in corporate governance. Further debate about whether these responses will be enough to prevent a change to the system as the result of a legitimization crisis will be left to later chapters.

The British framework of corporate governance

The British system of corporate governance exists in a nexus of social and economic relationships which have a distinctive history and pattern of development that was sketched out in chapter 1. Both joint-stock companies and private companies, which started from different roots, are in the UK governed by the same set of laws which are contained in a series of companies acts, the latest version of which is the 1985 Company Act. Different kinds of companies can be created under this law: companies limited by guarantee, unlimited companies, and limited joint stock companies. Of the later, there are two types: limited (Ltd) and public limited (PLC). A company limited by guarantee requires its members to pay up a fixed amount if the company is wound up. A limited company cannot issue shares to the public, a PLC can, as long as its capital is in excess of £50,000. The law requires that public companies have a statement in the memorandum of association which contains the name of the company, the location of its registered office, its objectives, that it is a public company, and the amount of nominal capital, with its division into shares of fixed amounts. The objects clause is likely to take up the main proportion of the memorandum's text. This sets out the objectives of the company and gives it the power to buy land, borrow money, acquire other businesses and anything necessary to further its objectives. In practice these are often standard clauses written by lawyers which allow the broadest interpretation and the maximize scope for director discretion in the operation of the business. If a company were to engage in activities outside its objects clauses then the action could be held by a court of law to be ultra vires, beyond its powers and voidable. Companies also need to have articles of association which set up procedures to govern the internal affairs of the company. Unless it registers a different set of articles with its memorandum, a company is automatically governed by the model set of articles in the Companies Act 1985. The articles constitute a contract between the company and its members. The members of the company are its shareholders who have agreed to enter their names in the company's register of members. Besides the law companies must also conform to other rules and regulations: the Stock Exchange's on 'Admission of Securities to Listing'; the Take-over Panel's code; rules of good practice on accounting issued by the accountancy profession; and increasingly new codes of conduct issued by various committees (Cadbury, Greenbury, Hampel).[3]

Under the Companies Act, assets and liabilities are owned by a company which in turn is owned by the shareholders. The shareholders appoint directors to run the company as agents on their behalf and the directors are then required to report annually to shareholders on their stewardship. Directors can in turn delegate their powers to managers but they are still ultimately responsible to the shareholders. Each component in this system is analyzed in more detail below.

Rights and duties of shareholders

One of the reasons why the company system is so attractive to investors is that they get to limit their exposure to risk by forming joint-stock companies. The shareholders are not liable for the debts of the company beyond the fully paid-up price of the shares, nor are they duty bound to take any interest in the running of the company. However, they do enjoy a number of rights: to dispose of the stock at will; to declared dividends; a share of any surplus capital should the company be wound up; voting rights in the AGM (annual general meeting); information on the fortunes of the company; and the right to subscribe to new share if more capital is required. Shareholder rights tend to be proportional to number of shares held in a company but not always, particularly when different classes of share are issued with different voting rights attached to them. The small shareholder has the opportunity to influence the directors of the company at the AGM albeit that all the directors are not obliged to attend nor does the chairman of the board have to answer shareholders questions. Institutional investors and large shareholders often enjoy private meetings with managers and directors, but these meetings should not disclose information that would contravene the rules of insider trading.

At the AGM shareholders vote on the report and accounts presented by the board and accountants, the re-appointment of members of the board and the auditors and their remuneration, and on other motions that are to be put to them. The right to call general meetings is in the hands of the directors and if 10% of the shareholders wish it the directors must call a meeting on their behalf. If companies do not hold AGMs then they can be fined by the courts. Shareholders do not have to attend in person at the AGM but may vote by proxy. There is no requirement that AGMs are quorate. Shareholders can demand that directors circulate resolutions in advance with an accompanying statement of up to a 1000 words if 5% of the shareholders wish it or a hundred shareholders owning capital of over £100 each request it. The auditors who are appointed by and for the shareholders have no right to address shareholders at the AGM and even if requested to speak they must be allowed to do so by the chairman of the board.

Banks in the UK, while lending significant sums of capital to companies on both a short and a long-term basis, tend not to take equity stakes in companies.[4] When they have been acquired this is often by historical accident rather than by design. On the whole banks do not play a significant role as shareholders in corporate governance decisions.

Information reported to shareholders is limited under the Companies Acts and the accounting conventions of the accounting professions. Most of the disclosure requirements are to do with numerical information rather than qualitative information which provides a true and fair picture of the companies activities over the last accounting period and what its future prospects are. Pressure to improve the reporting of a companies' position and impact upon the world has been growing in recent years as we shall see later on.

The board of directors

Most registered companies are required to have at least two directors. But many have more than two and often make distinctions between different types of directors albeit that these distinctions are not recognized under the Companies Act 1985. Most boards designate a chairman of the board of directors to chair the meetings. He is often separate from a managing director who in turn is often the senior executive director as opposed to non-executive directors who have little managerial work to do in the company. Under the law all directors are treated equally as having a duty to prepare annual reports and accounts and provide sound stewardship of the company regardless of what particular functional responsibility they may be designated. The board of directors is collectively responsible for all the company. The Companies Act has nothing to say about the way a company is to be run. In actuality, the chairman of the board tends to play an important role in reporting to the shareholders and others through the issuing of a chairman's statement and other comments. The Cadbury Committee felt that the roles of chairman and chief executive officer or managing director should be separated to prevent an over-accumulation of power on the board but did not make this a firm recommendation. They did make non-executive directors mandatory in quoted companies since it recommended that they have at least a three-person audit committee with at least three non-executive directors. Employee representation on company boards has been a dead letter since 1978 and the rejection of the Bullock Report on industrial democracy despite the EC Fifth Directive which requires employee representation at board level in large companies.[5]

The appointment and dismissal of directors is meant to be by the shareholders. However, the managing director tends to have the dominant say in the appointment of executive directors. In turn the chairman and non-executive directors have the power to dismiss the managing director by a vote in the board. But in law, the directors can only be dismissed by the shareholders which is their main source of power in corporate governance. Of course, if one of the directors is the controlling shareholder then no director can rest easy, the board being nothing more than an advisory committee with real accountability to the other shareholders is lost.

Most large companies have a sub-committee structure to help the board fulfill its role. The audit committee helps with liaison between the company and its auditors, the remuneration committee on the pay and benefits to be given to the executive directors, and nominating committees to help with the selection of non-executive directors for endorsement by the shareholders at the AGM.

In private companies the protection of shareholders is not as extensive since the shareholders are insiders and are often family members and relations. However they still enjoy the privilege of limited liability and legal personality.

Company law in other countries

Comparative studies of the corporate governance systems in other competitor nations have shown that there are often interesting differences between the institutional arrangements in the conduct of corporate life.[6] Law review bodies are often charged with a duty to examine the governance regimes of what appear to be successful nations in terms of their economic performance to see if alternative structures can bring better results. A brief mention of some of the major characteristics of the different systems of corporate governance will now be given.

In the USA, company law is a matter of state jurisdiction and the laws in these states can differ considerably, although there is some federal oversight on securities regulation and a general willingness to follow the leading states: New York, California and Delaware. Consequently, the Model Business Corporations Act which came into force in 1984, together with the American Law Institute Principles of Corporate Governance 1994, tend to guide most aspects of US practice. However, states compete for incorporations and Deleware is one of the most competitive centers for this administrative activity. This competitive contest has tended to give favorable terms for directors, enabling them to claim indemnity for breaches of duty, and scope for the preferment of outside interests over those of the shareholders in some circumstances. In comparison with the UK the interests of shareholders are not as closely protected but in terms of the performance of share values this does not seem to have caused any detrimental impact. Company law in Deleware is very flexible in other ways: parts of the proceeds of a capital issue can be distributed, and there are extensive provisions for informal operations and decision-making in small firms. There is a willingness to experiment with different versions of the corporate form such as closed companies and limited liability to be favorable to business development.

In Europe, there is an attempt to harmonize company law under Article 54 of the Treaty of Rome. This provision requires member states to enact into their own laws certain substantive requirements: that a company's constitution and the amount of capital subscribed are disclosed in a public register; that minimum requirements on the formation of public companies and the maintenance of their share capital are laid down; that accounts are prepared and published containing certain provisions regarding the content of these accounts; and that minimum and maximum requirements for branches established in a member state by limited companies formed in another, or in a third country, are imposed. The non-discrimination directive of Article 52 of the EC Treaty does not allow member states to discriminate against any company or firm which wishes to move within the EU. The European Convention on Human Rights also in effect places constraints upon the operation of company law by guaranteeing freedom of association and to the peaceful enjoyment of possessions.

In terms of individual European countries the German system is the most highly developed and has had an impact on other countries companies acts, including the French legislation in 1966. German company forms are divided between 'share' companies (Aktiengesellschaften) and limited companies (Gesellschaften mit beschrankter Haftung). The former tend to have detailed and prescriptive constitutions and are similar to public companies, with power to raise funds publicly; the later have limited numbers of members and allow for more flexible internal constitutions, the nearest equivalent to the private company in the UK. An important feature of the larger German companies is the dual board structure composed of a management board and a supervisory board, the later with co-determination. Made up of half employee representatives and half shareholder representatives, with a chairman entitled to cast the deciding vote in favor of shareholders, the supervisory board is responsible for strategic decisions, for supervision of the audit, and for the appointment and the dismissal of members of the management board. The management board is responsible for the operation of the company. The duties of the company directors are more broadly expressed to include employee interests and the public interest. German law also allows highly complex and distinctive arrangements to be made for groups, enabling holding companies to exercise control over groups of companies in the 'group interest' by means of a group contract, and requiring compensatory payments to outside minority shareholders. Dual boards with employee representatives have been introduced as an option into French law but are, as a rule, little used. French company law has been under review with a view to making it more flexible in recent years.

Until the 1970s most commonwealth countries tended to follow UK company law with adaptations of the 1948 or 1927 Acts. However, since then a process of reappraisal and simplification has been taking place in many of these countries moving them in the direction of the US model. Canada was one of the first to break away and mix provisions from the USA and UK philosophies of company law. Canada has: abolished the distinction between public and private companies; abolished shares of par value and authorized share capital limits; simplified capital maintenance requirements; allowed single shareholder companies; abolished the ultra vires doctrine; codified directors' duties and liabilities; enabled own company share purchases; and enabled companies to change their jurisdiction more easily. Accounting rules were removed from the legislation and made subject to professional regulation, and the procedures at elections and meetings considerably simplified. New Zealand moved in a similar direction in 1994, and in addition abolished company requirement to file a constitution. In Australia, the First Corporate Law Simplifications Act was passed which made major relaxations for small businesses including: single member companies; accounting exemptions; liberalizing share buy-backs; and relaxing requirements for company registers. Another Company Law Review Act in 1998 allowed for formation of a company without the need for a constitution; simplified the process for conducting shareholders meetings; facilitated the use of electronic technology for meetings; eased changes to share capital values; and reduced administrative burdens for company returns . South Africa and Hong Kong are in the process of reviewing their framework of company law in order to make it more flexible as in the USA.

The framework of corporate governance

The framework of corporate governance is based upon certain assumptions. The traditional rationalization for the privileges allowed to companies under incorporation is often based upon two sets of arguments about how the public good is served by these devices. The first argument is that incorporation is a public concession by the state in return for benefits, and the second is that there is a valid contract which entitles a company to exist as a private entity and so should, in a liberal democracy, be defended by the law.

The first of these is often labeled the 'concession' view because it regards the company as an existence granted by the state as a benefit to its members which in return has to be justified by the performance of public welfare functions such as the creation of wealth. The state is therefore entitled to intervene to define and ensure compliance with corporate objectives. However, this argument has been increasingly undermined by the proliferation of companies and other forms of wealth-creating organizations. Parkinson's view regarding validity of this argument as a supporting assumption of company law is that it is now limited, and he goes on to note that, 'it is not the legal qualities of limited liability or separate personality in themselves that justify intervention, but the concentration of power in private hands that has come about partly as a result of their existence."[7]

The second argument is labeled the 'contract' view because the owners of property are thought to have the moral and legal right to form corporations for their own mutual benefit and self-interest. Companies are then purely private organizations and should not be interfered with unduly by the state; their power is legitimated by property rights and the natural rights theory that property entitlements, if justly acquired, should not be interfered with without good reason. This view sees freedom as founded upon inalienable property entitlements that, if legitimate, should be protected by the state. However, this argument, whilst likely to justify private property entitlements in personal possessions, has to be stretched too far to legitimize the power of shareholders over corporate property who exercise very little control over that property beyond its purchase and disposal. Modern company law makes use of a refinement of the contracts model, namely the 'nexus of contracts theory' which will now be outlined below.

The nexus of contracts theory does not rely upon the property owner to exercise close control over the company's activities but makes the important assumption that corporate form is a useful construct for the coming together of self-interested individuals to pursue a collective endeavor. The company as a piece of owned property then in effect disappears; it is a device to facilitate contracting relationships for mutual benefit. Shareholders are not so much owners of the company but one of its contracting parties which includes suppliers, employees, creditors, and customers. Corporate governance arrangements are then seen as economic considerations where the 'agency costs' have to be kept within limits. Agency costs are the losses that can be incurred by the shareholders when their interests do not match those of the management of the company or other contractors and the costs of monitoring these divergences. The role of the law is to help reduce agency costs to what is acceptable to the contracting parties in the competitive market place. Over time, it is supposed that market competition will have led to the evolution of the most efficient mechanisms of corporate governance acceptable to the contracting parties. If present arrangements did not adequately protect shareholder interests then they would withdraw their investments and put pressure on management for a change in governance procedures. Likewise, if suppliers or employees were unhappy with their contracts they would refuse to enter into contracts with the firm and instead hold out for contracts more to their liking. The weakness in this theory, if the other contracting parties are brought into the picture, is now evident. The power of the contractors is different and clearly this theory does not take adequate account of the disproportionate power of the shareholders and management in the nexus of company contracts. The power of these contractors to determine the purposes and direction of the company is felt by many commentators to be overbearing and can no longer be justified, particularly if it is to the detriment of the common good. [8] The legitimacy of corporate governance arrangements has in recent years become threatened for this reason: the power disparities are such that they cannot be ignored and so they are being openly challenged by other contractors, now termed other stakeholders, in the corporate enterprise.

Problems with the operation of the present structure

Criticisms of the governance structures in companies can be placed under a number of headings: they are out of shareholder control; they allow for too much management self-dealing; and they are detrimental to the environment and to human rights.

Lack of shareholder control

In practice, at most AGMs shareholders are unable to make management accountable for the running of the company. [9]   As most companies have thousands of shareholders the voice of each shareholder is inconsequential. Moreover, with a portfolio approach to investment, the individual shareholder has little incentive to be very knowledgeable or concerned about the management of the company beyond the payment of the dividend or the share price. Management accountability is not secured by the AGM. Even institutional directors (pension funds, insurance companies, and investment trusts who own over 70% of equity stock) who have the collective shareholding to put pressure on the management are in practice found to be reluctant to do so and tend to confine their role to selling the shares of underperforming companies or encouraging   merger and takeover activity in the market for corporate control. [10]   On the whole they do not see it as their function to interfere with managerial prerogatives especially when the results over the long run have been very beneficial financially. In the main, institutional investors have allowed the market for corporate control to flourish as a mechanism for bringing under-performing managements into line with their expectations. The process is as follows: companies performing below par will experience a fall in their share price as shareholders grow disillusioned and sell their shares on the stock market; market analysts will see that the company's shares are undervalued compared with assets or opportunities, and so they will encourage rival companies or investors to buy the companies shares with a view to unseating the present management and to unlocking the profitability that is a present not being realized by the incumbent management. Moreover this mechanism need not be brought to bear all the time. The mere threat of this eventuality by company boards is enough to keep them on their metal and ensure that shareholder expectations are met. This in turn has lead to the criticism that the management of UK companies is too much focused on the need for high short-term returns rather than making investments that will bring in greater longer-term results. This means that investments in training, research and development and innovation are often neglectedwhich in the longer run puts UK firms at a competitive disadvantage with firms in Germany and Japan who have financial arrangements that allow them to make longer term investment commitments.[11] This view is further supported by research on takeover and merger activity which tends to show that these do not necessarily lead to improvements in company performance or improvements in the competitive position of UK industry.[12] Moreover, pervasive short-termism is often blamed for the detrimental impact of companies on the social, human rights and ecological environment.[13]

Management self-dealing

If managers are to be the agents of the shareholders then the problem becomes that of exercising control over their behavior. Managers are in all likelihood going to pursue their own interests. They will seek high and rising remuneration, security of tenure, substantial compensation for loss of office, executive surroundings and status symbols. Much of the evidence in recent years is that executives have been lining their own pockets at the expense of shareholders and often in a way unrelated to the performance of their companies or in relation to the improvements in pay and conditions of their workforces.[14]

Fewer than a quarter of UK companies have any formal process for evaluating the chief executive. A study by Korn/Ferry International found that many boards of directors were focusing primarily on strategy and achieving financial goals which meant that other issues, such as corporate social responsibility, industrial relations and environmental responsibility were given a low priority.[15] It also indicated that there had been little movement in increasing the representation of women in the board room. Women make up 5% of directors in the UK.

Damage to the environment and to human rights

Attention to wider social responsibility by the public company is, according to economic theory, something that can only be done by companies that are under weak competitive pressures, are acting with the approval of shareholders, or are enjoying a monopoly position in the market. Social activism or concern above and beyond that required by the law or regulations of the state is not thought to be the responsibility of business. However, in many ways because the market is not perfect and increasingly managers are in a controlling position, corporate largesse has increased in recent years and the strictly laissez-faire view has diminished as a guide to corporate conduct . In fact some commentators wonder if the role of business in the community has gone beyond what can be rightfully expected. Nevertheless there are a number of criticisms made about the functioning of corporate social responsibility in practice.[16] First, there is the point that in aggregate terms the level of expenditure is much less in the UK than the USA (0.5% compared to 2.5%). This expenditure is often not properly accounted for and the return to the company is not measured. It rests upon the sentiments of a beneficent management but is not treated seriously as a business investment or an expense. This approach to the issue does not encourage the company to build social responsibility into its strategy and operational processes; it treats it as the equivalent of whipped cream on top of the cake. This can mean that there are disincentives for the firm to move beyond the minimum in terms of environmental or social responsibility. Some commentators have therefore suggested that we need to include the notion of an integrated approach to social responsibility into the system of corporate governance.[17]

Attempts at reform

The Committee on the Financial Aspects of Corporate Governance under the chairmanship of Sir Adrian Cadbury, was established in May 1991 by the Financial Reporting Council, the London Stock Exchange and the accountancy profession. These bodies were concerned about the drop in confidence in financial reporting and in the ability of auditors to reassure the public about the financial viability of some companies. The Committee reported in 1992 and recommended that changes in the corporate governance system were needed to help raise standards in the system.[18] It therefore made proposals to try to establish confidence and trust in the system and to improve the voice of shareholders in governance.

The committee put forward two principles for consideration. First, that self-regulation, rather than statutory regulation and enforcement, was the best way forward; and second, that financial markets, rather than independent regulators, provided the most appropriate means of dealing with those companies which fell below the accepted standards of corporate governance. The recommendations were, consequently, that the unitary board of directors should be strengthened so that the respective responsibilities of directors, shareholders and auditors were clearer, making all directors responsible for the stewardship of the company's assets. The effectiveness of the board should be determined by its procedures and structures. It was recommended that there should be separate audit, nomination and remuneration committees.

The Cadbury Committee also advised that the role of chairman and chief executive should be separated. The chairman has the task of accepting responsibility for the board, for its workings, membership, balance, agenda, and communication with shareholders. The chief executive position should be held by a separate person who is responsible to the board for the operation of the company and is accountable to it on matters of policy. All boards in Cadbury's view should appoint a minimum of three (including the chairman) non-executive directors who are able to exercise independent judgment. They should not participate in share option schemes and should have information provided to them by the company. It was recommended that shareholders too should be kept well informed by the company.

At the heart of the Report was the suggested Code of Best Practice designed to encourage high standards of corporate behavior. The code stresses the need for integrity, openness and accountability. Public companies that require a listing on the stock exchange must publish a statement to indicate how they are in compliance with the code. The Committee remained responsible for implementing and monitoring its recommendation until 1995 when the Hampel Committee was set up to review progress and to continue the review of corporate governance arrangements.

Hampel Committee Report

The interim report of the Hampel committee criticized the Cadbury report for its 'tick-box' approach to corporate governance reforms, but it turned down more radical ideas for reform such as two-tier German-style boards, and the appointment of directors to represent workers' and other stakeholders' interests. It urged the government to introduce a shift in regulations towards a system of broad principles in an attempt to ease the compliance burden imposed on companies by the Cadbury and Greenbury Reports. It did not want a lighter approach for smaller companies but said that the basic principles should be the same for all businesses, especially as shareholders often need more assurance about smaller companies.

These recommendations were tempered slightly in the final Report of the Committee which was published in 1998.[19] The theme of the recommendations was that self-regulation rather than legislation in corporate governance was still to be the preferred approach and that recent changes had to be given more time to bed down. The Report in outline recommended the following principles of corporate governance. That companies should include in their annual reports a narrative account of how they apply the broad principles of governance and that they should explain their governance policies and any departures from best practice. Directors should receive appropriate training. That the majority of non-executive directors should be independent, and boards should disclose in the annual report which of the non-executive directors are considered to be independent. They recommended that the roles of chairman and chief executive should be separated and that companies which combined the role needed to justify this decision. A senior non-executive director should be identified in the annual report, to whom concerns could be conveyed. Also when directors' names are submitted to shareholders for re-election they should be accompanied by biographical details. Directors who resign before they are due to need to offer and explanation for this decision.

In regard to audits and accountability, the report suggested that the audit committee should keep under review the overall financial relationship between the company and its auditors to ensure a balance between the maintenance of objectivity and value for money. There are a list of proposals with regard to directors remuneration. The payment of directors in the form of company shares is to be allowed but is not recommended as a universal practice. Company boards were advised to set their directors contract periods to one year or less rather than the two to three years which is the present norm in many firms. Directors who are asked to leave a company early are advised to agree in advance what payment they may be entitled to in compensation. Boards should establish a remuneration committee made up of independent non-executive directors, who would then decide upon the remuneration of the companies executive directors. However, the decision on the broad framework and cost of executive remuneration is to remain the preserve of the full board under advisement from the remuneration committee. Shareholder approval should be sought for new long- term incentive plans, but the Hampel Committee did not favour obliging companies to seek shareholder approval for the remuneration report.

In regard to shareholders and the AGM, the report recommended that institutional investors be responsible to their clients for the use of their votes in AGMs and that they exercise this voting power. Also institutions should make available to clients information on the proportion of resolutions on which votes were cast and non-discretionary proxies lodged. These recommendations were included in a best practice code of corporate governance issued after the final Report.

The Government and DTI welcomed the report and in turn set up a company law steering group to consider what legislative response was needed to ensure that there was a proper balance struck between a voluntary governance code and the framework of company law.[20] Many company directors welcomed the Hampel Report because of its retention of a light touch and the principle of voluntary regulation which would allow business to flourish. However, some shareholder groups criticized the Report as being weak and as having significant omissions. For example, there was no definition of what makes for an independent director, and non-independent directors are not to be listed. There was also concern expressed that the retreat from flexible rules into broad, unenforceable principles would set back many of the improvements put into place after the Cadbury Report.

The TUC remained skeptical about the ability of the recommendations to reform the excesses of boardroom pay particularly as the majority of companies failed to comply with Greenbury's recommendation that performance criteria should be challenging. Despite the fact that business was going to enter into a period of market uncertainty some commentators wondered if it was appropriate that the hand of regulation be loosened if the control of institutional investors was not tightened in compensation. The danger, as the *Financial Times* commentator John Plender sees it, is, that the 'rotten borough ethos saddles wealth creation with a bad name and erodes the legitimacy of British business in the public mind.'[21]

The modern company law review

The New Labour Government in 1998, announced the launch of a fundamental review of the framework of core company law to be conducted by the Company Law Review Steering Group and funded by the Department of Trade and Industry.[22] The terms of reference for the review are to modernize the framework of company law to take into account the globalised economy and the competitiveness of British industry. The process is being conducted by the Steering Group which in turn is setting up working groups, a consultative committee and is commissioning research. It is hoped that a wide-ranging review that enjoys the support of many interested parties will lead to the publication of a white paper detailing a programme of legislation in the year 2001. The consultation document issued on the announcement of the review contained its own summary of what it saw as the drawbacks of the present

1985 Companies Act: it is couched in over-formal language; is complicated by excessive detail; tends towards over-regulation; and has a complex structure making it difficult for businessmen to understand and costly to interpret. The most serious problems identified however, were its obsolescent or ineffective provisions, such as requiring companies to keep a register of their members and the requirement for a statement of objects in the memorandum of association; and the obstacles it put in the way of business enterprise by not allowing for the introduction of information technology or for the adoption of codes of conduct to guide company practice. The review group did signal early on that it sees the need for new legislation to define the proper role of company directors in what is at the present time a very vague area. They also wanted to see the shareholders' position at annual general meeting improved and stronger voting powers given to shareholders over the question of directors' remuneration.

In February 1999, a consultation document was issued by the review group setting out a series of questions that the public were invited to comment upon.[23] It also gave some indication of the review's approach to its task and what it sees as the main issues. It analyses the interests which company law is meant to serve. The case of ensuring that company managers have regard to the need to ensure productive relationships with a range of interested parties over a long period is recognized. A distinction is drawn between the 'enlightened shareholder value' approach, which claims that this can be achieved within the present framework of law without harming shareholders interests, and the 'pluralist' approach, which claims that trusting and productive relationships will only be achievable where directors are permitted (or required) to balance shareholders' interests with those of others committed to the company. The review group has acknowledged that the current law is not widely recognized as embracing the enlightened shareholder value approach. They are also examining the alternative pluralist approach and its implications for legal discretion, duties, remedies and boardroom structures. The group is considering the importance of transparency in achieving a wider satisfaction of interests as well as investigating the case for enabling or requiring directors to satisfy wider social or philanthropic objectives. The review is keen to explore the needs of small and closely-held companies, which it does not consider are well served by the present Companies Act. They are assessing the merits of new free-standing legislation for such companies, as opposed to an integrated rewrite of the existing law. The group has expressed a provisional preference for the later option: a rewriting of the proposed legislation on a 'small business first' basis, with appropriate flexibility to suit the needs of such small companies, while retaining integrated legislation which provides for all companies.

The review is examining proposals for simplifying the law relating to company formations and maintenance of share capital. The aims are: to clarify and reform the rules relating to the capacity of companies and their agents and the validity of transactions with third parties; to remove the need for court approval of capital reductions; to simplify financial assistance regimes that are dependent on member approval and solvency certification; and to introduce no par value shares. The regime for the establishment of foreign companies in the UK is also under review, as is the attractiveness of the UK law to bring in foreign companies. Progress is expected to be made in introducing information and communications technologies into company meetings and in the presentation and holding of company information. The form and contents of accounts, the directors' report and the possibility of making it more accountable, and the responsibilities of the auditors are being reviewed. The role of accounting standards and international standards is to be reviewed together with the possibility of making exemptions for small and medium-sized companies.

One of the key debates in the review group, and one that the consultation document describes as 'at its heart', is the question of whether to propose the 'enlightened shareholder value' approach or the 'pluralist' view. However, three of the leading advocates of the pluralist view are members of the Steering Committee so it can be expected to be put forcefully. It is important to appreciate what a movement in the pluralist direction would mean for corporate governance. It may be best to think of pluralist responsibility as something that has to be taken into account at the decision-making stage of a company's operations rather than as a set of compliance requirements that are enforced by external authority. The enlightened shareholder value model of corporate governance puts the management of the agents of the shareholders in a simple but definite fiduciary relationship. The interests of the shareholders are meant to be paramount in the decision-making process as it its their assets that are at stake. The movement towards a pluralist view means that the fiduciary relationship will be broken or diluted as the interests of, or the impact upon, other stakeholders is taken into account in the decision-making process. Goodpaster has claimed that this is a step too far, in that it could allow management self-dealing back into the frame, as managers might put themselves into the position of the arbiter of the various stakes in the company.[24] The possibility exists that the interests of shareholders will be neglected to the point where there is effectively no fiduciary relationship at all. In these circumstances, it is unlikely that investors would want to put their funds at the disposal of companies run according to these principals. Goodpaster's own proposal is for the managers to exercise a non-fiduciary duty to other stakeholders' interests when making decisions. But in the last instance the judgment of management must be final in relation to fiduciary and non-fiduciary obligations.

Early speculations as to the final outcome of the Modern Company Law Review are that, even if the group comes out in favor of the 'pluralist' approach allowing directors to take into account the interest of stakeholders, it will opt for a permissive rather than a mandatory requirement. In other words, all directors will be allowed a discretion to sacrifice commercial advantage for public good purposes. However, the need to consider more radical solutions to the problems of company law could be placed upon the group if the climate of legitimacy continues to deteriorate. The possibility of other ways of conceiving the company may need to be considered as the nature of company institutionalization comes closer into the orbit of political debate.

In the next two chapters we will consider the other responses companies have been making in the face of growing criticism regarding their lack of social accountability and their environmental impact and reporting practices.

References

[1] Alborn, T., (1998), *Conceiving Companies*, London, Routledge, p82.

[2] *Committee on the Financial Aspects of Corporate Governance,* (1992) (Cadbury Report), London.

[3] Cadbury, op cit. *The Report of the Committee on Directors' Remuneration,* (1995), (Greenbury Report) London. Committee on Corporate Governance, (1998), ('Hampel Report'), London.

[4] Charkham, J., (1994), *Keeping Good Company: a Study of Corporate Governance in Five Countries,* University Press, p 297. Oxford

[5] *Committee of Inquiry on Industrial Democracy,* (1977) (Bullock Report), London: HMSO.

[6] Charkham, op cit.

[7] Parkinson, J., (1994), *Corporate Power and Responsibility: Issues in the Theory of Company Law,* Oxford, Oxford University Press, p 30.

[8] Hutton, W., (1995), *The State We're In,* London, Jonathan Cape.

[9] Charkham, op cit.

[10] Stapledon, G.P., (1996), *Institutional Shareholders and Corporate Governance,* Oxford, Clarendon Press.

[11] Hutton, op cit.

[12] Kay, J., (1986), *The Role of Mergers,* London: Institute of Fiscal Studies Working Paper No 94.

[13] Hutton, op cit.

[14] Gregg, P., Machin, S. and Szymanski, S., (1993), 'The Disappearing relationship Between Directors' Pay and Corporate Performance', *British Journal of Industrial Relations,* 31: 1, pp 1-9.

[15] The European Boards of Directors Study, (1997), London, Korn/Ferry International.

[16] Parkinson, op cit.

[17] White, J.B., (1985), 'How Should We Talk About Corporations? The Languages of Economics and of Citizenship', *Yale Law Journal,* 94, pp 1416 1425.

[18] Cadbury Report, op cit.

[19] Hampel Report, op cit.

[20] *Modern Company Law For a Competitive Economy,* (1998), London, Department of Trade and Industry.

[21] Plender, J., (1997), *Financial Times,* 7th July.

[22] *Modern Company Law,* op cit.

[23] *Modern Company Law For a Competitive Economy: The Strategic Framework,* (1999), London, For a competitive Economy, DTI.

[24] Goodpaster, K., (1991), 'Business Ethics and Stakeholder Analysis', *Business Ethics Quarterly,* 1:1, pp 53- 68.

chapter four

Developments in Company Social Accountability

' Above all it is to insist that all industries shall be conducted in complete publicity as to costs and profits, because publicity ought to be the antiseptic both of economic and political abuse, and no man can have confidence in his neighbour unless both work in the light.'[1]

Introduction

This chapter will outline some of the developments in company social accountability that have taken place over the past 30 years. The focus in this study will not be on the activity undertaken in the social responsibility area by companies; this is considerable and has been described richly in other studies. The intention here is to look at how this activity is reported upon and at how it is changing the company form. The trend has been for firms to become more open, transparent and accountable to non-shareholder interests in society. The slow pace of this response is perhaps an indication that we are still in a normal period of accepted company legitimacy. However, in recent years, the pace of change has noticeably quickened and more and more companies are making efforts to become more forthcoming about their social role and commitments. Accounting and reporting on social responsibility and activity is a new field. Many imaginative experiments are taking place in disclosure procedures and these are likely to help shape new conventions in the future and so become a pervasive feature of the company form.

A brief history of social accounting practice

Whilst there has always been concern about the social impact of business upon society, most notably from Ruskin onwards, the debate within orthodox management theory is more recent.[2] The general concern with greater social accountability began in the 1970s as part of the 'social responsibility debate' which had started in the USA and radiated outwards to Europe. Howard Bowen's book, *Social Responsibilities of the Businessman*, in 1953 opened up a debate on the wider social responsibilities of business to the community, as did the work of Peter Drucker who had come to question the purposes and responsibilities of the large corporation.[3] At about this time, environmental concerns about the impact of business in terms of pollution and the depletion of natural resources was starting to appear.[4] The development of this aspect will be given a separate treatment in the next chapter. The impact of the social responsibility debate on the form of the company in Britain was to slowly increase the disclosure requirements which had just been put in place under the 1967 Companies Act, which introduced the requirement that companies disclose their charitable and political donations.

The social responsibility debate in the USA had provoked some classic statements of the ideological rift between liberals and social democrats in politics. The neo-liberals Frederick von Hayek and Milton Friedman stood opposed to the social democrats Robert Dahl and Charles Lindblom. The liberals argued that businesses are to be understood as private property and are, as such, instruments of their owners designed primarily to make money. The common good is served by this narrow focus because the pressure of unintended consequences ensures that each business seeks out efficient allocations of resources, so generating the maximum amount of wealth in society, and the maximum amount of opportunity to engage others in the wealth creation process. This argument is encapsulated in the title of Friedman's article published in the *New York Times Magazine*, 'The social responsibility of business is to increase its profits'.[5] The other advantage of this definition is that business should not be not tempted to stray into other areas of activity such as politics or law making; this restriction of the scope of business power in a democratic society is thought to be a great virtue. The danger in the broader notion of social accountability is that managers may see this as an open invitation to begin making political decisions and exercising power for their own social purposes. This considerably loosens the notion of accountability   to shareholders and increases the agent's prerogatives. Those on the social democratic side of the debate consider these arguments to have been superseded by events, because large businesses are too powerful for shareholders to exercise real control and, today, business spends much time and effort lobbying politicians to make the business environment more favourable for its own interests. Some commentators have argued that the large corporation should now no longer be considered to be private property but instead should be publicly regulated on behalf of a range of stakeholders. This debate is the new form of joint-stock politics that is being played out at the end of this century much as it was when the question of whether to allow the creation of joint-stock companies was being discussed in Victorian society. We will be exploring this debate in more detail in later chapters. A movement in the direction of the social democrats position in the last 30 years on both sides of the Atlantic is detectable.

In the early 1970s, the American Accounting Association issued a series of reports on aspects of the social responsibility debate: employee reporting, employment reporting and industrial relations information disclosure. This debate crossed the Atlantic and, in the UK, the CBI accepted some of these points and provided some support for changes in company law. The Accounting Standards Steering Committee published its Corporate Report in 1975, which tried to establish a programme to develop accounting disclosures for the wider public.[6] The report recommended that firms publish: a value added statement; an employment report; a statement of money exchanges with government; a statement of transactions in foreign currencies; a statement of future prospects; and a statement of corporate objectives. However, the oil price crisis of the early 1970s triggered the worldwide recession and the impetus was lost, as survival and competition became the business and political priorities.

The notion of including the employees on the decision-making bodies in the company was largely accepted and implemented in continental Europe, with a strong determination that post-war reconstruction would include a place for co-determination in the company. When Britain entered the EC this debate was broached, and a Royal Commission (Bullock Report 1978) was set up under a Labour Government in 1975 to consider the mechanics of implementation. However, the notion of a unitary board with compulsory employee representation was an anathema to the CBI which campaigned vigorously against the Commission's proposals, which in the event were never taken up by the Labour Government and were then dropped by the incoming Conservative Government in 1979.

Some firms, at this time, did attempt to produce employee reports. There was very little standardisation of the content or format of these reports, which were often produced sporadically. The purposes of these reports was equally diverse: some were designed to communicate with the firm's employees; others were blatant attempts to forestall strike action; and some were designed to influence the collective bargaining environment. Some of the reports contained abbreviated financial statements; some a review of the organisation's progress during the year; and some reported on a wide range of personnel management indicators such as health and safety, labour turnover, and strike levels. Only a few reports contained a 'value-added statement' detailing the increased wealth added by employees to the assets of the business during the year.[7] However, as the industrial relations climate changed in the 1980s, the frequency of publication of these statements declined and except when the law required certain statements on employee matters, the general employee report disappeared as a feature of company accountability.

Several companies during the 1970s tried to implement some of the new concepts from the academic studies on social accounting. Deutshe Shell in 1975 issued a report containing a set of social accounts in an attempt to assess the extent to which the company contributed to social welfare. Its report identified corporate social objectives and then the cost of trying to meet those objectives. The US firm, Atlantic Richfield, in 1977 issued a report of more than 60 pages on its social responsibilities and invited the journalist Milton Markowitz to provide a critique of the report, which then appeared alongside as a sort of commentary on the accounts. For example, in regard to the firm's assets, the report contained the following statements on minority affairs: 'Atlantic Richfield has worked hard to provide job opportunities for minorities. Minority group members account for 13% of the total workforce, a ration that ranks Atlantic Richfield at the top of the petroleum industry. Jobs formerly restricted to men - such as refinery work - have been opened up to women. ...'[8] Nevertheless, aspersions were cast about the real purpose of this report, when it was revealed that Atlantic Richfield had been responsible for a major environmental pollution incident where nuclear waste had leaked into ground water in the USA. The Atlantic Richfield social report made no mention of this catastrophe.[9]   In many respects, the early attempts at CSR (Corporate Social Reporting) were often driven by fashionable trends in accounting theory, but this is not to say that valuable lessons were not learnt in these experiments and that, in some areas, general progress was made in identifying appropriate reporting criteria, as in the case of the employee reports.

Recent practice in social accounting

Recent years have witnessed an increase in company social reporting and disclosure. The reporting on employee matters will be examined first followed by the more general topic of social responsibility reporting. Reporting on the environment and the company's human rights record will be covered in the next chapter.

Employee reporting practice

Some of the most important stakeholders in the company are thought to be the employees. Although they have often been treated in accounting terms as costs, new systems of accounting are trying to treat them as potential assets. New attempts to recognise accountability to the employees have been revived again in recent years. One theoretical attempt to take account of the contribution of employees to the firm is that of Human Resource Accounting (HRA).[10] The concept is that the contribution of employees to the firm will be identified and measured and this information will then be published. Investments made in training and development can then be related to improvements in operating performance and the payback on these activities, previously only classified as a cost to the business, can be noted. The concept and implications for practice have been developed most fully by Likert, and have been applied to some companies in the USA.[11] However, the use of these techniques in wider accounting practice has generally failed to materialise, although the movement towards knowledge-based companies may, in time, rekindle this interest. There is already a lot of debate about this topic in the accounting journals. For example, new ideas have been put forward for assessing the 'worth' of employees to the company, and trying to estimate what it would cost the company if an employee were to leave.[12] This technique would require the use of 'soft' accounting information which puts a value upon the employee's tacit knowledge, skills and contribution to organisational knowledge and learning. It has been argued that this form of accounting is beneficial to the employees by showing them as valuable assets of the firm in the hope that it might lead to a more considerate leadership style and a more sophisticated system of personnel management.

The disclosure of information to employees and their trade unions gained great deal of support from the Employment Protection Act 1975. This put on a statutory basis the requirement to disclose information to trade unions that would help them in drawing up their claims in the collective bargaining process. However, the encouragement to disclose information which was in the interests of promoting good industrial relations did not have much effect. Despite the hardening of the relationship between the government and trade unions in the 1980s and 90s, these regulations have remained in force, but are only used in a perfunctory way. National Power, the energy company, for example, in its 1999 report has three paragraphs reporting on employees: the first mentions its commitment to continuous staff development, second that the company has adopted an 'Investors in People' scheme, and the third that it puts a lot of effort into maintaining good communications with its staff.[13] Railtrack has one item about employees regarding the extension of the employee share saving scheme and the performance-related profit sharing scheme.[14] Many companies in Europe have been obliged to go much further in terms of information disclosure to employees, and this has greatly assisted the role of trade unions in collective bargaining and more general representation within the company. In Britain, little progress has been made in extending the disclose of information beyond that giving details about the contractual terms and conditions of work. Little attention, so far, has been paid to the nature of employee information which would make it useful for trade unions, or would make employees feel more involved in the decision making of the firm or that will help them to hold the management accountable for its human resource management policies, particularly when it comes to fighting or challenging redundancy issues. Trade union researchers have suggested that the lack of ambition in trade union demands for information disclosure from companies is one of the factors that is holding the development of this legislation back.[15] Trade unions need to become much more sophisticated in dealing with company information in order to build better partnerships with the companies of its members and in order to hold managements to account for human resource decisions. This is one reason why central organisation and expertise is still an important requirement for modernising the trade union movement in Britain; a development at the moment greatly hampered by the large number of small unions and greater decentralisation in British trade unions than compared to with their counterparts in Europe. Nevertheless, in recent years, the TUC has taken a greater interest in the environmental impact of company activity, and in 1989 established its own

Environmental Action Group, with a remit to devise and facilitate the negotiation of 'green agreements' with employers. In 1991, the TUC published a policy document on its environmental stance entitled *Greening the Workplace*, which urged its member unions to take a more proactive stance on these issues in their bargaining activities with companies.[16]

It would seem that as a matter of general accounting practice in Britain companies do not appear to make significant disclosure of information to employees. Lyall's survey of 60 employee reports drawn from some of the 1000 largest UK companies, showed that only basic information was the subject of disclosure to employees: profits 57 companies; value-added 43; divisional information 29; financial resources 21; and capital investment 21.[17] No report contained information on budgets or future cash flows, or on production, selling and administration costs. This was despite the recommendations in 'The Corporate Report', published by the UK Accounting Standards Steering Committee, which tried to identify the groups and people for whom financial information should be prepared in relation to their interests in the firm.[18] The Report notes that in relation to employees: 'Nothing illustrates more vividly the 19th century origin of British Company Law than the way in which employees are almost totally ignored in the present Companies Acts and in corporate reports.'[19] It was the Committee's recommendation that special purpose employment reports should be published that contain the following information: numbers employed; broad reasons to be given for changes in the number employed; the age and sex distribution of employees; the functions of employees; the geographical location of major employment centres; major plant and site closures, disposals and acquisitions during the past year; the hours scheduled and worked by employees; employment costs concerning fringe benefits; the costs and benefits associated with pension schemes and ability of such schemes to meet future commitments; the trade unions recognised for collective bargaining purposes, bargaining units and whether bargaining information has been made available to the trade unions; information concerning health and safety including the frequency and severity of accidents and occupational diseases; and selected ratios relating to employment and a value-added statement. Despite these recommendations being included in the Department of Trade's Green Paper 'Aims and Scope of Company Reports 1976' they did not get very far as the Stock Exchange and CBI vigorously opposed them on the grounds that this would violate the duty of stewardship to shareholders.

The subject had not been the topic of debate again until recent discussions where a working party were set up on corporate governance issues by the New Labour Government in 1997. However, a study by Gray, Owen and Adams has shown that the number of UK companies disclosing information to employees on issues such as health and safety, pensions, and employee share ownership schemes has increased in frequency every year since the late 1980s.[20] It could be that a movement closer to EU standards will bring British companies into line with the practices of their European counterparts which are much more extensive. In the case of Germany, there is a long tradition of reporting on employee matters, with many firms producing social reports which contain: descriptions of goals, actions taken and achievements in the fields of employment and social concern; a value-added statement indicating the distribution among the various stakeholders; and a social account providing a quantitative presentation of all measurable employment and societal orientated corporate expenditures and revenues. Despite these extensive disclosure requirements many pressure groups in Germany, including the trade unions, are pushing for the development of social reporting to be taken further. A general review of reporting trends in the EU has concluded, however, that there is still much to be done to take these issues forward on a mandatory basis rather than allow some companies to make all the running with innovative voluntary initiatives.[21] Consequently, what is needed is EU wide social policies and laws that cover corporate accountability and greater responsibility. The EU has been trying to resolve the disputes about the proposals for a European company statute for some years. Its aim is to allow companies with operations in more than one member state to establish themselves as 'European companies' governed by one law, but applicable in all the EU. At present companies have to tailor their activities to comply with different company laws in the member states which adds to administration costs. The proposals have been blocked largely over disputes concerning the issue of worker involvement and differences between the UK and Germany over how far companies should be obliged to consult workers.

An interesting development which could increase the need for employee reporting still further by companies in the EU is a proposal by the Commission that a performance league table for large companies based upon best employment practice should be created; it would also be used to penalise 'bad' employers who fail to comply with notions of good practice.[22] Penalised companies would be denied access to grants, public procurement and public aid for research and development. Private companies employing more than 1000 employees inside the EU would also be denied state aid if they offended against 'good' employer practices. The European company league table would be compiled on the basis of an annual company report on 'managing change'; it would not be statutory but a voluntary undertaking. These reports would lay out corporate plans for structural change, education and training, health and safety, and equal opportunities, and would have to show what the company is doing in practice to implement the plans.

Social responsibility disclosure

In Europe, reporting upon social impacts and issues has taken a number of themes: community involvement and welfare; equal opportunities; customer services; socially beneficial products and services; and linkages with government policies. Some of these themes have been specified because they are of particular interest to the new and growing ethical investment funds. The first ethical investment fund in the UK was launched in 1984, and is called the Friends Provident Stewardship Fund. There are now around 35 funds managing over two billion pounds on behalf of 15,000 investors.[23]   These funds choose which companies to invest in on the basis of how they match up to as series of 'ethical criteria'. The majority of ethical funds specify lists of negative criteria which prevent them from placing money in a company if it has indulged in certain activities such as intensive farming, arms manufacture and distribution, child labour malpractices, nuclear power, pornography, etc. Some funds specify positive criteria which will make a company more favourable for investment if they engage in or promote activities such as better than average equal opportunity policies, community involvement, a strong commitment to sustainable development policies, etc. Most of the ethical funds choose the criteria they will use from a list of some 300 provided for them by the Ethical Investment Research Service (EIRS), which tracks companies and attempts to identify compliance with them. It can pay some companies to be mindful of these criteria in its business operations as they will attract potential investments from these investors. The ethical funds have been criticised for not putting enough resources into tracking the companies they invest in and in response to these criticisms several funds have improved their policies and commitments to measuring companies against the specified criteria. This trend if magnified will in turn will put even more pressure on the companies to report their activities against these criteria and make even more information available to the EIRS. In 1996, another variation of the ethical investment fund was launched. This is a fund that will only invest in companies that are in compliance with the corporate governance requirements set out in the RSA's report on 'Tomorrow's Company'.[24] The fund is managed by Kleinwort Benson Investment Management and has a governance committee chaired by Sir Anthony Cleaver, the chairman of AEA Technology, and the RSA's committee of inquiry into 'Tomorrow's Company'.[25] The report recommended that adversarial attitudes in relations to employees and suppliers had to be overcome, that dependence on financial measures of success had to be reduced, and that directors be encouraged to broaden their understanding of legal responsibility. Over £100 million is to be invested in around 70 companies who are prepared to fulfil the 'agenda for action' set out in the report. This requires company directors to adopt a statement of purpose, to develop a 'success model' for the company, and to review their measurement system each year against their ability to support its goals, purpose, values and key relationships.

One of the early drivers to encourage reporting in this field came from the EC Code of Conduct applying to companies with operations in South Africa. This Code required that information on consultation and collective bargaining, pay, trade union rights, migrant labour, equal opportunities, fringe benefits and desegregation should be submitted to national government agencies, and a statement that this report was so lodged in the firm's annual report. Ordinarily, in the UK, the Companies Act only requires disclosure on firm's policies towards disabled employees, and the donations made to political parties and to other charities.

Despite the limited requirements of EU and UK law on the need for social accountability statements in company annual reports, some firms have ventured to go further by making disclosures on a voluntary basis. A useful survey made in 1995 by Gray, Owen and Adams gives some indication of the efforts made by companies in this new activity.[26] Their study of 129 companies across western Europe found that the major items disclosed by most firms were customer relations(63%), and political donations, activities and statements (51%). Few companies made any comment at all about community involvements and other welfare activities (27%), equal opportunities (31%), sponsorship and advertising (18%), product safety and testing (16%), and charitable donations and activities (2%). On the question of reporting on ethical issues they noted that this aspect of reporting was very underdeveloped, and they did not detected a growth trend from their survey respondents. Most ethical reporting was entirely ad hoc with great variation on what was disclosed and how this was done. Even customer-related disclosure showed no clear patterns, and only 30% of firms' had any kind of policy statement in relation to their customers. An example of this is taken from the French company, Valeo: 'To satisfy its customers' expectations, Valeo has developed five core strategies. Their simultaneous implementation in all units of the group will enable us to design and produce innovative, quality products, delivered on time at the lowest cost.'[27]   Only a few statements were found regarding product safety and testing claims. One such example was that made by Volkswagen which highlight the car's safety features including the air bag system. Very few examples were found of statements aimed at stakeholders in the wider community. One notable exception, in the UK, was the community report of Grand Metropolitan which detailed aspects of its involvement with community groups, schools, and the operation of the Grandmet trust. Also highlighted were its partnerships with TEC's, schools and teachers, the scope and nature of its charitable donations, and the innovative programme of employee volunteering operating in the company. As Gray, Owen and Adams conclude in their survey, 'The lack of detailed attention given to community and ethical reporting by companies speaks of the relative lack of power wielded - or lack of interest exhibited - by non-environmental and non-employee stakeholders.'[28]

Nevertheless, the frequency and volume of reporting on these aspects of company impact has increased in recent years and looks set to increase still further in the future. Legislation emanating from the EU will be an important driver for change, as will the growing size and scope of the ethical investment funds which are searching for companies to place their funds in if the companies are prepared to be more transparent about their operations. Several pace setting and visionary companies can be identified as pushing the frontiers forward in their approach to social accountability and have already built up a reputation for imagination and ambition in this area.

The Body Shop's social auditing

The Body Shop, as guided by the enigmatic Anita Roddick, committed itself to a formal social audit process in 1993 and has since produced two Values Reports, one on 1995 and another in 1998. In the first social audit the company tried to measure its own performance against its mission statement, trading charter and other policies that existed on health and safety, human resources, and fair trade.[29] The company had already set up auditing processes to report on animal testing and the environment, so its first social audit was restricted to human stakeholders who it thought might be affected by its actions. The stakeholder groups included for the purposes of evaluation were: directly employed staff, international and UK franchisees, customers, suppliers, community trade suppliers, shareholders, the local community in Littlehampton, UK non-governmental organisations and charity applicants. Its method of performance measurement involved holding focus groups to identify issues for each group, and then distributing questionnaires. These were then analysed and added to documentary information in the company. The process was developed partly in collaboration with the New Economics Foundation (NEF) with the aim of establishing a new standard for conducting social auditing. The NEF also provided the Report with a verification statement. The format chosen for the Body Shop's first Social Statement was based on a stakeholder model, with each group given its own section in the report. In summary the report noted that the company needed to pay more attention to its relationships with franchises. The employees strongly supported the Body Shop's ethical stance, but they were not satisfied with the level of staff development they were receiving. Its Values Report was published in 1995 and in addition to the Social Statement included the Environmental and Animal Protection Reports. The process was undertaken again and a second Values Report issued in 1997 as a single document, structured in a stakeholder format but with an attempt to integrate the information on environmental and animal protection alongside. The Body Shop has invested considerable amounts of time and resources to the process and comprehensive reports have been produced. It is questionable whether the Values Report is a feasible document for other firms to emulate, but the Body Shop claims to have learnt a lot from the process. It claims it has led to an increased understanding of the company's identity, greater understanding of various stakeholders needs and aspirations, better communications, and improved business decision making. Nevertheless, it cautions others who are following in their footsteps to plan the process carefully, get expert advice on how to conduct the audit, and not allow one stakeholder voice to outweigh others. Interestingly, key personnel who helped conduct the audits have published a book on how to conduct this process and have been seconded to KPMG to set up its own social auditing service. KPMG, one of the 'big five' accounting firms is, in conjunction with the Body Shop, also setting up a new group, Sustainability Advisory Services, which will offer advice on risk assessment, supply chain management, and social and green reporting.[30] KPMG has agreed to meet all Body Shops non-financial audit needs for the next four years in return for its know-how in what is an expanding area of professional services. A survey conducted by PIRC in 1999, of 98 of the FTSE 100 companies found that 79 reported in some way on social and community issues and 14 had produced a dedicated report.[31]

The Co-operative Bank's partnership reports

The Co-op Bank was created in 1872 as part of the Rochdale Pioneers Co-operative Movement. In recent years it has re-invigorated its appeal by becoming one of the first banks to offer free banking and in 1992, after analysing some market research on ethical attitudes, launched an ethical banking policy aimed at securing its long-standing customers and at gaining new business. The bank committed itself to a range of self-imposed restrictions on its investments. For example: it will not invest in repressive regimes abroad; finance the manufacture and sale of weapons; provide financial services to tobacco product manufactures; invest in exploitative factory farming methods, fur trading, blood sports, drug trafficking or money laundering. It also aims to seek out and support fair trade and firms that have a pro-active stance on the environment, and pledges not to speculate against the pound in the currency markets. The policy has been aggressively marketed and has been spectacularly successful, generating a lot of new customers and improving the profitability of the Bank in every year since the policy was declared. In 1997, the Bank won a prestigious Corporate Conscience Award from the Council on Economic Priorities in the USA. Its first Partnership Report was published in 1998 so that its ethical claims could be held up for scrutiny.[32] The report was conducted by an outside consultant in an audit process that considered the various Bank partners: staff, customers, suppliers and the wider community. The Report attempts to measure the extent to which the Bank delivers value to its partners and assess whether it lives to its social responsibilities as well as meeting the claims made in its ethical mission statement. The audit process involved the conducting of interviews, sending out questionnaires and then analysing the results. The staff response to the survey was low; only 30% sent the 12 page questionnaire back. The results were that: the Bank appears to do very little recycling of waste products; only has 1.8% of its staff drawn from ethnic minorities; only 20% of its middle managers and 8% of its mainly female workforce are women. However, 89% of staff said they were proud to be employed by the Bank; 67% of current customers said they were very satisfied with the service; and all of its suppliers rated the Bank as very or quite prompt in paying its bills. In terms of the ethical policy, the Report concludes that the Bank follows through on commitments not to finance the arms trade, oppressive regimes, exploitative factory farming, the fur trade, blood sports or businesses that use animals for testing cosmetics. The procedures for implementing the Bank's ethical policy were also checked and the decisions to refuse to take on new customers scrutinised to see that it was for reasons specified, such as involvement with environmental damage or animal welfare.

Conclusions

For companies that trade upon their ethical reputations, the auditing and reporting of the veracity of their claims is a very important part of preserving their reputation, which will always be under scrutiny as it represents a high-risk business strategy in very competitive markets for reputations and brands. Research from the Future Foundation in 1997, found that companies operating in a responsible way are nearly always more successful in commercial terms because this has an impact on customer trust and perceptions.[33] Corporate community involvement has grow markedly in the past few years with many businesses claiming that it is not just philanthropy but also good for profits and company morale. Business in the Community has seen its membership increase to include three-quarters of the FTSE 100 members.[34] Many firms are working with schools, communities, development agencies, and charities in partnership to help and improve their reputations. Among the many spin-offs claimed for this activity are that it improves relationships with governments at home and abroad, improves the quality of the workforce the firm is able to attract, can be a useful vehicle for staff development and importantly can create better relationships with customers. The scale and scope of this activity is now considerable. However, the Institute of Business Ethics also found that many companies failed to put into effect their codes of ethical practice, and often its content was unknown to staff or customers.[35] Another drawback from the accounting perspective is that company annual reports are becoming very unwieldy documents containing not just information for shareholders but increasingly stakeholders, environmental reports and marketing communications. The average number of pages in a report is now 42, sending up the costs of printing and distribution.[36] It is, therefore, highly likely that reports in electronic format will be used in future and an attempt made via the Internet to make them more user friendly and interactive.[37]

In competitive global markets consumers are interested in more aspects of the purchasing decision than just the price; they are increasingly interested in the ethical stance of the company behind the brand name they buy. Many companies are building a reputation based upon higher standards of social responsibility which need to be verified and reported upon. The movement to audit this activity and account for the expenditures and investment involved is bound to increase, and it will probably become a formal requirement of the accounting system for larger companies. All the trends are moving in this direction, driving the company form into new areas of activity and disclosure. Social Accountability Standards are coming into existence for this purpose. SA 8000 was launched in 1998, and is awarded to companies that meet verifiable standards of social accountability in the areas of child labour, forced labour, health and safety, freedom of association, discrimination, disciplinary practices, working hours, compensation and management systems. It is modelled on the ISO 9000 and ISO 14000 Standards for manufacturing quality systems and environmental quality systems. It can only be a matter of time before other standards for corporate community involvement are developed and they are made a formal accounting requirement for companies. This is likely to take the issue of social responsibility into the main stream of corporate strategy thinking in larger companies, particularly if the legitimacy crisis continues to develop.

References

1   Tawney, R.H., (1921), *The Acquisitive Society*, London, G.Bell and Sons, p82.

2   Ruskin, J., (1860), *Unto this Last*, London, Dent.

3   Bowen, R. H., (1953), *Social Responsibilities of the Businessman*, New York, Harper.

4   Carson, R., (1962), *Silent Spring*, Boston, Houghton Mifflin.

5   Freidman, M., (1970), 'The Social Responsibility of Business is to Increase its Profits', *New York Times Magazine*, pp 32-33, 122, 124, 126.

6   Gray, R., Owen, D. and Adams, C., (1996), *Accounting and Accountability*, London, Prentice Hall.

7   Ibid.

8   Ibid, p 111.

9   Ibid, p 112.

10 Ibid, p117.

11 Likert, R., (1967), *The Human Organisation*, New York: McGraw Hill.

12 Roslender, R. and Dyson, J., (1992), 'Accounting for the worth of employees: a new look at an old problem', *British Accounting Review*, 24:4, pp 311-329.

13 National Power Report and Accounts (1999), London.

14 Railtrack Group PLC, Annual Report and Accounts (1999), London.

15 Lane, T., (1987), 'Economic democracy: are trade unions equipped?', *Industrial Relations Journal*, 18: 4, pp 322-329.

16 Trades Union Congress, (1991), *Greening the Workplace*, London, TUC.

17 Lyall, D., (1982), 'Disclosure practices in employee reports', *Accountants Magazine*, July, pp 246-248.

[18] Accounting Standards Committee, (1975), *The Corporate Report*, London, ICAEW.

[19] Ibid, para 6.12.

[20] Gray, et al, op cit.

[21] *Financial Times*, (1997), 'Drive to end company law deadlock', 14th May.

[22] *Financial Times*, (1997), 'Call for companies league table', 12th November.

[23] Cowton, C., (1999), 'Playing by the rules: ethical criteria at an ethical investment fund', *Business Ethics: A European Review*, 8: 1, pp 60-69.

[24] Royal Society of Arts, (1995), *Tomorrow's Company*, London.

[25] *Financial Times*, (1996), 'Fund to target corporate governance', 18th November.

[26] Gray, et al, op cit.

[27] Ibid, p 207.

[28] Ibid, p 211.

[29] Wheeler, D. and Sillanpaa, M., (1997), *The Stakeholder Corporation*, London, Pitman.

[30] *Financial Times*, (1998), 'KPMG and Body Shop link to offer ethical auditing', 7th December.

[31] *Observer*, (1999), 'Canny companies come clean', 27th June.

[32] *Financial Times*, (1998), 'Holier-than-thou bank's ethical audit', 15th April.

[33] Future Foundation, (1997), *The Responsible Organisation*, London.

[34] *Financial Times*, (1999), 'Business in the Community', 16th July.

[35] *Financial Times*, (1998), 'Ethical codes of practice not being implemented', 1st December.

[36] *The Company Report Report*, (1997), Peter Prowse Associates, London.

[37] *Financial Times*, (1998), 'Interactive annual reports urged', 3rd March.

5

Responing to Green and Human Rights Challenges

'The best modern businesses know that consumers and employees are interested in the good they did as well as the goods they made.'[1]

Introduction

This chapter will examine the changes in company accountability brought about in the face of challenges from the environmental lobby and human rights activists. The trend has been for firms to make incremental changes in their approach to environmental reporting and policies over the last 30 years, and major changes in the past five years as pressure has mounted for greater corporate responsibility in this area. The human rights record of many multinational companies is now coming under the spotlight and looks to be developing in much the same way. The significance of both these trends will be assessed in terms of the kind of changes this is impressing upon the company form. In this respect the focus of attention will once again be upon formal reporting requirements and the development of procedures and standards that are likely to become mandatory for all companies.

The development of green awareness in companies

Environmental management has been emerging for some time now and can be said to have passed through a number of stages in the consciousness of companies. The response of companies to this issue lends some support to the theory of evolution of the company form outlined in chapter 1. Pressure on companies to reply to environmental concerns can be seen to have evolved from industry-focused concerns to government regulation, to pressure from environmental activists, investors, insurance companies and competitors. In response, companies have begun to shift from a reactive stance aimed at the resistance of environmental concerns in the 1960s, to trying to actively manage them in the 1990s. The company's interest in greener management has in turn shifted from being the ancillary duty of a small sub-section of the engineering department towards the centre of corporate strategy-making by the senior executives. A brief explanation of how this change has come about will now be given, based upon the pioneering analysis of Andrew Hoffman in the USA.[2]

Hoffman, in trying to account for this widespread change of stance on the part of large numbers of western companies, dismisses the orthodox explanation that this is just a response to the cost of regulation and the need of companies to prevent further regulations. He claims this factor may be part of the explanation but the pattern of change is so dramatic that it marks out a fundamental shift in the behaviour of companies. His study of the chemical and petroleum industries in the USA shows that the changes in corporate environmentalism bear little correlation to the trends in the costs of regulation. Instead of the trajectory of the cost of regulation rising in a linear fashion, it has risen in a cyclical way more in relation to public opinion than anything else. This research indicates that public concern over environmental issues rose dramatically in the 1960s and reached a peak in the early 1970s, but that it declined considerably in the later 1970s. Then, in the 1980s, a significant and steady increase in both public awareness and public support for environmental campaigns is apparent, a trend which has gone on rising in the 1990s quite markedly. These trends in public opinion correlate closely to the trends in company attention to environmental issues and the initiatives they have taken on green management. Hoffman thus claims that a more plausible explanation for these events is that the 'greening of industry' follows public opinion rather than changes in costs and the regulatory framework. This contention is quite the contrary of conventional economic explanation of the trends in this field.

Hoffman's second argument to support this contentions is that, if the costs or regulations were the primary drivers of green initiatives in industry, then it might be reasonable to expect that most companies would move in step in technical expenditures to comply with the law on regulatory matters, but that there would be less of a common line in moving beyond the requirements of a regulatory regime. In fact, it appears that most firms made shifts beyond the requirements of the regulatory requirements in relative unison, by establishing environmental management teams with often the same structures and purposes at almost the same time. Hoffman characterises firms as seeming to behave in a 'clannish fashion', evolving through waves of common structures and responses. This explanation supports the conjecture that the greening of companies is more socially determined than economically determined.

Hoffman's own thesis is that, in companies where the environment is changing rapidly, issues are not 'objectively defined by individual firms but are socially defined by the firm's external environment - the collection of organisations that are influential in the formation and allocation of individual norms.'[3] He goes on in his study to claim that the key assumptions of economists about the profit-maximising nature of the firm should be rejected and the institutional view taken. This is, that 'the firm is a socially based organisation, seeking the subjective goals of survival and legitimacy.'[4] Executives in the determination of strategy and structure in a company may choose from a repertoire of possible actions, but although they may think they are making autonomous actions they are in fact often bounded by a range of rules, norms and beliefs in the organisations field. Various actors make up the organisations field, pressure groups, leading companies, government, competitors. It is from these groups that dominant conceptions of environmental management emerge. As the membership of the organisations field grows, the rules, norms and beliefs in this field evolve to reflect their combined interests. These institutional norms are in turn reflected in the operation cultures of the companies in this field and manifest themselves in decisions about the internal structure of the company in relation to these norms. Consequently, a study of organisational fields and these institutional processes gives an interesting insight into the limits on the range of options available and helps us understand the degree of uniformity to the behaviour of individual companies in environmental management amongst other areas.

Hoffman's account of how this change has progressed relative uniformity in the USA can be summarised as follows. From 1960 until 1970, industrial environmentalism was the main response of the corporation which existed alone in the organisations field, defining environmental management according to its own perspectives. The company took initiatives on environmental matters on an ad hoc basis and assigned responsibility for these actions to an ancillary department in relation to the mainline operations of the business. In 1970, this approach was replaced by regulatory environmentalism, a regime which lasted up until 1982. During this period government in the form of the Environmental Protection Agency (EPA) became the legitimate arbiter of what was defined as acceptable environmental management. The agency was, in fact, a mediating body that helped to negotiate between the pressures of green activist groups and the interests of industry over what constituted acceptable environmental practices in industry. Companies, in response to the agency, tended to set up special departments to deal with the agency along segmented lines (air, water) and they in time became departments of regulatory compliance. From 1982 until 1988, company environmentalism was redefined but this time in the guise of social responsibility. The legitimacy of the EPA was challenged by green pressure groups and companies began to seek cooperation with the government to find internally-based solutions to environmental problems. Consequently, within the company, environmental management became more integrated into operations functions and new management structures were created to manage these affairs.

In the most recent period from 1988, Hoffman characterises this phase as a movement into strategic environmentalism. The companies organisational field has expended to include investors, insurance companies and industry competitors. These forces have resulted in firms adopting a proactive strategy towards environmental management, taking them beyond the objectives of regulatory requirements to begin setting environmental objectives based upon more ambitious aspirations. Consequently, environmental responsibilities have began to diffuse into most departments in the company, so that economic competitiveness and environmental management are beginning to be the joint concerns of many executives.

Hoffman does not claim that this model of understanding the trajectory of the development of environmental management can lead to firm predictions about the future. However, he does note that the embrace of greater environmental concern in companies is not a signal to dismantle regulatory requirements. In the institutional perspective these regulatory regimes are an important part of the system of forces which, if removed, would upset the balance of pressures in the system and lead to unintended results. In this respect, regulative and normative institutions form a kind of base line upon which more imaginative initiatives can grow. In terms of imaginative developments in environmental management, Hoffman does offer some speculative comments on the prospects of achieving sustainable development. Sustainable development tries to take concern with environmental wastes one step further by also analysing process inputs and product development. An analysis has to be made not only of the damage that the by-products of industrial activity make on the environment but also the damage that all human activity inflicts on the resource base that future generations will inherit. However, there are different concepts of what sustainable development will require of companies. At the moment they are often outside the present organisational field. But Hoffman contends that, in time, the tensions will mount and a crisis will emerge that could result in a change in the organisation field and a change in its norms which will begin to bring about further changes in the company's response and strategies of environmental management.

External events are likely to determine when this crisis will take place and who will win out. Hoffman puts forward three scenarios. First, different views about sustainable development could enter into the organisational field by the force of an unpredictable event, one that shows up the contradictions in the existing institutional balance, such as the Bhopal disaster in 1984. In this respect the process of change could be rapid and chaotic with companies responding to events rather than being proactive. Second, the unorthodox perspectives on sustainable development could force themselves into the organisation field by careful campaigning and by utilising events opportunistically. The outcomes in this case will be more certain and the adjustments be more predictable amongst the contending groups in the organisation field. The third scenario is that the alternative views on sustainable development will remain outside the organisational field, will not achieve the necessary support and backing of public opinion and will eventually subside. Hoffman does not indicate which scenario will most likely win out; the movement of history is too uncertain. Nevertheless, his analysis of the process of change is encapsulated in his concluding remarks:

> How companies define their responsibility toward the environment is a direct reflection of how society views the environmental issue and thus of how the organisational field defines the role of business in responding to it. Evolving perspectives of what constitutes heresy and what constitutes dogma in a given industry depend not just on costs and regulation but on the full social, political, and economic system of which the industry is a part.[5]

The test of a good theory is to apply it to another case; in many respects the evolution of the company form in recent year would appear to be following the concerns of public opinion rather than economic imperatives. In the following section the development of environmental reporting in Europe, and in the UK in particular, will be briefly surveyed to see if it moves in a similar way to Hoffman's model.

European environmental reporting

In 1972, the state of the world's environment as a whole was discussed for the first time at a United Nations Conference on the Human Environment in Stockholm. Since then the publication of numerous reports on the limits to pollution growth, and resource depletion, and environmental damage and pollution have been presented in world forums, such as the Earth Summit in Rio de Janerio in 1992 and Earth Summit 2 in Kyoto in 1997. Environmental reporting in Europe began to develop in significant terms in the 1980s and early 1990s. In the late 1990s there has been a very marked increase in this kind of reporting as more and more groups have entered the organisation field of European companies. Most importantly, the development of the EU itself and cross-national regulations are a major spur in this trend; together with the green pressure groups, green political parties, insurance companies, ethical investors and national governments. The formulation of a common environmental policy in the European Economic area in 1992 was a key development. This policy required the signatory nations to preserve and protect and improve the quality of the environment; contribute towards protecting human health; and ensure a prudent utilisation of natural resources. Where possible preventative action should be taken, environmental damage should be restored as a matter of priority and the principle rule is that the 'polluter should pay'. However, the position regarding the acts of individual companies was not included in the regulations. More company-specific proposals from the EU have been included in the Commission's Fifth Action Programme on the Environment called 'Towards Sustainability 1992'. This asks companies to:

- disclose in their annual reports details of their environmental policy and programmes and the likely effects of the company's impact on the environment;
- detail in their accounts the expenses on environmental initiatives;
- make provision in their accounts for environmental risks and expenses;
- introduce product pricing based upon full cost of production including the use of natural resources.

In 1993, the EU introduced its Environmental Management and Audit Scheme (EMAS) to be adopted on a voluntary basis and enabling companies to use a eco-logo when in compliance. Under this initiative companies are asked to:

- set their own objectives for environmental performance and develop management systems to meet these objectives;
- begin a series of eco-auditing to assess their environmental performance and to provide the information to improve their environmental management systems;
- demonstrate commitment to externally validated assessment of their progress in meeting their objectives, and publish reports to interested parties.

The publication of environmental statements by companies should include:

- a description of the company's impacts on various locations;
- an assessment of all the significant issues in relation to the environment;
- the company's environmental policy, strategy and management systems;

- the date of the next statement;
- a summary of the statistics on pollutant emissions, waste generation, consumption of raw materials, energy, water and the generation of noise;
- other significant environmental aspects as appropriate;
- and the name of the company's accredited environmental verifier.

Despite the fact that these requirements were not compulsory, by the mid-1990s national regulations requiring company disclosure on environmental matters were appearing in Denmark, the Netherlands, and the Scandinavian countries. In the UK, requirements for environmental reporting are moving more slowly. A statement of good practice was issued by the Hundred Group of Finance Directors, which was later endorsed by the Department of Environment, this required companies to issue a minimum of one page of environmental information in the firm's annual reports.[6] The CBI , London Stock Exchange and professional accounting bodies have also called for practices of voluntary environmental reporting. However, as yet, there is no legal requirement to do so. In terms of actual disclosure, the most widespread reporting takes place in German companies followed by Swedish companies.

In the UK, surveys of environmental reporting by firms points to the fact that this activity was mainly confined to large companies in the early days.[7] But since the 1980s, there has been a clear rise in the proportion of large firms disclosing environmental information and some increase in the quantity of information disclosed. A comprehensive survey of more than 600 UK company's annual reports in 1996 by the Edinburgh-based financial reporting monitor, Company Reporting, indicated that there had been an 'explosion' of environmental data reporting but that much of this was not very useful information.[8] The survey noted that there is no inherent discipline in environmental reporting, many of the disclosures are a 'free-for -all' of statements, percentages, volumes, and monetary figures, carefully selected but not necessarily enabling comparisons among companies to be drawn. A striking example of the problem was highlighted in the report, regarding how much companies spend on environmental protection. These figures were often difficult to identify in the accounts. Shell for instance issued this statement, 'The costs of prevention, control abatement or elimination of releases into the air and water and disposal and handling of wastes at operating facilities are considered to be an ordinary part of carrying on business...'[9] They were therefore not accounted for separately. Many types of environmental disclosure were found in the survey: 29% of the sample made environmental disclosures; 18% made substantive statements; 14%, while setting targets, did not quantify them; 6% mentioned environmental audits; and just 2% of companies quantified targets in non-monetary terms. Different disclosure trends were apparent in various industrial sectors: most sectors tended to provide information on energy reduction, raw materials, recycling, waste management and emission of harmful substances; the building industry and engineering sectors gave the most substantive statement; the oil and gas sectors had the greatest tendency to disclose costs and provisions linked to environmental protection. Over 50 companies in the sample issued separate environmental reports and another 50 planed to do so in the near future. However, only 26% of the sample companies mentioned an audit or the use of external verifiers for the information disclosed; this makes the meaningful comparison of data in these reports difficult to make. Calls from the Association of Chartered Certified Accountants for common standards to be adopted in environmental reporting were made to government in 1998.[10] In its study of the matter, the ACCA recommended that a common standard could be achieved by a combination of government action, initiatives by international standards and rating organisations, and inter-firm competition. This process could mirror the development of standardised financial performance measures from similarly unpromising circumstances in the last century. The ACCA have asked the government to set basic standards on raw materials, energy consumption, emissions of waste and pollution, as there is no agreement on how to measure and report on these environmental issues. The government duly responded by asking companies to make greater disclosures on a voluntary basis otherwise legislative action would be forthcoming. However, the use of environmental performance indicators is bedevilled by the difficulty of finding standard measures that are appropriate for different sorts of companies.

A survey of FTSE 100 companies published in 1999 by Business in the Environment which puts its findings into an Index of Corporate Environmental Engagement, found that the average score for these companies on the ten environmental management parameters measured by the index had risen to 75% in 1998, from 60% in 1996, and 67% in 1997.[11] The parameters range from whether the company has a board member with environmental responsibility to whether it considers the environmental impact of its products and processes. Business in the Environment concluded that 'the index is achieving its primary aim of helping to encourage environmental management integration into mainstream business.'[12] However, participation in the exercise has been patchy; fewer than one in five of the FTSE Mid-250 companies responded to the survey, and around 20% of the FTSE 100 companies refused to take part.

There is a variety of different systems of environmental reporting in European companies at the moment. Gray, Owen and Adams group them into three categories for analysis: descriptive and performance reporting;

quantitative environmental accounts; and financial environmental reporting.[13] Companies in the UK tended to have the mainly descriptive environmental reports setting out policies, and activities, and some statistics on emissions control and energy savings. This kind of report was also prominent in other European countries. The main weakness of these reports is that they do not enable the reader to assess the extent of the firm's impact on the environment and the degree of progress to be made. In terms of quantitative environmental reporting, which attempts to provide a more comprehensive picture of the company's environmental impact, the more innovative reports are German, Swedish, Danish and Austrian. Reports produced by some companies in these countries not only described the firm's environmental policy and its production of eco-friendly products, but also tried to show the resources used and the efficiency with which they were employed. In other words, some kind of input-output analysis; showing all the inputs of energy and raw materials and then the outputs of products and emissions to the environment. In the final category, financial environmental accounts, some pioneering companies had attempted to account for their environmental impacts by putting a financial cost on them and then subtracting this from the financial gain arising from its activities.

In the UK the Body Shop PLC in its ground-breaking set of social accounts has perhaps taken this process to a new level. Although an excellent example of what can be achieved with leadership support, the more widespread adoption of these practices will clearly need a more statutory/regulatory spur, together with a further heightening of public opinion on green issues. Answering the question of whether it pays to be green could also provide another spur for companies to take action. A study by a European consortium of companies is trying to gather evidence on the matter.[14] The members are ICI, Volvo, Unilever, Monsanto, Deutsche Bank, Elextrolux and Gerling. The study has been underway for two years and an interim Report, 'Sustainable Strategies for Value Creation', was published in 1999, showing that improving environmental compliance and developing eco-friendly products can enhance earnings per share and profitability. The report notes that 'Investors are beginning to look at the downside risk of investing in companies that are either only just complying with environmental law or those companies that make empty mission statements about it.'[15]

Another factor putting pressure on companies to increase their levels of environmental reporting is the growth of ethical and environmental investment funds in the USA and Europe. These funds were launched onto the market in the USA in the 1970s and then into Europe in the 1980s and 90s. In the UK, one of the first funds was Friends Provident Stewardship, created in June 1984.[16] Fund managers have declared to investors that they will adhere to certain investment criteria in addition to rate of return for the investment of these funds; typically performance factors considered are heavily weighted in terms of environmental issues. Fund managers have to conduct or rely upon expert research to guide them on their investment choices. Consequently, the more companies that are prepared to disclose and can provide verification about their environmental claims, the more attractive these firms will be to the fund managers. As the size of these investment funds grows more and more companies will probably want to be the recipients of this kind of investment, creating a self-fulfilling cycle of environmental and sustainability reporting. Whilst the impact of these funds could be exaggerated in relation to the market for investment funds available worldwide, it may be that a snowball effect can be created as pension funds and national and local government funds are increasingly more sensitive to the social impact of their investments. In 1999, pension funds in the UK reversed their opposition to rules requiring the disclosure of their ethical and environmental stance to pension fund trustees.[17] Friends of the Earth immediately announced a campaign to encourage members of company pension schemes to write to their trustees and withdraw the investment made in some companies with poor environmental records. Some estimate that the pool of funds that is directed towards socially responsible investment is now in the region of 10 billion sterling in the UK today.[18] Collectively, this pool of financial pressure will act as another driver for the improvement of accounting information on the company's environmental impact.

Another factor moving companies in the direction of greater environmental and social reporting is the Social Audit Movement. Social Audit Ltd was formed by the great social entrepreneur Michael Young in 1971, as a not-for-profit organisation concerned with improving government and corporate responsiveness to the needs of the public. A variety of interested parties have made use of these reports over the years, but they have not had the lasting impact that the founders of the movement hoped they would have. However, a whole host of other groups have come onto the scene since then to put pressure on company environmental disclosure and accountability: Friends of the Earth, Greenpeace, the Consumers' Association, New Consumer, the Prince of Wales Business Leader Forum, the World Bank, the World Business Council for Sustainable Development, and Pensions and Investments Research Consultants (PIRC). The latter organisation presented a shareholders' resolution at the London meeting of Royal Dutch Shell company demanding the oil group publish externally verified reports on its environmental and ethical conduct.[19] Even when such resolutions are defeated the pressure group argues that it makes other institutional investors take note and brings informal pressure to bear upon the company. In fact the case of Shell and its volt-face on environmental consciousness is worth exploring in a little more detail.

Shell's green baptism at the hands of Greenpeace

In 1995, Shell was forced to abandon plans to dispose of, in the Atlantic, its partly-owned oil storage platform called the Brent Star used in the North sea. This was as a result of the actions of the environmental campaign group Greenpeace.[20] The company had gained agreement that this course of action was the 'best practicable environmental option' with the government in Britain by carrying out a full environmental risk assessment on the consequences for maritime pollution in the Atlantic ocean. However, Greenpeace in an imaginative and daring campaign occupied the rig at sea and conducted a publicity campaign against the dumping with the full glare of the world media upon them. As events unfolded consumer boycotts and arson attacks on petrol station forecourts put pressure on the company, particularly in Germany. It became apparent that this was not just a local UK issue but a European issue and in the event Shell was forced to cut its losses and back down in the face of the campaign much to the embarrassment of the British government and the company's own board of directors, shareholders and employees. The controversy was compounded a few weeks later when Greenpeace admitted that it has made mistakes in publicising the amount of oil residue left in the rig. Nevertheless, Greenpeace's successful public relations attack was a unique event in British environmental politics. For the first time, an environmental pressure group has catalysed international public opinion to bring about the kind of change that unsettled the very basis of management authority. The lessons have rippled out into the boardrooms of other multinationals such as Monsanto, Dow Chemical, Unilever, and BP.

Shell's plight was compounded a few months later when the company found itself on the defensive again after the execution by Nigeria's military government of minority rights activist Ken Sarowiwa. The company's record in Nigeria came under intense public scrutiny and it was even mocked for not withdrawing its investments from the country by Anita Roddick the founder of the Body Shop, in the *Financial Times*.[21] The battering of Shell's reputation has resulted in a fundamental company restructuring programme to change the corporate culture and transform its approach to strategy and performance. The change programme aims to reduce the company's bureaucratic organisation, focus more closely on customers and markets, take personnel diversity more seriously and increase the number of senior women managers from 4% to 20%, and pay much more attention to public relations and stakeholders.[22] In 1998, it published a new statement of General Business Principles accompanied by a values report, 'Profits and Principles', launched by an expensive advertising (£15 million) campaign to bring it to the public's attention on the Internet, and print media. The Report emphasises that Shell cares about what its customers think about them and expresses the intention to enter into a process of dialogue with its customers and listen to their concerns. A second report, 'People, Planet and Profits: an act of commitment', was published in 1999 providing extensive detail on Shell's approach to sustainable development, social investment and a verification statement.[23] The reader is invited to judge Shell on the progress it makes in keeping to a 'road map' it set itself in its first report. In public relations terms and from the point of view of management thinking this is a dramatic turnaround in approach and responsiveness to the new agenda. Only time and rigorous verification statements will show if this is merely window dressing or real commitment on behalf a new Shell.

BP also gets the message

Shell's predicament was noted with concern by the other British oil company, BP, in 1997. The chief executive, Sir John Browne announced in a speech in California that BP was committing itself to creating a new and more environmentally-aware approach to sustainable development.[24] It had just faced problems over alleged violations of human rights in its operations in Columbia, and a brush with Greenpeace in the Atlantic over its camp perched on Rockall to prevent BP from being allowed to search for oil in the western approaches. A new statement of environmental and ethical principles was published soon afterwards and a regional directorate created to ensure that its principles are adhered to by all its operations. The company called for energy conservation measures and argued that precautionary action in the short term be taken to meet any public targets on carbon dioxide and other greenhouse gas emissions. The motivation for the change in stance was described by Sir John Browne in an interview as arising from four reasons: first that they appreciate that action to improve the environment needs to be taken; second that BP staff want to work for a firm which reflects their view of the world, third that BP's customers and host governments want the company to be green; and finally that it has the technical capacity to rise to the challenge.[25] The Company has therefore declare it has a responsibility to act to reduce carbon emissions and contain the risk of global warming. This is when most oil companies in the world are still in denial about the very existence of climate change and are lobbying hard against curbs on the burning of fossil fuels. BP is committing itself to monitor carbon dioxide emissions, rather than rely on simulations, as a first step to controlling them. Second, it will develop its solar activities into a going concern within a decade. Thirdly, BP will support scientific exploration of cause and effect in global warning. And finally, it will back policy instruments such as carbon taxes to reduce petrol consumption more generally. Once again if these changes are followed through by BP then public pressure will mount for them to become more universally applied and the company form will be pulled out further in this direction.

Reporting on human rights issues

Towards the end of the apartheid regime in South Africa there was some concern to establish the degree of involvement and relationship of European firms to this country. The EC issued a Code of Conduct applying to firms with operations in South Africa that required them to submit information on trade union rights and collective bargaining, pay, migrant labour, equal opportunities, fringe benefits and desegregation to the appropriate government departments in member states, together with a statement in the annual report that this report was available for inspection. Apart from this, the attempts to limit trade with countries or regimes that are in violation of international treaties on human rights has been limited and piecemeal with little common agreement in the EU as an economic and political entity.

In the UK in recent times, an ethical policy for companies doing business overseas has been proposed by the Labour Government's Foreign Secretary, Robin Cook. The Foreign Office's global citizenship unit is to produce a manual to advise on best practice for companies on protecting the environment abroad and in taking responsibility on matters such as human rights and child labour.[26]

Most of the pressure to get companies to take their responsibilities seriously on human rights protection is coming from pressure groups and customers. For example, the pressure group the World Development Movement recently claimed that Rio Tinto, the world's biggest mining group, was steamrollering through the lands of the indigenous peoples of Indonesia and wanted the government to step in and take action against the company in the UK.[27] Amnesty International has asked consumers to avoid British retailers who are buying their produce from exploited third world farm workers on multinational company plantations.[28] Human rights concerns are set to become a growing issue and, in the case of Shell and BP, one that they are already taking very seriously. Human rights violations have often been regarded as a product of domestic politics and therefore beyond the sphere of influence of international companies. But with the globalisation of the economy and the sourcing of consumer products in the developing world and the increasing role and influence of multinationals as the engines of economic development, companies can no longer stand aside with impunity in a critical world in which communications of what they do is immediate. Retailers who contract to buy products from tens of thousands of sources in the developing world, confront in their supply chains potential problems of child labour, debt slavery, hostility to trade unions, sweatshops, starvation wages and discrimination. Companies making direct investments in foreign countries face the threat of their security arrangements having an adverse impact and of being accused of complicity if they are seen to benefit from silence in the face of oppression. So far only a few companies such as Body Shop, Levi Strauss, Toys R Us, Avon Cosmetics and the Co-op Bank have built human rights commitments into their decision-making policies, but slowly this number is likely to be increasing as campaigning groups search for the way to make this a Brent Spar-type campaign. Some pressure is coming from consumers through the supermarkets and other stores in the field of clothing, footwear, toys, sports goods and cosmetics. The initiative of the Council on Economic Priorities, a New York based research consultancy, has drawn up the SA 8000 Social Accountability Standard for measuring the ethical commitment of companies in this area.[29] SA 8000 sets out specific provisions on issues such as trade union rights, the use of child labour, working hours, health and safety at work, and fair pay and conditions, as well as the necessary management systems to deliver them. Each company applying for certification will be given independent verification by an outside auditor such as SGS-ICS, the world's largest certification company. The standard is modelled on the quality standards and based upon conventions laid down by the International Labour Organisation, the Universal Declaration of Human Rights, and the United Nations Convention on the Rights of the Child. SA 8000 has other elements to help with social auditing: the auditors are required to talk to and learn from interested parties - trade unions, workers and charities etc., and a complaints and appeals process allows for interested parties to bring up issues of non-compliance at certified companies. Accreditation is valid for a span of three years, with surveillance and observation audits every six months, covering each and every country where the certification body audits ten or more companies. It can only be a matter of time before the call for companies to publish comprehensive information on their compliance with the likes of SA 8000 will be felt in the corporate world more generally. The leading charities, Save the Children, Cafod, and the Worldwide Fund for Nature made a joint submission to the Modern Company Law Review calling for the government to make companies comply with the standard in 1999.[30]

Conclusions

It may take some time for it to happen but it is very likely that companies will come to accept that they should care about human rights and the environment because that is the best way for them to go on making money. This is not an ethical position but a pragmatic one. Some companies will commit themselves to caring about these principles because they are genuinely motivated by an ethical concern, but these firms will probably be in the minority. The demands of many pressure groups, investors, governments, and customers may well, in the long run, put the requirements of social accountability into the framework of company law either through offering incentives or by making such requirement compulsory. Larger companies will then be obliged to consider the environment and show respect for human rights as a condition of operating in the company form. Public companies will not have simple objectives; their management's will have to make trade-offs and strike balances among the objectives that are pursued. The company form will become a complex and sophisticated mechanism in which privileges and obligations will have to co-exist. The institutionalisation of the company may well have evolve into a much more sophisticated form of semi-public property.

To understand the momentum that is building for a reappraisal of the company form, an examination of the trends leading towards the creation of an information society, is the task of the next chapter.

References

[1]   Blair, T., (1999), 'Blair praises social responsibility', *Financial Times,*London, 16th July.

[2]   Hoffman, A.J., (1997), *From Heresy to Dogma: An Institutional History of Corporate Environmentalism*, San Fransisco, The New Lexington Press.

[3]   Ibid, p 7.

[4]   Ibid, p 13.

[5]   Ibid, p 197.

[6]   Gray, R., Owen, D. and Adams, C., (1996), *Accounting and Accountability*, London: Prentice Hall., p 98.

[7]   Ibid.

[8]   Company Reporting, (1996), *Environmental Reporting*, Edinburgh.

[9]   Ibid.

[10]   ACCA, (1998), *Environment under the Spoltlight*, Glasgow, ACCA.

[11]   *Financial Times*, (1999), 'Measure of progress in the works', 21st June.

[12]   Ibid.

[13]   Gray, et al, op cit, p 174.

[14]   *Financial Times*, (1999), 'Greener profit drivers', 28th April.

[15]   Ibid.

[16] Cowton, C.J., (1999), 'Playing by the rules: ethical criteria at an ethical investment fund', *Business Ethics: A European Review*, 8: 1, pp 60-69.

[17] *Financial Times*, (1999), 'Pension funds end opposition to rules on ethical stance', 2nd July.

[18] Gray, et al, op cit, p 252.

[19] PIRC, (1998), *Environmental and Social reporting: a Survey of Current Practice at FTSE 350 Companies*, London, PIRC.

[20] *Financial Times*, (1995), 'Greenpeace admits Brent Spar blunder', 6th September.

[21] *Financial Times*, (1996), 'Body Shop challenges Shell to confront new business reality', 31st October.

[22] *Financial Times*, (1998), 'Oiling the group's wheels of change', 31st March.

[23] Shell Report, (1999), *People, Planet and Profits: an act of commitment*, London.

[24] *New Statesman*, (1997), 'Interview: John Browne', 4th July.

[25] Ibid.

[26] *Financial Times*, (1999), 'Cook plans ethics guide for companies', 2nd January.

[27] *Financial Times*, (1999), 'Multinationals attacked over child labour', 5th July.

[28] *Financial Times*, (1998), 'Amnesty questions ethics of multinationals', 22nd April.

[29] *Financial Times*, (1998), 'Standard to verify business ethics launched', 11th June.

[30] *Financial Times*, (1999), 'Companies urged to issue social performance data', 8th June.

6

chapter six

Forces shaping future companies

'Predictions? No. These are the implications of a future that has already happened."[1]

Introduction

The evolution of the company form has been examined historically, and some of the pressures mounting in the contemporary scene have been noted. It is now time to look towards the future and at the drivers of change that are likely to shape the company form still further. The relationship of companies to society is very important for determining their form and operations; if society changes then so will the company. It is important therefore to try to understand the nature of the social forces that are shaping our society and then to try to gauge the implications for the trajectory of the company. Engaging in speculation about the future is always a dangerous and foolhardy exercise but it can at least help stimulate thought and debate. It is the contention of this book that we are entering a new period of discussion about joint-stock politics and the contribution companies can make to the common good. The reasons why this is an important debate and some speculation about the various positions taken in this debate will be outlined at the end of the chapter. First, a brief overview of the changes that are shaping our society.

The new informational society

There is a bewildering array of literature on the nature of modern society and whether we should describe it as post-modern or not. However, some accounts of the nature of society stand out for their scholarship, clarity and depth of vision. One of the most accomplished works of sociology in recent times, leading to its comparison with the works of Max Weber, is the three volume study of Manuel Castells, *The Information Age: economy, society and culture.*[2]

According to Castells we have entered a new era: the era of informational capitalism. There are several distinctive features of this new society; one of its defining structures is the network. Today, the   generation of wealth, the exercise of power and the generation of cultural symbols all rely upon the information-processing capacity of society. The main mechanism forming the material foundation of this change is the move towards networking as a form of organisation in economic and social life. Networking came to prominence after the need to restructure capitalist economies was begun in the mid-1970s. This has, through a number of emergent processes, led to the creation of a new form of capitalism, 'global capitalism', which is characterised by rapid change, dispersal of production centres and much greater organisational flexibility. These changes have in turn lead to changes in the nature of the welfare state, the weakening of the trade union movement, and the fragmentation of the labour market. Information technologies have helped to facilitate this change by providing tools for networking, distant communications, storing information, coordinating the composition of work, and both concentration and decentralising the decision making in companies.

The movement to globalization has allowed new areas of the world to become competitive and to take a bigger share of world trade. The Pacific Rim countries, despite a recent recession, have become world players in the new world capitalism. In contrast, areas of the world have remained excluded from these changes, isolated from networks of capital, labour, information and markets. This has meant that sometimes the only connection they can make to the world market is, in Castells' term, a 'perverse connection', that is, through criminal activity in the supply of drugs, sex and other outlawed commodities. In the second world of communism, the difficulties of restructuring the command state led to economic stagnation and a weakening of its military power and the collapse of the Soviet empire. The only remaining statist regime, China, has had to open itself up to try to incorporate global capitalism on the basis of a nationalistic policy of modernisation. Whether it will be able to make the transition to informationalism with in the parameters of statism remains to be seen.

It would seem that for the first time in history common patterns of economic life are developing.   However, cultural differences remain and societies react to these developments in different ways: in some cases a cultural elite have broken away from the mass of society with values based upon cosmopolitanism and internationalism and an apparent autonomy from the rest of society; on the other hand there are increasingly insecure and uncertain social groups, excluded from information, resources and power and forming resistance identities against the processes of globalisation. According to Castells, a new society is taking shape, based upon new relationships of production , power and experience.

The relationships of production

These have been changed in social and technical terms. The key drivers of change in the global economy are competitiveness and productivity. Competitiveness comes from flexibility and improved productivity comes from innovation. Firms in the economy try to generate the maximum degree of innovation and flexibility with the use of information technology. Castells calls firms that have mastered the changes needed 'network enterprises' as they strive for adaptation and enhance coordination at the same time in their operating systems. The labour factor of production is much more differentiated into what he calls 'self-programmable' and 'generic' labour, the difference between the two being the degree of education and cultural adaptability. The generic labour is much more likely to be replaced by machines or by competitive pricing in the world labour market and so has a less secure and poorly remunerated outlook. Organisational flexibility in the network firm requires subcontracting and a wide variety of contractual arrangements, making the labour factor much more individualised and difficult to organise into trade unions.

Besides the transformation of workers in the labour market, capital is also transformed into three categories: holders of property rights, the managerial class and the global financial markets. The holders of property rights are of mainly three sorts: shareholders of companies, family owners, and individual entrepreneurs. Whilst Schumpeter thought that the latter would be an extinct class in the future, the creation of informationalism has meant that those who can innovate and display flexibility have been able to flourish in the new global markets, adding to the ranks of the entrepreneurial class. The second rank of capital is, however, that of the top management of both private and state-owned companies who are often highly remunerated and major share owners in their companies. The third level of profit appropriators is that of the global financial markets, which have the technical capacity to scan markets in search of the best returns and the ability to enter and leave at the click of a mouse. A new form of uncertainty begins to plague markets that can be scanned by restless capital funds and on occasion a market collapse can be triggered by these massive movements of capital. Castells calls global financial markets the nerve centres of informational capitalism because their movements determine the value of stocks, bonds, and currencies, bringing about booms and busts. The logic of these markets is uncertain and at times irrational, exhibiting a mass psychology and great turbulence owing to the speed at which computer-generated selling can take place.

The relationship between capital and labour has changed in a number of ways: a greater increase in social inequality and polarisation in the labour market; greater social exclusion of some workers; and the generation of a new class of workers who own their own capital in the form of knowledge.

The relationships of power

The nation state as an entity is under question and this is leading to a crisis of political democracy. Globalisation reduces the power of the state over many aspects of economic life and this tends to frustrate the electorate who wish the state to take action on their behalf to manage the welfare of the people. This in turn puts the institutions of politics into question and various strategies of decentralisation and internationalisation make the geometry of power relationships ever more complicated. Under these conditions informational politics using the mass media become the dominant mode of politics. Politics becomes more like a theatre and political institutions become bargaining agencies rather than cites of power. This, in turn, tends to make citizens cynical about the political process and less interested in participation. Power is therefore vested in cultural codes through which people and institutions represent life and make decisions, including political decisions. The fears of an electorate can be manipulated through the media and associated with various images and meanings, for example immigration and crime, race and poverty and conflict. Culture is the new form of power and is manipulated through the mass media which is a source of capital.

The relationships of experience

There is a criticism of patriarchalism, which in turn takes the form of a change in our notions of family, gender, sexuality and personality. Patriarchal authority is being challenged throughout the world because of the structural changes in global markets (calling for many more women workers) and because of the impact of social movements (feminism, and sexual liberation). The future of the family is uncertain as patriarchal authority looses state support and new egalitarian forms of the family come into being. Networks of people are replacing nuclear families as primary groups and centres of emotional support but single parent families are also growing in number. These new patterns will alter socialisation and consequently the nature of characters in society. Castells sees this leading to the development of 'flexible personalities' who are able to engage endlessly in the reconstruction of the self, rather than to define themselves through adaptation to what were once conventional social roles, which are not longer viable and so have ceased to make sense.

Changes in these three types of relationship (production, power and experience) slowly begin to transform the material basis of social life and space and time. Castells claims that the space of flows of information begins to dominate the spaces of people's cultures. By this he means that time in a society can be put out of sequence and its history disrupted creating a culture of 'virtuality'. Where previously history was created by a people in the same space and time in the new era of informationalism, a new sense of history is emerging from the superseding of places and the annihilation of time. A good example of this was the series of events that were triggered off after four Los Angeles policemen were accused of viciously beating Rodney King, a black motorist, who was being arrested for motoring offences. When this incident was captured on video tape by a passing witness and then shown on television, riots broke out in cities across the USA and in some other parts of the world in protest at the treatment of this black man. A local event was the cause of national and international spontaneous rioting. People's sense of reality can now be grounded in the setting of virtual images that are outside of their local sense of space and time, in symbols that are actual rather than metaphorical. In the network society, all societies are to some extent penetrated by the logic of the virtuality of space and time. Challenges to this order are arising from the reactive construction of autonomous identities of groups who feel themselves at odds with these trends. The logic of the information age is so pervasive that the only way of opposing it is to stay out of these networks and construct new lifestyles on the basis of different values and beliefs. Most prominent therefore are religious fundamentalism and new forms of nationalism based upon ethnic identity; their strength lies in their separation from the state, and the logic of capitalism and technology. They are hard to co-opt into participatory institutions and even in defeat they bring about a change in society. In network society, social classes are diminished and instead we have the rise of tribes and a fragmentation of life styles and experience.

In terms of the future, Castells outlines in broad brush strokes how things might develop. The new millennium will be dominated by a global information highway and by mobile computing and telecommunications technology. These will increase the power of interactive computing and allow for the grater decentralisation of informational power in society. The century will also see the fruits of genetic engineering harvested through the manipulation of biological matter, allowing us to heal the sick and improve the fertility of the earth. However, all technologies, it ought to be acknowledged, give man the potential to do evil as well as good. Biological and computing power can also be used for the purposes of death and destruction if we are not careful. The particular danger is that these new sources of power are not under centralised control, and so could fall into the hands of fanatical groups with few inhibitions about using them against civilian populations.

The technological productive power of the new information economy will increase enormously. New concepts and procedures for accounting in industry will be needed to measure the performance of this new economy. More will be produced from less labour input and a much higher levels of quality. As Drucker predicted, 'knowledge workers' will replace manual workers in most areas of the economy. Consequently, the distribution of the rewards from work will depend to a large extent upon levels of education and skill and the redistribution mechanisms made possible by the welfare state in a society. The global economy will continue to expand and grow to take in most countries in the world, but in a selective way. Valuable sectors in a economy will be linked into the global network but unproductive sectors will be left out. Valuable and left-out sectors will be found everywhere in the world, in all countries. Rather like the difference between some street blocks in New York, in the space of a few meters the complexion of the neighbourhood can change dramatically from relative affluence to intimidating squalor. The world may be split into segments and distinct spaces defined by different time regimes, some local, some global. Those in the excluded spaces may connect with global capitalism through a criminal connection, or may turn completely against the included and re-affirm their excluded identities and alternative lifestyles.

In the face of fragmentation, nation states will lose sovereignty, but will gain power by grouping together in multilateral networks, the most complex of which is likely to be the EU. The global economy may be governed by technocratic elite who preside over a set of multilateral institutions such as the G-7, IMF, WTO and World Bank, who are to oversee regulation and crisis state interventions on behalf of the world players in global capitalism. International politics will probably be steered by a set of multilateral institutions guided by the UN and other regional and international institutions. Security alliances will come to dominate and take on a policing function in international and national conflicts. Three issues are likely to be important for peace: the first is the place of China as it grows in power and seeks to influence its region of the Pacific; the second, is the integration of Russia into the global market system as it begins to stabilise; the third, is the threat to peace posed by small groups and criminal gangs at odds with the prevailing regime and prepared to use the new forms of terror and warfare that new technology will make available. Informational society may be sophisticated, but could be vulnerable to disruption from many sources, particularly from groups who are prepared to take risks and inflict terror and uncertainly on the many. The only global superpower for a long time to come is likely to be the USA, and few international peace keeping actions will be able to take place without their support or participation. Other nation states may be still influential, but will have to contend with the intricacies of regional and devolved power structures, as well as the negotiations of multinational alliances. Globalisation of the economy is likely to be matched by localisation of politics within the nation state. Local and regional areas will become more flexible and use the power of networks to maintain their competitive positions in the economic sphere. People will be more individualised in their working lives, and have less confidence in political participation as forces to influence their lifestyles. There will be more inequality, and less support for traditional patterns of experience. Castells does not see the future as the coming of a new dark age, but more likely the dawning of an informed bewilderment.

This outline of the changes that are taking place in social structures and experience together with Castells' informative speculation about the trends at the highest level of politics, provides some broad parameters for a consideration of the impact this might have upon the corporate form. The next section will attempt to answer the following question. What are the key features of the global economy that will influence the nature of tomorrow's business practice, and how will these impact on the debate about the best way to institutionalise business organisations in society? As was noted, one of the key players in the global economy, in Castells' view, will be the 'network enterprises' and the characteristics of these will be described in more detail below.

Networks and business

The intensification of economic competition together with the development of information technology are driving the search for new business strategies and organisational forms. Two key responses can be identified: uncertainty in markets has been coped with by the creation of flexibility in production, operations and marketing; and, management changes have been introduced aimed at creating lean production, and producing higher quality with less inputs.

First, the movement from mass production to flexible production noted by many commentators has been labelled the transition from Fordism to post-Fordism. The former was based on productivity gains from economies of scale and assembly line production and mechanised processes leading to standardised products and mass consumer marketing. The company form best suited to this was the large company based upon a functional division of labour and specialist functions. When demand began to fluctuate and became less predictable, with greater expectations and more market segmentation, a more flexible production system was felt to be needed. One approach to this was to develop flexible specialisation where production is made adaptable to market changes by producing small batches and changing designs more frequently. Another approach was to introduce high-volume flexible production systems which enjoy economies of scale, but are reprogrammed to produce new products when required. This system allows the large company to dominate the industry. However, the large company has not managed to stay dominant in some sectors of industry. Small and medium-sized firms in many sectors have gained an edge by innovation and flexibility. The experience in northern Italy has been that the movement to flexible specialisation may be best handled by a return to smaller, customised craft production firms working in close networks. To accommodate this, many large firms have taken advantage of sub-contracting processes to ensure that small firms deliver the innovation and cost benefits that can be incorporated in the large firms production functions. The large firm therefore adopts the form of a holding company or multi-divisional structure, to ensure that it can retake advantage of the flexibility and adaptability needed to face uncertain and highly competitive markets.

The second development that has changed companies has been the adoption of new management methods, most of them originating mainly from the example of Japanese companies.   The 'lean production' ideas from the Japanese car producers have been labelled 'Toyotism' in contrast to the 'Fordist' and 'Taylorist' ideas that dominated mass production systems in the west. Toyotism is said to have begun in Japan in 1948, and is composed of several elements: a just-in-time system of component supplies, eliminating the need for inventory stocks; total quality control of the production process aiming at few, if any, product defects and the most efficient use of raw materials and waste reduction; worker involvement and participation in the management process, worker empowerment and team working and rewards for improved performance. Whilst the model may have been developed in Japan, it does not need to be practised in Japan for its benefits to be realised. It is Fordism improved. The firm in this model sits upon a network of supplier relationships which allows for greater differentiation of the labour and capital inputs and at the same time allows greater incentives and responsibility to be exercised without the need for vertical integration within the company. Of course the model relies on there being little or no disruption in the production and distribution process: that is, no defective parts, no breakdowns in machines, no inventory, no delays, and no paper work. Consequently, to manage this system efficiently requires that uncertainty is reduced and that relationships run smoothly. This is not an adaptable system but one that controls uncertainty by putting flexibility into the process, not into the product. Workers are not just specialists in a division of labour; they are put into multi-functional teams, are able to cope with local problems and are able to use their initiatives. They are workers, who work hard, and think hard too: they are 'knowledge workers' in Drucker's sense of the term.

These ideas, in the hands of other commentators, have also been described as those that characterise the 'learning company' which maintains its competitiveness throughout its use of knowledge.[3] This phrase is born out of the realisation that knowledge in a firm is of two kinds: explicit and tacit, each of which is discovered at the point of production. The knowledge accumulated in the company is gained from personal experience and cannot be articulated by workers controlled in a formal hierarchy. When workers are managed in teams with a sense of empowerment, bridges between workers are built along which this tacit knowledge can travel, leading eventually to the accumulation of knowledge in the company as a community which can then be used to advantage against the competition. In an economic system, where innovation and efficiency are critical, the company's ability to increase its sources of knowledge that can be shared and stored becomes an important component of competitive advantage. But the sharing of this tacit worker knowledge when combined with explicit knowledge requires the generation of trust inside the company, which implies good industrial relations and job security for the workforce. In some societies these are difficult aspects of the management process to get right.

'Knowledge management' also means that companies derive competitive advantage from learning faster than their competitors.[4] It can cover a wide range of activities in a wide range of business sectors, but its common attribute is the sharing of information in the firm. At its most mundane, it can be a simple as writing down contact telephone numbers on a list and sending it to everyone who can make use of it in the company. Or it can mean that management attempts to capture the unwritten routines that make the organisation function, attempts to code them, and then attempts to make them into an expert system on a computer to be used as a general organisational resource. In theory, this should then be of use to other workers to help them improve their own performance and, accumulatively, the collective performance of the firm. The company has to appreciate that knowledge is not a 'thing', but a constant flow of information. It is essential, therefore, that the firm has a strategy that brings together people, processes, and technology in a programme of cultural integration. Once the data base of knowledge has been created, it then has to be applied creatively to improve customer service and the business' performance.

What is new about this approach is that knowledge is being used and managed like any other asset; in fact, it becomes 'the' asset. This raises issues regarding the estimation of value in the firm because the problem is now about how to account for this asset in the balance sheet. 'Intellectual capital' to coin an expression, will need to be measured and reported. Performance indicators in this area such as customer satisfaction, staff turnover, market share, attainment of quality targets need to be developed. As yet there are few accounting standards or conventions in existence to deal with these issues. The companies knowledge management systems have to make information available at the right time, to the right people and at the right price. Turning tacit knowledge into explicit information in data bases is very challenging, because workers must be persuaded to input and share their own knowledge. The firm has to move from the orthodox patterns of organisation towards flat structures and team-based working in order to get the right culture for sharing, and for information to flow freely. If the main asset of the company is knowledge rather than financial resources, this can only be partially owned in the old sense of the term. Consequently, the notion of shareholders as the property owners of the capital in the company may have to be compromised, and the new owners of the intellectual capital in the firm enfranchised. If this knowledge is mainly in the worker's head then they may have to be included as the intellectual capital of the business, but if it can be stored on computer then this might not be the case. Labour may then, under the right circumstances, change its status as a mere factor of production into a key capital asset and might, therefore, have to be accorded a partial ownership stake in the company. This could herald profound changes in the nature of corporate governance appropriate to informational capitalism.

In the new global economy, flexibility of response to market demands as a firm's competitive edge can also be gained from inter-firm networking. This is potentially a useful strategy for the small firm in its contest with bigger firms, and involves linking the firm up in a network of small firms, and finding market niches and cooperative ventures to pursue. This is the model of business that has succeeded so well in Hong Kong and amongst the wider Chinese Diaspora in the Pacific Rim countries.[5]

Larger companies are now exploiting the power of networks by forming strategic alliances in some business sectors. They are particularly useful in areas where the cost of research and development is high, or where capital investment is 'lumpy' and needs to be substantial. Some companies have been encouraged to enter into alliances as the result of government incentives and subsidies, as in the case of microelectronics and defence products, for example. The strategic alliances of the large firms can also include those of their smaller firms as sub-contractors. Few companies today are totally self- reliant; most have a cooperative relationship with other firms and, therefore, need to be able to develop the capacity to foster trust relationships as well as competitive strategies.   The ability to work with others requires that the governance mechanisms of the firm are more transparent and predictable and, as such, configured so that one firm will not take advantage of the other firm's openness for self-seeking reasons. The implication here is that other stakeholder interests, such as alliance firms or suppliers, will need to be recognised and their interests taken account of in relation to the shareholders' proprietorial rights in the governance system of the company. The cultivation of the relationship with the network will be as important as the cultivation of the relationship with shareholders.

Many companies are changing their models of organisation to partly reflect these trends of market volatility, uncertainty and rapid technological change.

Their models of organisation structure have moved from vertical bureaucracies to flat collections of teams: the latter are characterised by a process focus, low hierarchy, team coordination, sharp focus on customer satisfaction, the close management of suppliers, attention to information sharing, and intensive employee training at all levels. To be able to internalise the benefits of network flexibility the company has had to become an internal network itself and energise each element in its organisational structure. An element of internal competition is often required within the organisation that is striving to meet a common objective. This may sound like the management of a contradiction, given the need to share information mentioned above. However, this is the long-standing advice contained in the writings of the management gurus, who have for some time been encouraging companies to make these changes. As early as 1982, Peters and Waterman's advice to managers in their best selling book, *In Search of Excellence*, was to operate a 'loose-tight' control structure in the company.[6] Strategy formulation also had to be different and the notion of cross-border strategies were being urged upon the company. Companies that operated in a variety of domestic markets were advised to use this information between markets in their business strategies and trade across market borders. The term the 'individualised corporation' has recently been coined by Ghoshal and Bartlett to describe this new approach, where the actual operating units of the corporation become the focus of strategy formation, and are then combined into an inter-company network.[7] This type of company is then able to innovate and adapt itself to markets that change in a relentlessly changing configuration of units. Information circulation in these companies become a crucial central management task; in essence, the creation of the inter-company network within the company. Information technology is decisive in allowing such networks to develop, with the operating units held together by the efforts and shared culture of its leadership elite, who must travel relentlessly in this role and try to build the trust and commitment across the organisation to keep the network together and functioning efficiently. The company in this model has to work effectively as a network of multifunctional decision-making centres which, if successful, is an extremely flexible structure, and avoids the problem of lack if fit between what the market wants and what resources were available in the company.

Most of the new thinking in strategic management is concentrated upon the challenge of combining organisational flexibility and coordination capabilities to ensure both innovation and continuity in a fast-changing market place. These new models of business organisation are all variations on utilising networking concepts.[8] Networked enterprises will increasingly come into competition with each other and with older types of organisational models, whether the network models or only one version of it will become dominate, or whether they all will merely co-exist with each other, only time will tell. If the network models become the dominant business organisations, then the challenge of having to reshape the framework of corporate governance and company law to recognise the stakeholders' interests that these new models have to balance, will have to be taken up. A new era of joint-stock politics may be dawning, where the interests of owners of factors of production in the company are having to come to new agreements. It is towards furthering this debate that the final chapters of the book will be devoted. Prior to this, however, an important feature of informational capitalism needs to be focused upon as it might provide some indication of what might be one of the decisive factors in shaping the joint-stock politics debate. This feature is the role of social capital in maintaining an informational society.

Social capital recovery

From the picture that has been sketched out above, it can be seen that the trajectory of global capitalism will be different from its past, and that the nature and form of the company is likely to change under pressure from the market, and as the result of changes in knowledge and technology. However, it will be argued, that these are not fully-determining processes. Besides the economic and the informational dimensions of society, there are the political and social dimensions that will also play a part in shaping the company of the future. It is contended that the role of social capital in furthering the development of the information age could prove to be decisive.

Social capital is a term that has been coined by many commentators to describe the norms of trust and social reciprocation that are essential to maintain a civil society. The recent work of Francis Fukuyama has brought it to a much wider audience but he, in turn, acknowledges that the concept is derived from the sociological theory of James S. Coleman, the writer on architecture and urban affairs, Jane Jacobs, and more recently the political scientist Robert Putnam.[9] If capital is understood to be property and money, and human capital is the investment in human knowledge and skills, social capital is the term now used to describe the relationships of trust which bind people together. Social capital is intangible and relational but nonetheless as important for social welfare than property capital. Fukuyama's definition of social capital is 'the existence of a certain set of informal values or norms shared among members of a group that permit co-operation among them.'[10] He points out that the sharing of values and norms does not necessarily produce social capital because the values may be perverse and the cooperation used for malign purposes, as for example in the case of the Mafia. The bonds the produce social capital must be more virtuous (such as truth-telling, promise keeping, and reciprocation), and must be directed towards worthy ends. Social capital is not a pervasive feature of all societies; it tends to reside in affiliation groups and is distributed in various amounts in different societies. The family is a very important source of social capital generation, and this is so in many other types of centres of affiliation such as clubs, churches, trade unions, political parties and, importantly, companies.

Robert Putnam's interesting study of civil engagement in different regions of Italy showed that the quality of governance was determined by the longstanding traditions of civil engagement, or its absence. He measured voter turnout, newspaper readership, membership in choral societies and football clubs as the proxy indicators of a successful region. He concluded: 'In fact, historical analysis suggested that these networks of organised reciprocity and civic solidarity, far from being an epiphenomenon of socioeconomic modernisation, were a precondition for it.'[11] When he returned home he set about trying to measure the degree of civil engagement that existed in contemporary America. His now famous article, 'Bowling Alone: America's Declining Social Capital', announced that the quality of collective life in the USA was in decline because the post-war generations were weaned on television and were forsaking the traditional forms of organised activity (bowling clubs, etc.) on which their parents and grandparents had spent their free time.[12] Whether television is the simple cause of this decline is debatable, but his general thesis, even if partly correct, has serious implications for society because membership of networks comprising formal associations or informal patterns of sociability are vital components of social connectedness. A connected community can alleviate many social problems and facilitate the implementation of various kinds of public policy, for instance by using trade unions to administer social welfare schemes. If social capital is depleted then society looses a valuable resource that can help to ameliorate the social disruption and disconnection that capitalism tends to leave in its wake. The current problem in Britain of the social exclusion of some sectors of the population is difficult to deal with because this social and moral infrastructure is lacking in many inner cities and poor rural areas. Many years ago, Jane Jacobs noted the failure of urban regeneration programmes in the USA; the philosophy of 'salvation by bricks' through re-building projects was ineffective without attention being paid to the cultural and moral depravation of the inner cities inhabitants.[13] Low levels of social capital tend to go hand in glove with low levels of political involvement and high levels of social cynicism. If families and other affiliation groups are allowed to erode generally, and the margins of society become completely disconnected as Castells has indicated, capitalism as a whole will eventually suffer. The task of maintaining and generating social capital is an important challenge that faces all social institutions, and particularly business institutions, for they are the main engines of creation and destruction in the global market.

Schumpeter's contribution to the development of the notion of social capital should be noted here. Although he did not invent this term, it is a recognisable concept in his work. Schumpeter derived an important insight from Marx in this respect, in that the economic process tends, over time, to become more socially dependent and this is reflected in peoples' characters. As Schumpeter notes:

> Capitalism does not merely mean that the housewife may influence production by her choice between peas and beans; or that the youngster may choose whether he wants to work in a factory or on a farm; or that the plant managers have some voice in deciding what and how to produce: it means a scheme of values, an attitude towards life, a civilisation - the civilisation of inequality and of the family fortune. This civilisation is rapidly passing away, however.[14]

What he meant by this is that modern societies have succeeded only because they have been able to live off several centuries of accumulated social capital. If capitalism cannot regenerate this stock of social capital then the technological and organisational aspects of economic activity are likely to become more socially controlled over time, and this in turn will change the psychology of people in business organisations. He anticipated that industrial property and organisation would become depersonalised, and that ownership would degenerate to stock and bond holding, with the executives of the firm acquiring the mind set of administrators. Over the course of time, the capitalist order would tend to destroy itself because of the operation of certain destructive processes, the most corrosive of which was the erosion of the scheme of values that underpins family life and social civilisation. This then leads to a loss of motivation and identity with capitalist values not only amongst the general population but amongst the business class itself. This change he felt would give rise to the general tendency in capitalist society for even greater demands for equality, security and regulation. Schumpeter's insight remains that the legitimacy of business firms is always under scrutiny, there is likely to be a growing critical public regarding the distribution of risks and rewards from business enterprise, and increasing pressure on governments to regulate and provide for the problems and insecurities generated by capitalist society. Legitimisation crises are possible focal points for the forward march of socialising tendencies upon the fortress of private property in the form of the company. The challenge that constantly faces businessmen is to justify and build the foundations of legitimate companies.

The legitimate company

The restoration of social capital and the legitimisation of contracts between business companies and society depends upon the maintenance of trust relationships. Trust is a risky investment and selfish behaviour has to be guarded against. One of the best ways to build trust and gain protection from deception is to make a commitment to abide by moral rules and restraints. In this way the feared war of all against all can be avoided and a cooperative improvement in conditions can be secured. Although we have not solved the free-rider problem implied by the question, 'why should I be moral?', there are good reasons why we, collectively, should be moral, based upon game theory and 'tit for tat' player strategies. If the reasons for a collective morality are compelling then, as members of affiliation groups, the question of individual conformity is less likely to arise. This may build into a general social demand that all the citizens abide by a moral code; this demand can also be made of society's corporate citizens too. Companies may be increasingly required to be socially responsible, and actively engage in building trust relationships in society. To be allowed to become public institutions they will have to show concern for and contribute to the public good as well as private gain. The example of Norman Bowie's recent book on *Business Ethics* is a good indicator of the nature of this important new social demand.[15] The question the book seeks to address is 'how would a business firm in a capitalist economy be structured and managed according to the principles of Kantian ethics?'. Bowie uses the three formulations of Kant's categorical imperative to address this question and argues for the following conclusions. First, that market interactions are morally permissible as long as they are consistent with the universalizability criteria and do not violate any other moral principles. Business is a morally acceptable method of creating and distributing wealth in society. Second, that the principle of respect for persons provides a set of moral obligations for those engaged in business such that they cannot treat employees as a commodity, like other assets of the business. This means that employees are worthy of respect and should not be coerced or deceived in any way: they should not be 'lied to', or 'cheated', or have 'their trust' undermined. He also argues that firms have to respect imperfect obligations towards employees to provide them with meaningful work. By this he means that work is to be freely chosen and will provide opportunities for the employee to exercise autonomy on the job; that the level of remuneration for the job is sufficient to help support the independence and well-being of the employee; that the work will help the employee develop rational capacities and not hinder moral development; and that the governance of the firm is not paternalistic but democratic and open to deliberation. The third formulation of the categorical imperative is that business should be a contributor to the kingdom of ends; that is it should be viewed as a collective effort and as a moral community as well as an instrumental association. This concept requires that stakeholder interests are considered prior to and during decision making. As Bowie formulates it, the company should comply with the following principles:

1. The firm should consider the interests of all the affected stakeholders in any decision it makes.

2. The firm should have those affected by the firm's rules and policies participate in the determination of those rules and policies before they are implemented.

3. It should not be the case that for all decisions the interests of one stakeholder take priority.

4. When a situation arises where it appears that the humanity of one set of stakeholders must be sacrificed for the humanity of another set of stakeholders, that decision cannot be made on the grounds that there is a greater number of stakeholders in the one group than in another.

5. No principle can be adopted which is inconsistent with the need to universalise principles or violates the humanity in the person of any stakeholder.

6. Every profit-making firm has an imperfect duty of beneficence.

7. Each business firm must establish procedures designed to insure that relations among stakeholders are governed by rules of justice. These rules are to be developed in accordance with principles 1-6 and must receive the endorsement of all stakeholders. They must be principles that can be publicly accepted and thus be objective in a Kantian sense.[16]

If these principles are to be taken seriously then the organisational implications are that authoritarian hierarchical structures and the extreme division of labour are no longer morally permissible. The inclusion of other stakeholders' interests and their representation in a more collegiate type of organisation are strongly implied by these moral arguments if the company is to be regarded as legitimate in society.

A period of transition

Social capital recovery and moral arguments may not be persuasive enough, however. Political and ideological considerations based upon property interests are probably the more powerful forces that will shape the future of the company. Some of the impetus towards a greater concern with business ethics, and the demand that companies learn to become more socially responsible, will be countered by calls for business to become more innovative, risk-taking and, ultimately, wealth generating. Supporters of the capitalist ethos and interests will argue strongly for the restoration of shareholder power over their property rights in the company, and that management accountability to shareholders, regarding how this property is used, are still essential prerequisites for the generation of wealth in society and ultimately for the preservation of political freedoms. This position can also be defended in democratic terms because it is claimed we are all, in some form or another, shareholders now. Widespread vicarious shareholding in the form of pensions, insurance policies and savings give most people a stake in the efficient management of the capitalist system, and, it is argued, the best way to serve the interest of everyone with such a stake is to ensure that more attention is paid by the company's management to delivering shareholder value.

The new joint-stock politics regarding corporate governance issues may well in their essentials revolve around the debate about property rights versus the need to rebuild and maintain social capital. If we put these together as two dimensions and divide each dimension into two positions, there are four possible scenarios that will indicate what the possible trajectories of the company form may be. These can be mapped out in a two by two matrix below.

The four possible future trajectories of the company form

Conditionality of property/ Social capital maintenance	Liberal	Communitarian
Low contribution	Restore	Reform
High contribution	Replace	Radical

The first dimension is the degree to which property rights are considered to be held under social conditionality. At one end of the dimension there is the liberal view that property is to be the exclusive and unalienable possession of the individual, that this right is absolute because it was acquired either by a contractual exchange under the law in the market place, or the property has been brought into being by an act or effort of the owner and therefore has become is his property. Or in addition that the entitlement is long-standing and of proven provenance, so that a challenge to such ownership would be doubtful and ultimately fruitless. In other words, the holding of property by the owner is exclusive and final. It follows from this that the holding of such property shall be also unconditional: that the property is to be undivided and the owner's right of use or appropriation of the property is only to be challenged if it interferes with the property or personal rights of other people. Owners shall be at liberty to destroy, change, and increase their property at will, and be under no restraint from the public or other citizens. In the case of property in the company in the form of shares, they can buy and sell this shareholding at any time, and without prior consultation with others. Shareholders may then create or wind-up companies at will under company law without reference to employees, customers, communities or other parties. The principle relationship between the owner of company shares and the management of the company is a fiduciary one, of the agent/principle sort. The form of the company is best understood in the liberal view as a nexus of contracts.

At the other end of this dimension is the view of a more communitarian political philosophy that maintains that property is to be owned and appropriated under various degrees of social conditionality. Personal property, cars, stereos, wrist watches, etc., are to be held in an unconditional and exclusive sense. But then other types of property which have a bigger impact upon social and communal life are to be held under various conditions of restraint and forbearance. These will restrict the degree of ownership and the rights of the owner to appropriate and do what they wish with this property. For example, owners of large tracts of land will be able to sell the land under certain conditions but will be restricted to whom they can sell it, what uses it can be put to, who can or cannot be allowed access to the land. When it comes to the company form, this could mean that, whilst shareholders are entitled to dividends and nominal ownership of the company, the sale of shares is a conditional process that will involve consultation with various stakeholders, rights of veto and delay to the sale and perhaps even the denial of sales in certain circumstances. Indeed it might involve the separation of shareholders' property rights and ownership and the collective ownership of the company form which is constituted as a trust with overriding powers over the shareholders.

The other dimension is the degree of social capital maintenance that the company is expected to contribute towards and help recover: a low contribution or a high contribution. Low social capital contributions on the part of the company will involve moderate changes to the form of the company which will modify its present constitution under the law, but not substantially change its function in society. Low levels of social capital maintenance might moderate social discontent to some extent and help to re-legitimise the company in society in the short term, but will not necessarily undermine its destructive tendencies over the longer term. High aspirations for business organisations in the rebuilding of social capital based upon them taking a greater role in supporting the social communities of society, and the need for moral order within it, will be more difficult to achieve, but would in the long run change the nature of capitalism more fundamentally. Which view comes to prevail will, to a large extent, depend upon which political processes and structural drivers gain dominance during periodic legitimization crises, where the powers of the state are often invoked to appease democratic discontent and the force of property interests in society are at their weakest.

Putting these two dimensions across each other, property against social capital, gives rise to four scenarios for the trajectory of the movement in the company form. The next four chapters will explore each scenario in turn and outline the arguments of some of the leading projectionists in each position.

References

[1] Drucker, P., (1998), *Peter Drucker on the Profession of Management*, Boston, Harvard Business School Press, p x.

[2] Castells, M., (1998), *The Information Age: Economy, Society and Culture*, (3 Volumes: The Rise of the Network Society; The Power of Identity; End of Millennium), Oxford, Blackwell.

[3] Senge, P. M., (1990), *The Fifth Discipline: The Art and Practice of the Learning Organization*, New York, Doubleday.

[4] Nonaka, 1. and Takeuchi, H., (1995), *The Knowledge-Creating Company*, London, Pitman.

[5] Redding, S.G., (1990), *The Spirit of Chinese Capitalism*, Berlin, de Gruyter.

[6] Peters, T. and Waterman, R., (1982), *In Search of Excellence*, New York, Harper Row.

[7] Ghoshal, G. Bartlett, C., (1997), *The Individualised Corporation*, London,Heinemann.

[8] Nohria, N. and Eccles, R., (1992), *Networks and Organisations: Structure, Form, and Action*, Boston, Harvard Business School Press.

9 Fukuyama, F., (1995), *Trust: the Social Virtues and the Creation of Prosperity*, New York, Free Press. Coleman, J. S., (1990), *Foundations of Social Theory*, Cambridge, Mass., Harvard University Press. Jacobs, J., (1992), *The Death and Life of Great American Cities*, New York, Vintage. Putnam, R., (1993), *Making Democracy Work: Civic Traditions in Modern Italy*, Princeton, Princeton University Press.

10 Fukuyama, F., (1999), *The Great Disruption*, London,Profile Books, p 16.

11 Putnam, op cit, p 251.

12 Putnam, R., (1995), 'Bowling alone: America's Declining Social Capital', *Journal of Demoracy*, 6, pp 664-682.

13 Jacobs, op cit.

14 Schumpeter, J., (1987), *Capitalism, Socialism and Democracy*, London, Counterpoint, p 425.

15 Bowie, N.E., (1999), *Business Ethics: A Kantian Perspective*, Oxford, Blackwell.

16 Ibid, p 90-91.

7

chapter seven

Radical Reform of the Company

'We are not what Hobbes and so many of his successors thought we were, isolated individuals pursuing self-interest, nor can a society be constructed on these lines. We have attachments and affiliations, loyalties and loves. These cannot be reduced to contractual alliances for the temporary pursuit of gain. They are covenantal, which is to say that they are both moral and fundamental: they enter into our identity, our understanding of the specific person we are.'[1]

Introduction

This chapter will set out the scenario for the position of the radical reform of the company form based upon a communitarian view of the conditionality of property rights, and the aspiration for a high contribution to the maintenance of social capital on the part of the company. The position of the communitarians on the question of private property and its conditionality will be outlined first. It is not possible to give a full literature review of all the contributions that might be loosely categorized under communitarian thinking, so a careful selection has been made of the work of three leading thinkers in this field. An exposition of these three proposals for the radical reform of the company should be sufficient for the character of this position to be appreciated and understood. A critique is not attempted in this chapter; this will be made in the final chapter, when all four scenarios will be evaluated, and the conclusions of this study will be drawn.

Communitarian property conditionality

Communitarians, on the whole, contend that the individual develops and can only flourish morally and politically within the context of a community.[2] In this respect, they dispute the liberal view that the principal task of government is to secure the liberties of private property and the rights of individuals. Their main criticism of the liberal stand point is that it takes an overly atomistic view of the individual in society by ignoring the fact that our sense of self is constituted by the various commitments and attachments that we enter into, which can only be set aside in abstraction and not in reality. Politics, for the communitarian, is, importantly, about the need to maintain and promote associations and commitments crucial to our sense of self, as well as trying to preserve the individual's powers of choice over their way of living. Communitarians are also aware of the importance of social context in the interpretation of principles and rules and are concerned that the liberal's abstract universalism will ignore these factors, leading to impractical solutions and policies out of kilter with the institutions and habits of people in a specific time and place. The communitarian political agenda, therefore, is concerned to rebuild the centres of association and community in our lives and to pay attention to the development of the virtues that are needed to make communities flourish. In the labour market, this makes them critical of 'greedy' employers who do not allow employees sufficient time or energy to be with and take responsibility for their families, and for the demands that firms make on employees for excessive mobility, and the weakening of company job security and the notion of loyalty in employment. Communitarians would like the firm to be recognized as an important community in the moral sense, besides its economic function of wealth creation. Therefore, the process of creation and destruction of firms is not something to be ignored, or its social and moral impact discounted. The company represents an important social institution in society, and is the concern of society if it begins not to deliver what is expected of it as a social institution. The incorporation of private property in the Companies Act is a necessary concern of politicians and the political process, and so, a balance has to be struck which will meet the needs of the community as well as the rights of shareholders. In this respect, the notion of property rights as overriding the interests of the community is a matter of secondary importance. A view, clearly at odds with the liberal position.

One of the problems communitarian thinking aims to overcome is the view of the firm which is institutionalized by economists and institutionalized by the law. This regards the company as a disposable and purely instrumental tool for the creation of wealth and ignores its aspects of endurance, community and substantive significance. The legal institutionalization of the company proscribes narrow accountabilities and limited responsibilities. The challenge for the communitarians is to open these up and to broaden our understanding of the social significance of business activity. The basic assumptions of the communitarian approach to the company is founded upon the notion of property not as a natural right and so at the foundation of all other rights, but of property rights as a social convention, the nature and extent of ownership being something that is defined by social norms and not something that is not fundamental or foundational. The intellectual case for this argument has been set out in detail by the democratic political theorist Robert Dahl.[3] His case for changing the ownership and control of the company and putting it on a democratic footing is perhaps the most eloquent and authoritative in this literature.

The introduction of economic democracy

In Dahl's book, *A Preface to Economic Democracy*, the arguments about the extension of democracy to economic enterprises are explored. Dahl asks, in effect, is it possible to find an alternative to corporate capitalism that would be just as efficient and would at the same time enhance the values of democracy, political equality and political liberty. Dahl is a firm believer in the 'right' of people to govern themselves in a democratic process when engaged in an associative venture. He rests the claim to this right on the validity of the following assumptions about the nature of human associations: that the group has a need to reach at least some collective decisions that will be binding on all members of the group; that these decisions are to be debated and then decided upon, after which they become binding upon everyone; that binding decisions ought to be made only by people who are subject to the decisions; that the good of each person is entitled to consideration; that each person is entitled to be the final judge of what is in their own interests; that all members of the group are in principle equal in matters of decision; and that scarce and valued things should be fairly allocated in the group as far as is possible. Where these criteria are met the group will be required to engage in a democratic process to become self-governing. This will involve the following: equal votes, effective participation, enlightened understanding, control of the agenda for deliberation by the demos, and inclusiveness. His argument is that people as a matter of right should be able to have a democratic process in any institution where these assumptions about human groups are valid.

An important question with regard to business organizations is whether the decisions of a business are binding upon employees in a way that is comparable with the laws of the democratic state. The two arguments defending the right of private property owners to control a firm are considered by Dahl and are both rejected. The first of these is the utilitarian argument that private ownership is, on balance, beneficial because the firm generates wealth that is then distributed to owners, employees and society more generally. However, he notes that if private ownership of firms is a utilitarian proposition then this has to be subordinate to the fundamental and inalienable right to self-government.

It is therefore up to a self-governing group to decide how far they wish to subject themselves to the demands of private owners or whether other arrangements are preferable. The second argument is that the right of property ownership is itself a natural and inalienable right that should be protected by the government, and so this natural right is prior to any notion of self-government. He deals with this argument by pointing out that property rights are as much social as natural in origin, therefore they should be subordinate to societies decision-making process, if a conflict of rights were to arise.

He then goes on to consider whether the democratic process should apply to associations formed by an economic enterprise. The problem with the present position regarding the right of private shareholders to control the affairs of the company is that the ideological justification for an agrarian regime of private property control has been transferred to a corporate capitalist regime. Thus an economic order that produced inequality in the distribution of economic and political resources acquired its legitimacy by clothing itself in the ideology of landlords' and tenants' rights to property. As a result the alternative to this system of control has rarely been considered. He points out that the claims of private property owners to control of the firm are based upon arguments that contain several non-sequitors, if the premises are as follows: everyone has a right to economic liberty; the right to economic liberty justifies a right to private property; a right to private property justifies a right to private ownership of firms; a right to privately-owned firms justifies privately-owned corporations of great size; a right to private ownership of firms cannot properly be curtailed by the democratic process.

The first statement can be accepted but it does not follow that the other four statements necessarily follow. So, the assumption that shareholders, by supplying the firm with capital, should then control the decision making of the firm is open to question. The supply of capital to the firm can in principle be separated from the rights of ownership and control of the firm. The two can be separated as issues without apparent detriment to either party: shareholders and employees of the company. Shareholders are investors in the company and rightly enjoy the returns to their investment but the members of the company are not owned as such and so are at liberty to govern themselves according to democratic processes. From his analysis Dahl concludes that the arguments supporting the fundamental right of private property over those of the right to self-government are all flawed, and that the right to private property is only justified as a right to a minimum collection of resources, those necessary to life, liberty and the pursuit of happiness, the democratic process and primary rights. The arguments for private property as a right do not justify the private ownership of corporate enterprises. Therefore, the members of the enterprise are entitled to decide by democratic means how the firm should be owned and controlled to achieve democratic values such as fairness, efficiency, and the distribution according to necessary criteria.

Dahl goes on to advocate an alternative system for economic governance in the firm. His basic premise is that all firms that are beyond the small business should be institutionalized as self-governing through a democratic process involving everyone who works in them. Each person in the firm would be entitled to one vote and only one vote in a democratic process that would determine how the revenues of the firm are to be allocated. The firms employees would constitute its demos of citizens who would decide wages and how surplus revenues are allocated, but in relation to the need for investment and the competitive environment of the firm. The hope is that this kind of firm would improve the quality of lives within the firm and without it in society. Dahl claims that the distribution of wages and salaries would be less unequal and that this would reduce the adversarial and conflictual relationship within the firm and indirectly in society and politics at large. But his main argument for the introduction of self-governing enterprises is a moral one: if democracy is justified in governing the state, then it is also justified in the government process inside the firm. Moreover if the democratic process in the management of the affairs of the state has some imperfection in it, this is no reason to abandon the democratic ideal within the firm. The democratic process might lead to some inefficiencies and oligarchic tendencies but this is a poor reason for abandoning the democratic aspiration in favour of an authoritarian hierarchy.

Dahl advocates a system of cooperative ownership in which the members of a self-governing enterprise would not have the rights to posses, use, manage, rent, sell alienate, destroy, or transmit portions of the firm as individuals. They would have these rights collectively, so that a share of the firm and its assets would be personal property but not private property. The question of leadership in the firm would be tackled by the election of managers for the running of the enterprise by the citizens. If innovation were to prove to be a problem then, in an economy of firms, entrepreneurial activity should be given sort-term incentives; for example a grace period of five years before the firm is put onto a self-governing footing. In order to move towards this system Dahl thinks that the Swedish method of wage-earner funds would be helpful. This is where legislation requires that a percentage of the firm's revenues are paid into a fund which buys the shares of the firm and reinvests the profits until the firm is owned by the workers in it. However, one does not gain the impression from reading his various books, advocating self-governing enterprises, that he is very optimistic that his rational arguments will prevail.

Let us now consider two more pragmatic proposals for a radical transformation in company form that build upon these arguments, both based upon a communitarian perspective. The first is from professor Paul Hirst and is taken from his book *Associative Democracy*.[4]

The company as an associative democracy

This book sets out to identify a third way to organize an advanced society, given that state socialism has collapsed and democratic capitalism has so many problems. Hirst's response is to return to the thinking of the associationalists who flourished after the first world war (Figgis, Cole, Laski) but whose voices were all but ignored after the second world war, when social democracy came to the fore. In the book, Hirst sets out the broad themes of this approach and has some specific proposals to make about the governance structure of the firm.

Hirst claims that the collapse of socialism and the weaknesses of democratic socialist societies means that a new set of ideas is needed to overcome the growing problems of democratic legitimacy, corruption, poverty, crime and drug addiction. His solution is to return to the publicly-funded but voluntary associations that will be able to work in partnership with the socially excluded or, as it is sometimes called, the 'underclass'. He claims that the socialists have failed this class by identifying welfare with state provision, constantly wanting more of it, and by marginalizing voluntary welfare groups as unnecessary. The new task is to build security and welfare through mutual associations and so create a healthy civil society. Associations can assist the excluded by helping them organize themselves and then funding projects to try to transform ghettos and slums and the corrosive cycles of dependency.

Associationalism is not just a recipe for the poor; the principle of association democracy is to be applied to the whole of society. Hirst claims that associationalism makes representative democracy accountable by limiting the scope of state bureaucracy without diminishing the social provision needed by an advanced society. It should enable a market society to deliver the aspirations of its citizens by grounding the market in a social network of cooperative and regulatory institutions. He thinks that this could be the political ideology the our societies are looking for: that is the prospect of radical reform to mobilize the political will to rebuild our institutions in line with modern aspirations. The principles of associational democracy are that individual liberty and human well-being are both best served when many of the affairs of the community are organized and managed by democratic voluntary associations. A balance is to be struck between the maximum amount of individual freedom and the effective governance of communal affairs. Individualism is to be conditional upon the need for social fellowship and support; individual choice is to be combined with the public provision of collectivism. Associations are important checks on centres of power and need the protection of the law and a certain amount of public funding through taxation in order to maintain their independence. Associationalism allows for a plurality of groups, norms and values, as long as they are supportive of the framework for an associationalist society which has a common set of public rules and regulatory institutions that try to manage conflicts between different groups and see that individual rights and liberties are preserved.

Hirst proposes three principles that should guide the construction of an associationalist political agenda: that voluntary self-governing associations gradually and progressively become the primary means of democratic governance of economic and social affairs; that power should as far as possible be distributed to distinct domains of authority, whether territorial or functional, and that administration within such domains should be devolved to the lowest level consistent with the effective governance of the affairs in question - these are the conjoint principles of state pluralism and of federation; that democratic governance does not consist just in the powers of citizen election or majority decision, but in the continuous flow of information between governors and the governed, whereby the former seek the consent and cooperation of the latter.[5]

Hirst's exposition in his book deals with how these principles are to be given expression in the present context, but for the purposes of this analysis the substance of his proposals for company governance will be examined.

Hirst acknowledges that there is, perhaps, no one best way to govern the firm; it is such a complex phenomena that the best that can be done is to recognize this fact and propose general principles. He also notes that a position advocating democratic workers control is no longer tenable because it does not deal adequately with the interests of other stakeholders and the practical record of worker-controlled firms is not impressive. He is optimistic that the changes in industrial structure in recent decades have demonstrated that the growing concentration of industry and the dominance of the large corporation is not an inexorable trend and that competitive markets can be served just as well by smaller, less hierarchical organizations. However, he is concerned about concentration of power in some multinational firms which is based not necessarily on the economies of scale, but on large investments in research and development and financial support networks. These structures of corporate power could pose a threat to the independence of associationalist society but he argues that intervention must be based upon criteria of economic efficiency rather than the need to democratize these organizations. As nationalization and regulations have been tried and have largely failed, his answer is to promote a general policy of economic decentralization and self-government in these firms. In respect of the corporate form, the problems are that it has degenerated into a largely unaccountable form of private privilege that is given the protection of the law, on the basis of limited liability, legal personality and corporate personality. Such is the dispersal of citizens' financial assets in financial institutions that there is, in effect, a diversity of ownership from control and most of the power of corporate property is effectively in the hands of management. Consequently, many companies are too powerful to be regarded as private associations that need to be transformed into organizations, that are more open to those involved in them and are to be governed by the participation of their various stakeholders. Public policy must be to encourage these firms to evolve into self-governing associations that are representative of their stakeholders, to continue to enjoy the privileges of company status under the law. Hirst then puts forward a proposal for new structures of corporate governance.

Company governance structures are to be incrementally democratized using a wide range of new funding mechanisms: alternative financial institutions to provide funds for more stakeholder-oriented companies, the creation of new cooperative firms drawing upon mutual funds and credit union. The forms of finance would be supported by national legislation giving them a privileged tax advantage for investors and for these firms provided they remain non-profitmaking. It is envisaged that building societies, churches and environmental groups would be key generators of firms and funding in this sector of the economy. The tax laws would also be changed to accommodate incentives for investments in manufacturing and other sectors of industrial under-investment, but concessions would be conditional upon democratization measures being undertaken, for example the recognition of trade unions and collective bargaining and the introduction of employee share ownership plans.

Multinational companies would be tackled in a different way. Public opinion would be an important vehicle of pressure for change in their governance practices and international concern at environmental and human rights abuses may stimulate a process of incremental change even in the multinational corporation. Hirst would like to see these companies create an international corporate senate, which would be an advisory body composed of the great and the good with whom corporate managements could consult about their plans for social vetting, and to which unions and other aggrieved parties in different countries could bring their concerns.

These measures will demand that the state carefully monitor the degree of power and fiscal autonomy that is devolved to regional governments and other public agencies that will support the cooperative firms sector of the economy against the degree of power the state needs to retain to itself in order to regulate the activities of the multinational companies. After all, big firms need to be faced by big governments if their power is to be checked. The state needs to protect small property from big property and the threat of monopoly; it needs to be extensive in its scale of operations but functionally limited in the scope of its powers. The associational state, in order to promote a change in the company form, would need to operate against the following principles. First, it has to acknowledge that some economic activities does need to be organized on a large scale; second, companies should in the first instance be encouraged to follow their own strategies. In this last respect, governments need to try to lay down general rules that are applicable to all companies and not to discriminate too closely between companies, especially as the historical record of governments in picking industrial winners is so dismal. Third, legislation needs to be enforced on anti-concentration measures limiting the scope and number of mergers and take-overs unless they are in the public interest. Indeed, it should be public policy to encourage existing firms to de-centralize and create de-mergers where appropriate. Large firms should also be encouraged, through tax and investment incentives, to democratize their governance arrangements as much as possible. This process might also be facilitated by a decentralization audit to be required of all firms over 1000 employees and to offer appropriate sub-activities of the business incentives for worker buy-out or to extend the scope of contracted-out services. Networking, joint ventures and other forms of mutual cooperation are to be fostered in preference to vertical integration in the companies that need to undertake larger projects or greater levels of research and development activity. If existing firms did not take advantage of these encouragements to de-concentrate there would need to be public policy that would require firms to move in a more associationalist direction. Hirst suggests that this apply to all firms over a certain size (500 employees or $100m capital), and that, if necessary, the following requirements would be imposed.

1. They should establish a two-tier board, including a supervisory board representing shareholders (one-third shareholder representatives, one-third employee representatives elected by secret ballot of individual employees, and one-third community representatives - chosen from a list provided by regional or national bodies representative of consumers and other associations, and approved by a majority of the representatives of the first two groups), and that the board would appoint the management board charged with the operational running of the company but answerable to the supervisory board.

2. The members of both boards should bear the legal duty to consider and to give due regard to the interests of shareholders, employees, consumers, the community and the environment when making decisions.

3. The board should institute a works council charged with the codetermination of company policy and below it a comprehensive system of participation involving all employees.

4. The company should give a Japanese-style lifetime employment contract to all full-time employees with more than two years' service, and establish a single employee status with the same holidays, pension rights, terms of service and social facilities.

5. Part-time employees should be granted similar rights if they have worked for more than sixteen hours per week for two years and the management board should undertake to ensure that employment practices are not devised to evade the legislation, directors being personally liable.

6. New share issues and mergers should require a 60% majority of the supervisory board.

7. The company should institute an employee share ownership plan.[6]

Whilst Hirst claims these proposals might seem, to many, radical, he points out that they are little more than an amalgam of Japanese and German best practice and so should not in themselves lead firms into uncompetitive behavior. By aiming to include into membership of the company many of the members of society who have a stake in these institutions, the hope is that they will gain a renewed public legitimacy and a democratic mandate for the property rights they entail. It is also hoped that these reforms in the company form will be part of a wider agenda of change to bring about a richer civil society in which markets can flourish and in which the state is powerful but not too powerful to block associational diversity and creativity.

Whilst Hirst's reforms of are radical and far-reaching, involving the embrace of associational politics in wider society , there is not a clear analysis of how this transformation might come about or under what conditions a change in this direction might be started. For an analysis that takes the question of the conditions necessary and the stages needed to make such a transition, the underappreciated work of Jonathan Boswell and the proposals he put forward in *Community and the Economy* are worthy of examination.[7]

The theory of public cooperation

Jonathan Boswell's approach to the company form is again part of his scheme to establish a framework for society on the basis of democratic communitarianism, a political philosophy that will take the value of fraternity as seriously as equality and liberty. In his book Boswell gives an account of the routes of this line of thinking which today has now been labeled communitarian. His perspective is informed by the historical strands of this thinking, in particular Durkheim, Christian personalism, and the Oxford idealist social liberals. The thread that runs through these perspectives he considers to be the search for associativeness amongst separate beings: that if people have good relationships they will best develop their distinctive personalities and that the highest end is a form of communion. As a set of principles for guiding action he identifies three: firstly, there are distinct and unique components (individuals and groups) whose diversity and freedom are crucial; secondly, that these units are to be brought together in mutually fulfilling relationships of community; and thirdly, that since such a balance is never perfectly attained, it always needs to be striven for, so that the need to maintain a sense of community never stops. This is clearly a strand of thinking that is distinctive and rather unfashionable in the face of the prevailing philosophy of market individualism. The vision here is not one of separate individuals living in society, each seeking their own personal good and coming together in contractual and self-interested relationships as consumers or spectators, but a view which puts the cultivation of personal virtue in the community as its highest end, so that personal development and fulfillment are achieved in social relationships in the context of liberty, and people are connected in a plurality of fraternal groups and associations. In terms of property, this implies that it should be distributed as widely as possible, both to persons and to groups, and deployed in communal ways to support the common good. Every person should have a right to some property in the interests of security, creativity and justice. But with property rights should go social duties to the poor and to ensure the common good is pursued. Boswell's achievement is to take these rather vague notions and think through what they would mean for a modern economy and in particular for the corporate form. It is not possible to give a full account of this theory of the economy of public cooperation but his account of the company appropriate for this will be outlined in detail.

It is a difficult business to go against a strong orthodoxy which has many models and metaphors, which are deep-rooted in the public psyche, such as market optimality, material progress, and financial quantification. However, as a guiding metaphor Boswell puts forward the notion that associativeness in liberty is best thought of as attempting an ideal performance from an orchestra which has chosen to play a complex score. Each interpretation by the orchestra and its conductor is an approximation but it is unlikely that the perfect rendition will be attained, even assuming the composer could conceive of such an expression of his work. The interpretation of the orchestra involves an active, creative interdependence among a diverse set of players and their various instruments. The hope and possibility is that the work of the orchestra will create something above and beyond each member that will also involve the audience and create a transcending good for all concerned, a special act of communal togetherness which does not diminish individual worth and dignity. In economic terms, the requirement is for an ambitious programme of employee partnership, inter-enterprise co-determination and industrial democracy. This has to exist within an economy based upon general communitarian principles, with a clear role for markets and a regulatory state, but both subordinate to the notion of a greater economic community. The principle of firms both for and in the community is to be the organizing rationale of our economic life. This would have important implications for the form of the company, as Boswell notes:

...the ideal of economic community implies a new or renovated fabric of recognition's, connections and affiliations across the system. A nexus of mutual obligations and loyalties would stretch across the political economy or at least its leading parts. Public responsibilities would be enshrined in organizations' objects and codes, ratified by the democratic community, sustained through the economic culture.[8]

Boswell gives some historical evidence of how public cooperation has emerged in the economy, of how it can be encouraged and of how it can be used to supplement and supplant competition and state direction as methods of distribution in the economic system. He shows that capacities for contributing to extended fraternity, associationalism and democratic participation start with isolated acts and then move through single organization concentrations, to an economy-wide cooperativeness. The key forces for developing public cooperations are time, the size and number of organizations, transparency, continuity and ideological support. Within these forces the following processes are needed: that there is continuity so that there are incentives to cooperate; that organizational units are not too large; that there is organizational transparency so that other people know what is going on; and that the people in organizations have some elements of common background so that they have some shared values. Such as system would entail some costs, its institutions and personnel would be less mobile, some sub-optimal decisions would be taken, and the decision-making process might well be slower. The potential gains could be that it supports a greater diversity of organizations, the system is more stable, there is a marked reintegration of economic institutions and above all there is the chance for personal growth within a community.

Boswell admits that a transition towards this kind of economy is unlikely to arise naturally or to proceed smoothly and that some crisis factor will need to emerge if the changes he envisages are to win out. He thinks it likely that the following sequence is required: some initial favorable structures; the representation of a communitarian ideology by a political movement; a catalytic event like defeat in war, the aftermath or fear of a civil war, or a continuous eternal threat; and a coalitions government in which the communitarian movement acts as a fulcrum. It is fairly obvious from this analysis that a transition towards an economy of extensive public cooperation is unlikely to be a quick or likely event in the near future. What Boswell does is to show how things could be different in the longer term and that we have a very long way to go if we are to begin to embrace a communitarian approach to the economy and the operation of company form in the manner of a communitarian notion of property. Nevertheless, it is interesting to note that some of the requirements that he considers necessary for a move in this direction are beginning to become apparent in our company practices. The size of firms in terms of employment is reducing and cooperative networking is a much more important factor in the modern economy. Organizational transparency and social monitoring are on the increase in industry. The public relations function of many firms pays attention to internal communications and information disclosure as well as external information transmission. The growth in the publication and validation of social and environmental reporting is also a move in this direction. On some factors, social proximity and community forums there has not been so much progress. If anything in the UK the governments in the 1980s and 90s dismantled collective forums and reduced the togetherness of people in social proximity. On the whole, Boswell is more optimistic that continental European nations are further along the road towards public cooperation than the UK, and the USA is perhaps the furthest of the advanced economies away from this transition. In the case of the UK, he claims we have fallen between two stools of free competition and state control of the commanding hights of the economy. After the Conservative Governments of the past 17 years, the institutional supports and ideological background for a system of public cooperation are much diminished. But our connection with Europe and the election of a Labour Government with a strong mandate for social bridge building gives some ground for optimism in relation to the communitarian project for the economy. There is also an aspiration to find a 'third way' in intellectual circles and Boswell's prescription looks to be a promising candidate.[9]

This chapter has outlined the communitarian case for a change in the company form to be institutionalized in an advanced western economy as a social institution that generates social capital as well as depletes it. The arguments justifying this position were considered and two wide ranging proposals for change were outlined. An evaluation of this position will be given in the final chapter.

References

1 Sacks, J., (1997) *The Politics of Hope*, London, Jonathan Cape, p 170.

9 Etzioni, A., (1995), *New Communitarian Thinking*, London, Unversity Press of Virginia.

3 Dahl, R.A., (1985), *A Preface to Economic Democracy*, Berkeley, University of California Press.

4 Hirst, P., (1994), *Associative Democracy: New Forms of Economic and Social Governance*, London, Polity Press.

5 Ibid, p 20.

6 Ibid, p 151-2.

7 Boswell, J., (1990), *Community and the Economy: The Theory of Public Co Operation*, London,Routledge.

8 Ibid, p 55.

9 Giddens, A., (1999), *The Third Way*, London, Polity Press.

8

chapter eight

Reform of the Company

'We would not have needed the experience of the Great Depression of 1929-39 to show us that society must insist on the maintenance of the 'going concern' and must if necessary sacrifice to it the individual rights of shareholders, creditors, workers, and, in the last analysis, even of consumers.'[1]

Introduction

This chapter will consider the scenario of reform of the company from the perspective of a greater degree of social conditionality over property rights, but with less of an expectation that the company will be able to generate an extensive regeneration of social capital in society. We will first consider some of the internal governance changes that might be needed to make the company more suitable for the implementation of knowledge management and to become more like an internal network, labeled, in this instance, as the creation of a 'community of purpose'. We will then go on to consider some of the changes that might be needed in the institutionalization of the company suggested by the conceptual work of Coleman, and at a more practical level at changes in company law suggested by Parkinson and then by Kay. The intention, once again, is to outline the arguments and proposals for this position; an evaluation will be made in chapter 11.

HRM in the community of purpose

The conception of human resource management (HRM) in the community of purpose draws upon some aspects of communitarian thinking for its guiding principles and underlying values.[2] Its guiding principle with regard to the employment relationship is the need to balance economic interests alongside mutual moral responsibilities in the organization. It has a sophisticated and pluralistic concept of the nature and purpose of the business enterprise. Importantly, it has a moral foundation which guides its management practices and mechanisms of intervention. Conceiving of the company as a 'community of purpose' does not imply that it has only one purpose or that it should contain a harmony of interests; it is a collection of economic interests and a community of moral agents with different purposes. Alan Flanders' depiction of the firm was much the same.

> Although there is no inherent common purpose in industry its constituent groups are dependent on each other to achieve their own objectives, and the area of common intent and overlapping purposes can be extended as the quality of their relations improves. This depends, not on preaching co-operation, but on how inevitable conflicts spinning from divergent interests are resolved.[3]

Paternalism is flawed in ethical terms because it does not afford employees appropriate moral respect which, even if economic power is unequally distributed, need not mean that moral respect has to be unequally distributed. This argument was forcefully made some years ago in industrial relations by Alan Flanders.[4] After all, equality in moral agency is the principle of democracy in a civil society. Flanders accepted the view that businesses are primarily economic organizations but rejected the Hayekian view that they have limited responsibilities. The responsibility of companies is to take into account the consequences of their actions for all stakeholders as well as for the shareholders. In his view, the firm, in meeting its legal obligations, was not doing nearly enough; it also had to meet internal and external social responsibilities. The firm's internal responsibilities to employees are in addition to those that are created by the 'legal fiction' of the contract of employment, and arise because 'in return for the price which the employer is prepared to pay for his labour, the employee surrenders control over a large part of his life.'[5] Consequently, because companies direct the whole person and restrict his freedom, it is important that with management power must go responsibility. Management's power is not that of ownership but that of organization: the ability to control the setting and conditions of working life. At present, these are influenced by the forces of the market, the rule of law and sometimes by the countervailing power of trade unions, although Flanders considered these to be negative or reactive checks upon management power. He thought a positive control on management , by making them accountable to a wider range of stakeholders, was needed. Ultimately, he would have liked the laws of corporate governance to be have been changed to reflect the notions of the 'participative' company outlined by George Goyder and others. But, Flanders also noted that 'institutional controls over the uses of power have their limits and can never offer an adequate substitute for morality, however much they might be improved.'[6] In the interim, he advocated the practice of collective bargaining on the grounds that this was the best method of equalizing the economic bargaining power of employees against the employer   and, importantly, collective bargaining also helped to create 'industrial citizenship' rights for employees which would give people dignity in work. Consequently, collective bargaining fulfills a moral purpose in addition to its distributive role; in a democratic society it gives employees a share in the governance of the organization in which they work, and helps them maintain a sense of dignity underpinned by rights, participation and justice.

Flanders hoped that management would appreciate that a certain set of values should govern the way they treated their workers. He defined these values in Kantian terms, that people are to be treated as ends and not means and that their moral agency is to be respected. In concrete terms, this means not imposing values upon workers that they would not choose themselves. He was particularly critical of managerial paternalism where it imposed decisions by force, or where it resorted to manipulation of employees motivations because 'human dignity at work means that people should have some say over their own lives, some say in what is to happen and their own freedom to choose.'[7] Flanders' book on the pioneering productivity experiments at the Fawley refinery was an attempt to show that it was practically possible for management to avoid both paternalism and indifference, and instead act upon higher standards of conduct in industrial relations.[8]

Whilst it must be noted that the power relationship between employer and employee is unequal and probably always will be, the exchange of respect and bestowal of dignity between employer and employee can be equal and reciprocal. It will be argued that the moral trap of paternalism can be avoided by conceiving of the employment relationship as both an economic and moral relationship, in which economic power is best handled through mechanisms of countervailing power, and the moral relationship is constituted as a community of respect among equals.

In the domain of economic interests, it is clear that the trend towards the non-representation of employees in the firm has to be resisted by management, and representative and participative structures introduced and enhanced. Bargaining power cannot be equalized, but it is important that employee economic interests are recognized and given voice in the firm both on moral and pragmatic grounds. Industrial relations research suggests that, instead of hindering management from managing, responsible trade unions make them manage better.[9] Union voice asserts workers' rights and presses for best practice in companies, and helps prevent management from treating workers as a dumb factor of production. By keeping management on its metal, the slide into a low-wage low-investment economy is avoided, and businesses are stimulated into investments in training and technology that will increase productivity and competitiveness. Trade unions are, in fact, often lubricants of technological change rather than irritants: they help to raise important issues before implementation and help to overcome the difficulties of managing change in the organization. Indeed, it is often said that many managers would perform much better if they had to explain and justify their actions to their workforces more often. Through processes of collective bargaining, flexible collective agreements can be negotiated which cover issues such as personal development, technology, pay for skills, teamworking, security of employment, and other incentives for continuous improvement. HRM in the community of purpose must, therefore, include the representation and inclusion of employee economic interests in the management decision-making process.

In the moral domain, in a community of purpose, it is important that the moral agency of employees is both respected and given parity of esteem in HRM policies and practice. Employees are to be regarded not as the property of the firm to be manipulated as just another resource, nor as children in a family in which the managers are the parents and moral guardians of the children, but as adult moral agents who are capable of deliberation and decision for themselves. The indignity and condescension that many employees feel can be avoided if the wise advice of Mary Parker Follett is followed in respect of the giving of orders and on what basis authority is to be exercised at work.[10] Directions and instructions should be based upon the 'law of the situation' and not just on the manager's positional authority in the organization. Otherwise a system of order givers and order takers is created, which in turn leads to the dysfunctional effects of loss of employee initiative, loss of self-respect and a sense of responsibility, and loss of motivation to do the best work the employee can. Follett suggests that the disadvantages of the command and control organization can be overcome if orders are depersonalized; that is, if the logic of the task is followed to indicate what must be done, and in which sequence. The 'law of the situation' is determined by what reasonable employees would agree needs to be done to achieve the results required. In this situation, directions and responsibilities are arrived at through agreement between employees, and everyone should then understand what is required by whom and when, and, in turn, the task should be performed more effectively. Follett's advice went unheeded for a long time, but recent changes in organizations and new experiments with team working tend to suggest that, in high-performance teams work and responsibilities are usually based upon the team members assessment of what the situation demands and who will be best able to fulfill a particular task.[11] Often the leader of these teams takes on the role of facilitator or mentor rather than the authority figure who gives out the orders. Often the person who becomes the team leader is not necessarily the best qualified by a badge of ability, but by competence and interpersonal skills on the job. This advice on how to respect the voice and autonomy of employees in the organization may not be a quick or an easy system of management to operate, but there are signs that some firms are approaching ever nearer to this moral ideal in their HRM practice.[12]

This is not to say that HRM should be neutral towards the moral character of employees; it must undertake to continue to form their characters and help to foster the public virtues upon which society depends.[13] HRM policies and practice should seek to cultivate in all employees the qualities of character necessary to the common good of self-government and civility. Above and beyond the contractual relationship are moral bonds between employer and employees in a community of purpose which mean that a more collegiate approach to the management or the governance of the firm should be the long-term aim of HRM practice. A statement of the moral values which should underpin HRM is therefore required, but it need not be a new one. Such a statement was made very eloquently in one of the first textbooks on personnel management in 1945, by C. H. Northcott.[14] In his chapter on the aims and principles that should govern the practice of personnel management, the object of personnel management (HRM) is to 'secure the greatest degree of collaboration within each establishment, by ensuring that there is[15] : justice, implicit in the recognition by the employer of his obligations in respect of the workers' claims; personality, a principle which lies behind the need of the worker for satisfaction in work and service; the democratic principle which deepens the sense of partnership and the rightfulness of the claim of the workers for status in industry commensurate with position as members of a democracy; and co-operation, the establishment of a relationship so all-embracing as to be the governing factor in industrial relations generally.

Whilst these moral principles seem to have been dropped from later texts on HRM, the importance of paying attention to matters of dignity and respect at work today means that these values need to be revived and re-interpreted in contemporary organizations. The communitarian approach to HRM practice relies on the moral agency (virtue) of the employee to guide their behavior as much as possible, but should the employee fall short of accepted standards of conduct then management must step in and bring the employees' actions back into line. Naturally enough, management must keep and maintain these high standards of conduct themselves and lead by example. HRM policy and procedures are of secondary importance in managerial terms to the creation of cooperative relationships and shared conceptions of conduct that are to pervade the organization. HRM policy and procedures are to be drawn up to reflect and express these shared understandings. Indeed, it could be argued that one of the reasons for the deterioration in the climate of industrial relations in the 1970s was that the change in the moral order of the firm was not reflected in new-shared understandings, but instead led towards the creation of legal rights and contractual processes which undermined the firm's community of purpose.

The conceptualization of the company as a community of purpose is a reintroduction of a functional view of the organization that does not exist as a permanent or unchanging system, but one that has a negotiated order that can degenerate as well as flourish. Healthy companies need management that is balanced by democratic mechanisms, or they have a tendency to become more closed in the face of competitive pressures from outside. Without internal employee participation, firms tend to become closed and authoritarian, and unable to innovate and change. However, the company that is open and unstructured to the point of anarchy should also be avoided because a company that faces increased competitive pressures will have little reason to stay together. A good principle, therefore, to be observed in HRM practice would be that democratic mechanisms should be maximized and only limited when real and present danger exists in terms of productivity and profitability. Apart from this, openness, debate, participation and accountability are to be key objectives of HRM policy in a network enterprise. This implies that the role of the HRM professional is to act as the facilitator or mediator of corporate dialogue at all levels in the company. HRM professionals need to insist that the employee's moral agency is respected, and that they are given the chance to make decisions based upon discussion and deliberation, and to have their views included in the decision-making processes of the firm. Knowledge management and internal networking depend upon trust and cooperation that can only be achieved when employees are treated with the dignity and respect that they deserve as citizens of the company. But that is not to say that only their views will count, it is also important that other stakeholder voices are heard in the governance structures of the company, and that these are brought together around shared notions of the common good in society.

HRM practice in the community of purpose aims to broker a working agreement between a variety of stakeholders' economic interests and to mediate and show respect to all moral agents in the enterprise. In this way, an ethical middle path can be trodden between paternalism and contract, and the firm can become an enterprising network. If these reforms are to have any lasting foundation, however, they will need to be underpinned by an institutional framework that recognizes and supports the interests of other stakeholders. For some fresh thinking on how this might be achieved let us consider the conceptual work of the leading rational choice sociologist, James S. Coleman.[16]

James S. Coleman's conceptual analysis

In a monumental study representing the culmination of his lifetime work, James S. Coleman has, using rational choice theory, erected a unified conceptual framework for describing and quantifying both stability and change in social systems. As part of this study he as been thinking out the nature of corporate actors in the social system and has contributed some new notions of how it might be best to conceptualize them as actors in society.

If asked who might be regarded as an elementary actor in the social system, the common man might respond that there are only natural persons. Coleman points out, however, that under sets of rules and various constitutions, corporate actors are effectively now present upon the scene and their actions need to be understood. Business corporations are, in fact, often combinations of natural persons and corporations as shareholders. The natural person can be thought of as two selves: the object self and the acting self or, in other words, an agent and principal in one body. A corporate actor is created when principal and agent are two different persons. It is also possible for the principal to be a corporate actor, or for the agent to be a corporate actor, or for both to be corporate actors, as in the case where one company owns or controls another. A publicly held corporation can be thought of as having multiple principals who own the corporation as shareholders and multiple agents who are employed by the corporation. In the traditional depiction of the workings of a corporation it was assumed by Weber and others that the corporation is a machine with human agents as parts that obey the orders of the executive. It is now both more realistic and appropriate to acknowledge that the human parts of the organization have purposes of their own and are increasingly reluctant to give up control over their labour and submit to the will of the executive. This change has made it more difficult for the managers of the company to motivate the employees and impose constraints on the control mechanisms that can be used in the organization. Consequently, the Weberian model of organization is being replaced by the organization which acts as an investor, facilitator, and guide to the employment of the resources it marshals.

In the Weberian organization, a structure of positions is created that exists independently of the occupants of those positions. These are positions in relation, not persons in relation. This has the effect of freeing the persons from the positions they occupy. People appointed to a position take on the obligations and expectations, goals and resources associated with the position they would take a role in a play. As the nature of the corporation changes there is a blurring of the distinction between these two sets of positions. It makes it difficult to fully separate the two sets of rights and interests of the agents occupying the positions and the interests of the principals who direct the organization. The modern evolution of the corporation has made this agent principal concept inappropriate. As Coleman writes, 'The modern corporation can increasingly be seen not as a machine with parts but as a system of action comparable to an unconstrained market, a system whose organizational structure lies not in defining expectations and obligations and exercising authority, but in structuring reward systems and providing resources.'[17] Authority in the corporation is increasingly dispersed and problematic. How are the employees' interests to be taken into account by those who exercise authority in the corporation? Three possibilities are examined: that a period of employee indoctrination is needed to gain acceptance of the authority structure in the firm; the firm's authority structure be modified to include a degree of co-determination; and that ownership rights be shared with employees or groups of employees who make inventions and innovations in the corporation. The latter remedy would, in effect, rejoin to some extent the 'split atom of private property' which Berle and Means described as the major consequence of the joint-stock corporation. Rather than all the benefits of ownership going to the shareholders, they would be shared with the employees once again, giving a partial reuniting of ownership and control. What these changes represent is a moving away from the basic model of the corporation where the authority structure is disjoint between principals and agents: the employees have no interests in the purposes of the owners, but they agree to act in the owners' interests in exchange for compensation. The suggested new model for the authority structure of the corporation is, therefore, one where there is discipline exercised through a set of incentives which gives employees and owners conjoint interests. 'Employees' acquisition of interest in the corporation itself, through a kind of identification, and the decline of shareholders' interest in the corporation except as a source of return on capital move the conception of the corporation away from one in which there is an owner as principal and employees as agents.'[18] The appropriate conception for the modern company in Coleman's view is as 'a system of action composed of positions (not persons).' It is acknowledged that the occupiers of positions will pursue their own interests; the task of the management is to design the structure of the organization so that these pursuits will also achieve the purpose of the corporate actor.

If the corporate form effectively splits the atom of private property into two rights, the right to use the property for the pursuit of a lawful purpose, and the right to benefit from the use of the property, then the managers hold the use right and the shareholders the beneficial rights. The problem that was acknowledged in chapter three is that the control of the managers use rights is considerable and yet the oversight of these rights by the shareholders is fragmented and weak. The result is a society that is increasingly alienated from direct control over its resources and is increasingly supported by a set of corporations in whom it has vested that direct control. This problem could be addressed (see chapter 9) by strengthening the control of shareholders or by increasing the power of government to control the managers of the corporation. However, both approaches have difficulties and drawbacks. Another reaction to this situation that Coleman mentions is the general withdrawal of trust from corporate bodies that are unresponsive to the interests of its participants or beneficiaries. Whilst this is a difficult process to measure, it can have a large impact on the authority structure of the corporation in the longer term. In other words, its legitimacy can be undermined and political action is likely over the fate of the corporation in society. A very different form of company institutionalization might then be brought into being.

Coleman also examines the emerging responsibilities of society's corporate actors: to whom are they responsible, and how is fulfillment of this responsibility best ensured? He begins by acknowledging that it is not clear that companies are not intrinsically and irrevocably responsible to any persons. The owners are, in this respect, residual claimants and they cannot be the only actors to whom the company should be made responsible. Therefore, the question of defining the company's responsibilities in society is indeed a difficult one. When the company, by becoming detached from a natural person or group, became free-standing under the law, it became divorced from the ideas of the responsibilities of natural persons which are normally induced through a period of moral socialization. For a certain period companies that had strong connections with their local communities may have had a sense of responsibility for these communities. But, as companies grew larger and became more global, these links have weakened and are less likely to make the company act responsibly. Consequently, the issue of what other means are available for inducing responsible behavior by companies becomes more urgent. There is no one group to whom the company owes responsibility; the company has to satisfy the interests of various sets: customers, employees, the environment, suppliers, shareholders, and the community. Coleman proposes that changes are needed on three fronts if companies are to be made responsible: there need to be changes in the structure of corporate governance, changes to incentive structures confronting agents in the company, and changes in the investments of the company. He would like to see a movement towards the representation of employee interests on boards of directors, making them more responsive to the interests of workers. However, he acknowledges that this will not necessarily make the company more responsible to other parties; in fact it could make it less responsible, as workers seek to maximize their interests. It also seem unlikely that a broader distribution of corporate control would lead to more extensive socially responsible actions, such as establishing charitable foundations. These are usually created in circumstances where wealth and power are concentrated on one person or in a family, not firms, where the decisions are made through a process of internal democracy.

He then considers if the representation of external interests on boards would be appropriate. One measure that would help would be to ensure the company obeys the letter and spirit of the law. The law can be thought of as representing the interests of those actors in society for whom the company's actions have some consequence. Rather than have a board representative whose role is to monitor the firms legal compliance, it might be better if the job where given to auditors. The Companies Acts should contain a law which requires external functional audits addressing actions relevant to the various markets in which the company participates. In effect, this is to broaden and deepen the present role of the financial auditors into stakeholder auditors. Compliance with the law is one thing but making the firm responsive to its community is another and might be addressed with other measures.

Coleman suggests that the board of the company might be further socialized by the introduction of external interests directors for minority groups, the environment, and the local community. The difficulty here is that the Companies Acts would have to be changed to allow a wider view of the purpose of the company to be incorporated. A further problem lies in what interests the company should internalize. Coleman suggests that this might be decided in favour of the following: those whose interests are indirectly harmed by the corporation (housewives, the unemployed and children), and those who experience directly externalities imposed from the company (environmental groups, communities, customers). The extension of accountability through reporting on the actions of the company can also help to socialize the company in society. The use of ethical investment funds and policies is another means of inducing greater social responsibility for the company.

Changes to the incentive structure of taxation can also help. Relief from taxes can be allowed for activities which are not in the company's interest but are widely regarded as being in the public interest. Company contributions to charitable activities would reduce a tax liability; this would be the equivalent of creating tax havens for socially responsible behavior. Coleman has even suggested that companies could be induced to become age-balanced, with a distribution of ages that mirrors the distribution in society as a whole. The inducement to the company would be a tax credit equal to the cost the state of providing comparable services for children and the aged.

In the practical hands of the corporate lawyer, these notions of making the company more socially responsible take a more cautious path, which looks at the problems of constructing a workable legal framework for reform of company legislation. One of the more imaginative advocates of proposals in this direction who is a leading authority on company law is Professor John Parkinson.

The analysis of John Parkinson

In his book, *Corporate Power and Responsibility*,   Professor Parkinson presents a detailed critique of the conventional models of corporate governance and its supporting arguments.[19] He presents a very interesting analysis of social responsibility as a process, rather than concerned with any particular outcome. Social responsibility is an attribute of the decision-making processes in the corporate governance structure and can be understood in two ways. First, it is to try to moralize the company's decision-making process so that it acts in a similar way to a responsible person and takes into account the point of view of other people. But the aim is not to institutionalize some specific moral code nor to necessarily approve any particle outcome. The point is to take into account the interests of third parties in the decision-making process in the hope that a better judgment about the weighting of interests will result. The second meaning is to make the company more responsive to the interests of affected groups by increasing the ability of those groups to shape company conduct. This might be done by letting them put pressure on the company from outside or by giving them some constitutional status within the governance structure. In his view, the first mechanism of making the company more responsible is only likely to bring about modest changes in company behaviour because, even if the decision making brings a significant change in managerial attitudes and values, it is unlikely to take place. The second approach, may bring about some changes but again he is skeptical because the power of the stakeholders is likely to remain limited compared to that of the shareholders. He is also careful in his use of the term stakeholder and does not wish to imply that making the company more responsive to stakeholders' interests should imply that all stakeholders are equal. In fact , what may be due to a stakeholder depends upon the type of relationship the stakeholder has with the company. Shareholders have capital at risk and so should receive an appropriate return; employees need job security and to be able to share in the fruits of their own labour, customers and suppliers have certain expectations about reliability and quality. Therefore, the management of the company have to make an attempt in good faith to balance the stakeholders' interests rather than treat the shareholders' interests as paramount. This would obviously require considerable changes in company law and so he makes a series of proposals.

First, a reformulation of directors' duties so that they place greater priority on the development of the company's relationships and pay more attention to the welfare of groups affected by corporate activities. Second, he advocates the introduction of the two-tier board structure similar to that which operates in Germany. The advantage of this structure is that it improves the disciplinary framework within which the executive management operates and gives the stakeholders a place on the board of supervisors. The main task of the supervisory board would be to appoint the members of the executive board, who would be appointed to fixed-term contracts and their performance subject to regular review and reports. The supervisory board would have the power to renew contracts of the executive managers. The supervisory board also might make the hostile takeover of the firm more difficult and so this would give the management more scope to consider the longer-term development of the company. Reports could be made to the supervisory board regarding the company's performance on a range of issues: investment, research and development, training, health and safety, compliance with the law and regulations, and the quality of its relationships with customers, suppliers and community. Management would therefore have to satisfy a balanced scorecard of objectives as judged by the supervisory board. Improving the information collected and made available to the supervisory board is a very important part of trying to make the management more accountable. In this respect Parkinson advocates increasing the requirements regarding corporate reporting and disclosure to include social and environmental reporting and an audit process to verify these claims. The important point is that the supervisory board is independent of the executive board and is able to hold it to account. The supervisory board would have to nominate its own members, with appointment being conditional on approval of the shareholders in the AGM and the employees through works councils. He does not go so far as to suggest (as in the case of Germany) that members of the supervisory board are nominated by the workers as their representatives; he would prefer these to remain independent of the company. In fact he sees the development of the professional monitoring of directors as a desirable outcome, creating a responsible cadre of experienced and competent stakeholder representatives. In respect of the full democratization of corporate governance, he is more skeptical, and seems to consider this development to be outside the bounds of practical possibility, even if it were to take place within the context of the existing corporate form. This is because of the difficulty of balancing the need for profitability and wider notions of stakeholder welfare; these could be overweighed in favour of the welfare claims if the control of the employees in the company is too strong. He is also mindful of making changes in corporate responsiveness that are liable to add significantly to the cost profile of companies in what is an increasingly global marketplace, particularly if such changes are only addressed in one country. In this respect, the forum for more substantive changes in corporate governance are best to take place at the international level and the power block level of the European Union.

Another advocate of reform in company law in the UK, who is particularly mindful of the need to strike the right balance between the goals of accountability and yet for companies to remain competitive, is Professor John

Kay. He is also, like Parkinson, a prominent member of the review of company law due to report in 2001.

The work of John Kay

In Professor Kay's view, the large company is a social institution with a corporate personality rather than the creation of private contract and so is fundamentally incapable of being owned by any one.[20] He makes the point that, under the 1985 Companies Act in the UK, a distinction between a limited company and a PLC was made to bring us into line with European law. In France, for example, large companies have the status of *societe anonyme*, and this applies to all companies with over 50 shareholders. The governance of a *societe anonyme* is subject to detailed statutory regulation in many areas; if a small business wishes to operate with less regulation but still maintain a limited risk it must be formed as a societe a *responsabilitie limite*. A similar situation is operative in Germany. The large company in these societies is a public institution and is acknowledged to represent a wide range of interests and so is to be regulated in a way which makes it responsible to these interests. In the Anglo-American model the company is a private creation of contractors rather than a public body and so the distinction is not made between the two different types of company. The distinction between PLCs and limited companies is not perceived as having made much difference to the governance of these institutions. The principal-agent relationship, whilst subject to criticism, is still the main mechanism of control and most proposals for reform revolve around making it work better. Kay, on the other hand, does not think this is likely to happen as the reality of company operation is too far from the theory to be made a practical control model. He urges the consideration of an alternative approach, that of adapting the control model to the realities of company ownership.

Kay disputes the assertion that the company is owned by its shareholders because this is a meaningless statement in reality. Ownership normally is of an object and the owner can decide who may use it or not, how it is to be used, whether to dispose of it or not, and how much to trade it for. But, he notes, when you buy a share in a large company from the stock exchange, few of these rights pertain, except the right to sell it again. As the owner of company shares there is no right to enter or use the premises of the company, no right to prevent others from entering or using the assets of the company, and no right to take part in the decision- making process about the direction of the company, or when to buy or dispose of assets. All the shareholder can do is vote on a limited range of issues at the AGM, and agree to accept a limited dividend, or if not satisfied sell the shares. So shareholders own their shares, but only in a limited sense of the word own the company. Possession is absent from this meaning of ownership. He notes that the definition of ownership provided by Grossman and Hart is widely used in this context: the owner of an asset is the person who enjoys those rights over it that have not been given to others by explicit contract.[21] But he notes that, in relation to shareholders, they do not appear to be the owners. The board of directors exercises the major rights of control over the company assets. So, if ownership does not mean control, what do shareholders own? In his view it might be better to say that the company is not owned by any one, and that this is not of any real consequence as many institutions appear to function well without clear owners. For example, the BBC, universities, libraries, the River Thames. As long as disputes and direction matters can be solved, ownership rights may be unimportant. Indeed he notes that, according to the strict letter of the law, the company does not appear to be owned by its shareholders, because it is incorporated as a separate legal personality from its subscribers. The company is something separate from its totality of shareholders. This makes the shareholders important, but not necessarily exclusive, members of a stakeholder group with interests in the company. Whilst there are fiduciary duties to be respected with regard to shareholders' interests, this does not mean that on every decision the question of delivering shareholder value is to be uppermost in the minds of the directors.

Kay proposes a trustee model of corporate governance as a more appropriate form and draws his evidence to support this from the operation of companies in continental Europe and Japan. In this model the existence of a distinct corporate personality and its importance for commercial success is emphasized. It acknowledges that the large company is a social institution and that the management are not the agents of the shareholders but the trustees of the stakeholders. Of course the notion of trustees is an ancient one under the law of estates and they are defined as the settlers of the residual terms of the estate after the owner's death. In effect, Kay is pronouncing the death of the company's owner and the estate of assets is to be presided over by the management for the benefit of the stakeholders. The duty of these trustees is to preserve and enhance the value of the assets under their control and to balance the claims to a return on these assets fairly between the interested parties. This model has two distinct differences from the principal-agency model. First, the trustees are to sustain the company's assets not just the company's share value. This is a broader concept of the company's purpose and includes the development of the skills of employees, the expectations of customers and suppliers, and the company's reputation in the community. The notion of a company personality as a set of trust relationships that need to be cultivated is clearly distinct from the notion of a nexus of self-interested contractors. Second, the trustees have to balance the conflicting interests of current stakeholders and future stakeholders, which requires a longer-term perspective of the development of the capabilities of the company. Short-term shareholder gain and the temptation to trade company assets rather than grow them will, in Kay's view, become less prominent in company practice.

This new model of corporate governance would allow managers to pursue multiple objectives but hold them accountable for the company's performance. A key requirement is to make the content of stakeholder accountability substantive through a new Companies Act. This Act would establish the important distinction between PLCs and the small limited company. The former is a social institution with legal personality and the latter is for small firms and enterpreprenurial risk taking in the start up and development phase of company growth. The distinction is to be made on the basis of size and is to include very large private firms. In terms of corporate objectives and responsibilities the Act would prescribe as follows:

A director of a PLC shall at all times act in the manner he considers in the exercise of his business judgment best fitted to advance the interests of the company. The interests of the company include:

- the payment of returns to shareholders and investors sufficient to remunerate past investment and encourage future investment in the company;

- the development of the skills and capabilities of employees and suppliers of the company;

- the achievement of stability and security in the company's employment and trading relationships;

- the provision of goods and services of good quality to the company's customers at fair prices; and

- the enhancement of the company's reputation for high standards of business conduct.[22]

Kay's Companies Act would also contain a framework for corporate governance in a PLC. This would require a PLC to have a board, with an independent chairmen and a number (at least three) of independent directors (financially independent, that is). The Act would define the role and functions of the CEO (a distinct role from chairman of the board of trustees), and some of the other senior officers of the company. A careful process of selection of senior managers would be prescribed, overseen by the independent directors via a selection committee that makes use of other independent advisers and would be itself be obliged to consult employees, investors and suppliers and any relevant regulatory agencies. The appointment of the CEO should be for a fixed term of four years, and salary and bonuses should be determined at the beginning of the appointment. The contract should only exceptionally be renewed for one further term, and only modest termination payments should be allowed. The power to nominate directors to the board should rest with the independent directors, but they would be obliged to consult shareholders before appointing new independent directors.

Kay hopes that this model will allow sufficient freedom for the business to be successful and yet will make it more accountable to stakeholders. The main idea is to give the management the greatest amount of freedom to run the business over a period of years, but in a responsible way. Under these conditions, the number of hostile takeovers should be reduced in number since the ownership of a majority of the shares would not confer rights to appoint the executive management. And yet the four-year term of office for the management allows the opportunity for new ideas and proposals to be brought forward. The CEO would need to be fully accountable for the company's performance to stakeholders if their term of office is to be renewed.

Conclusions

What these approaches to the reform of the corporate form and the structure of corporate governance have in common is a desire to embrace change in the principal-agent control model and to begin to include a wider consideration of other stakeholders' interests. There is clearly some variation in the different proposals by Parkinson and Kay about how this can be best accomplished. The notion of allowing the managers to balance and weight the different stakeholders' interests and yet remain accountable to them for the performance of the firm and the satisfaction of their expectations is clearly a difficult issue to square, given the inherent contradictions and conflicts of interests that are bound to arise from time to time. The change envisaged by these writers is, however, incremental within the field of the institutionalization of company law and management practices. It requires a considerable commitment from political parities if these changes are to be embraced, but not the kind of change in the system which would put the company in the forefront of the drive to regenerate social capital in society. The prospects for the success of these proposals will be considered in chapter 11.

References

[1] Drucker, P., (1964), *The Concept of the Corporation*, New York, Mentor, p 31.

[2] Etzioni, A., (1997), *The New Golden Rule: community and morality in a democratic society*, London, Profile Books.

[3] Flanders, A., (1970), *Management and Unions: the theory and reform of industrial relations*, London , Faber, p 150.

[4] Flanders, op cit.

[5] Flanders, op cit. p 132.

[6] Ibid, p 146.

[7] Ibid, p 147.

[8] Flanders, A., (1964), *The Fawley Productivity Agreements*, London, Faber.

[9] Wadhwani, S., (1990), 'The Effects of Unions on Productivity Growth, Investment and Employment: a report on recent work', *British Journal of Industrial Relations*, 28:3, pp 371 385. Machin, S. and Wadhwani, S., (1991), 'The Effects of Unions on Organizational Change and Employment', *Economic Journal*, 101:3, pp 835-854. Sadowski, D., Backes-Gellner, U. and Frick, B., (1995), 'Works Councils: barriers or boosts for the competitiveness of German firms?' *British Journal of Industrial Relations*, 33:3, pp 493-513.

[10] Graham, P. (Ed.), (1996),   *Mary Parker Follett: prophet of management*, Boston, Harvard Business School Press.

[11] Herriot, P. and Pemberton, C., (1995), *Competitive Advantage Through Diversity: organizational learning from difference*, London , Sage.

[12] Heckscher, C., (1995), *White -Collar Blues: management loyalties in an age of restructuring*, New York, Basic Books.

[13] The argument being echoed here is that put forward by the communitarian political philosopher, Sandel, M., (1996), *Democracy's Discontent*, Cambridge Mass., Belknap/Harvard Press.

[14] Northcott, C.H., (1945), *Personnel Management: its scope and practice*, London, Pitman.

[15] Ibid, p 167.

[16] Coleman, J.S., (1990), *Foundations of Social Theory*, Cambridge, Mass., Harvard University Press.

[17] Ibid, p 436.

[18] Ibid, p 450.

[19] Parkinson, J.E., (1994), *Corporate Power and Responsibility*, Oxford, Oxford University Press.

[20] Kay, J., (1996), *The Business of Economics*, Oxford, Oxford University Press.

[21] Grossman, S. and Hart, O., (1986), 'The costs and benefits of ownership: a theory of vertical and lateral integration', *Journal of Political Economy*, 94, pp 691-719.

[22] Kay, J., (1997), 'The Stakeholder Corporation' in Kelly, G., Kelly, D. and Gamble, A., *Stakeholder Capitalism*, London, Macmillan, p 137.

9

chapter nine

Restore the Company

'The problem of business governance is not a problem of political philosophy; it is a problem of business philosophy...what we need is in fact a philosophy of business, because it is important to keep clear about what a business is and is not, especially today.'[1]

Introduction

This chapter will consider the liberal position on the question of private property and the form of the company and then go on to consider the issue of restoration of the shareholders' position in the constitution of the company. The contribution of the company to the recovery or generation of social capital in this position is expected to be very limited or perhaps negligible. The basic scenarios in this position are the development and variations of the classic arguments set out by the two doyens of neoclassical economics, Frederick von Hayek and Milton Freidman. A sturdy new defender of this position, specifically on the question of corporate governance, is Elaine Sternberg. The spread of shareownership and the development of popular capitalism have has been taken up by Jeffrey Gates in recent years. The careful monitoring of the company through the corporate governance system for the delivery of greater shareholder value is strongly advocated by Monks and Minow. All these writers are advocates of the liberal view of property rights that they consider to be fundamental to the maintenance of freedom in society.

A liberal approach to property

Liberals argue that the laws and other social institutions are neutral with respect to individual persons and their concept of the good life and how to live it.[2] Institutions, including business, exist to enable individuals to pursue their own ends as long as they do not interfere with others engaged in the same process. In questions of morality, liberals tend to the view that justice is a matter of procedural rights, and the question of substantive goals, such as the common good, should not be allowed to decide matters. Consequently, in the matter of property rights these are fundamental and basic to the rights of individuals to exercise freedom and choice in society and so have to be protected. The distribution of these rights is therefore a secondary matter and cannot be allowed to override the person's property rights. The establishment of private property in the company form is something that the state should refrain from interfering in and, apart from matters of procedural justice and the prevention of deception and fraud, should refrain from regulation beyond the necessary requirements of administrating contract law. The firm is conceived of as a nexus of contracts which is owned by the shareholders. The management are agents in the relationship with their investor principals. All others are contractors and can gain satisfaction and redress under the contract arrangements or by recourse to the courts and the law of contract. In the pursuit of each person's self-interest the common good will be served by the invisible hand of the market as Adam Smith forcefully advocated. In this respect a moral outcome miraculously results from selfish motives. If this spontaneous system of interaction and outcomes is interfered with in an intentional way, to try to pursue some other political purpose, then disaster will follow. The aim of the liberal is to vigorously defend this system and to see that malignant and benign intentions of intellectuals do not undermine what is a natural and spontaneous evolution of a civilized social order. When these doctrines are applied to the institutionalization of the company, then a vigorous defense of the status quo and a rolling back of its recidivist tendencies is the main quest of commentators in this field.

The views of Friedman and Hayek

In Milton Friedman's view, which was noted earlier, a business that has a social conscience is sliding down the long and slippery slope towards socialism which he considers will ultimately become totalitarian and undermine freedom in society.[3]   The notion of corporate social responsibility, he thinks, is analytically loose and, when subjected to a rigorous analysis, can be shown to be an oxymoron because only people can have responsibilities; corporations are incapable of being responsible. The executives of the corporation are responsible as agents of the shareholders' interest and, as such, their responsibility is to make profits for return in the interests of shareholder. The purpose of the business is not that of a family, church or club; its function and raison d'etre is to engage in business for profit. Without this clarity of purpose it would be difficult for the shareholders to hold the management of the business accountable for their actions. Managers might be tempted to spend the corporation's resources on all manner of schemes and interests that are for the management's or employees' benefit. This is, in effect, to deprive the shareholders of their rightful returns and prevents them from exercising their own choices over how their wealth is spent. Taxation is the role of the government, as is the funding of social spending; it is not therefore the duty of the corporation to usurp this function. It also frees management from strict accountability and allows them to pursue their own purposes with other people's money. If shareholder's want to support social causes then they should be at liberty to make charitable donations from their dividend income or realized share wealth; it is not the duty of managers to judge the social priorities of governments, charities or shareholders. The danger in the corporation becoming involved in social spending is that this is crossing the boundary into other institutions activities and so will attract the attention of politicians whose task it is to make choices about political priorities. If business gets involved in these activities then politicians will want to become more influential in the corporate decision-making process. The control and purpose of the firm will then become a political matter and subject to negotiation and bargaining that will distort the nature and independence associated with private property, and so in the long run endanger the freedom of individual in society. The function of business in society is to pursue self-interest but within the constraints of the law and the accepted boundaries of business custom. If the institutions of business are kept within these constraints, then corporations are fully accountable to their shareholders and the interests of other stakeholders are served in the normal contractual manner or via the government regime of regulation. The only reason to make investment in the field of social causes is to improve the profitability of the company in its markets or to prevent the attack of politicians who are trying to change the rules of corporate governance.

In essence, Friedman maintains that corporate responsibility is bound by the law, the ethical customs of a society, and the prevailing regulatory regime. The premises that underpin this argument are that of the agency-principal theory and that the institutional division of labour in society is best for the common good of society.

A similar argument is set out in Frederick von Hayek's article, 'The Corporation in a Democratic Society: in whose interest ought it and will it be run?' [4] Again the objects of the corporation should be limited to using shareholders' capital in the most profitable manner. Hayek believes that if businesses are not limited to this objective and begin to use profits to pursue 'socially desirable' causes, then two major problems will arise. In the short term, the managers of these firms will have greater powers over cultural, political and moral issues. In the long term, government involvement will be increased substituting regulations for self-regulation in business. Again, if managers are allowed to decide what social issues a company should fund, they will base their decisions on personal preference rather than on the cause's intrinsic value. This makes social spending an arbitrary business. It also gives a minority the power to decide what is beneficial for the majority outside of the political process. Consequently to avoid this problem, a company's primary goal should be to efficiently allocate its enduring resources. All other interests are transient or limit this efficient allocation of resources. This could cause the company to change from serving the needs of individuals into organizations which determine the needs to be served. Hayek believes that socially desirable causes should stay in the public sector and be paid for by the public, either from voluntary contributions or via taxation.

Hayek goes on to argue that when a corporation sticks to making profits the government will keep away from it, but if the corporation begins to fund social projects then government will begin to interfere. In fact, if anything, the shareholders' control of the company is not at the present time effective enough. He proposes that it be strengthened in two ways. Shareholders should be enabled under the Companies Acts to decide what proportion of the net profits is to be retained by the firm. This is to prevent the management retaining profits and spending them on unapproved (by shareholders) investment. Each shareholder, in his view, should be able to take away his or her full profit entitlement each year. The second reform in corporate governance he would like to introduce is the removal from companies of inter-company voting rights so that minority control can reside in corporate managers' hands. This has led to the separation of ownership from control to the detriment of shareholders' interests, in Hayek's opinion.

The need to strengthen shareholder control of the company has recently become the theme of other commentators in this area, most notably Elaine Sternberg, who has been keen to criticize the notion of stakeholding in matters of corporate governance.[5]

Elaine Sternberg

Sternberg's view of corporate governance echoes that of Freidman and Hayek in that this is, again, an activity which is very limited and specific. It is about 'ways of ensuring that corporate actions, assets and agents are directed at achieving the corporate objectives established by the corporation's shareholders.'[6] Because corporations are owned by their shareholders, absolutely, in her view, it is those shareholders they should serve, not stakeholders. Therefore, '...in business corporations, directors are properly accountable to shareholders for maximizing shareholder value.'[7] Directors are not on the board of the company to serve other interests, however worthy they may be. She goes on to argue that, though there are faults in the traditional Anglo-Saxon model of corporate governance, most of the recent criticisms are misdirected. Critics are often attacking the operations of business itself rather than the governance structures. Many critics, she claims, make false assumptions about what constitutes ethical conduct by corporations, and confuse issues about sort-termism, redundancies and high executive remuneration with corporate governance matters. What they really dislike, she claims, is the use of corporate assets to maximize owner value. In her analysis she makes the point that many critics of corporate governance are conflating the notion of governance with the political philosophy of government in society. It is not for companies to aim at achieving public policy objectives, or to give their stakeholders the rights and privileges commonly associated with citizenship. The German and Japanese approaches to corporate governance have few lessons for those in the UK and USA, because they are '...both theoretically and practically inferior to the traditional Anglo-Saxon system.'[8] This is because these systems are incapable of achieving the definitive purpose of corporate governance: the delivery of shareholder value. Nor do they protect sufficiently, in her view, shareholder property rights.

Sternberg devotes a chapter to a critique of the stakeholder theory of recent years, and describes it as 'fundamentally misguided' and says that it '...undermines both private property and accountability.'[9] In her view, it is unworkable because it involves multiple accountability and the impossible task of balancing stakeholder benefits which are unclear, differently weighted and difficult to reconcile. Regulation that attempts to limit shareholder rights and property interests will be counter-productive and encourage investors to move elsewhere.

Some criticisms of the traditional Anglo-Saxon model of governance are justified, in her view, however. The practice of accountability to shareholders falls short, in reality, in several ways. General meetings and corporate elections do not allow shareholders to control the pursuit of company purposes adequately. Directors are often ill-equipped to exercise their proper fiduciary duties, insufficiently accountable to shareholders and are not independent enough of the corporation's management. Institutional investors are often weak and unaccountable to managers of the funds that invest on behalf of their beneficiaries.

Sternberg proposes several ways in which the corporate governance system of the Anglo-Saxon type can be improved. The essence of the plan is to improve the accountability of the corporation to its shareholders by having companies compete for investment funds. This requires a clarification of the objectives of corporate governance and free competition in the methods for achieving them.

This implies an improved market for corporate control where companies compete for shareholders, and investment fund managers compete for funds, in part, on the degree and kinds of accountability they give to investors. In such a competitive arena, companies could differentiate themselves by identifying their corporate objectives more precisely. They could extend the scope and reduce the costs of voting to nominate directors, and they could allow shareholders to directly nominate directors. Other measures would include the election of boards of directors of all non-executive members, better reporting and wider disclosure to shareholders, and better methods of knowing whether the corporate purpose is on track. These measures would arise from a competitive framework of choice for shareholders for their investments, rather than from government intervention in regulatory provisions for corporate governance.

Sternberg is very keen on improving the market for corporate control as a way of improving practices of corporate governance. This is the market in which companies compete for shareholders, and investment managers for funds. The challenge, as she sees it, is to find new ways to extend the competition that exists in respect of operational performance to corporate governance arrangements. Active approaches to improving corporate governance are advocated, similar to those in the USA, targeted by groups such as the LENS group and Pro Ned and PIRC in the UK. Companies could differentiate themselves more by specifying their company objectives with precision, to deliver shareholder value within a particular industry, for example, or in the case of investment trusts, the types of investment and strategies they will subscribe too. Companies could also compete for shareholders by varying the extent to which their policies are truly performance-related and by having them translated into performance indicators and remuneration schemes. Various improvements could be made in company voting arrangements to extend the use of shareholder decision making in cost-effective ways, to appoint representatives and decide various issues. New technology could also be used to put shareholder resolutions onto the agendas of AGMs and EGMs. Shareholder approval could be sought for all takeovers and mergers and for all major shifts in strategy, the sale of major assets, and for all major corporate dispersments, for example donations to political parties and charities. Shareholders could also be given the power to alter, as well as approve, reorganization plans in the face of bankruptcy. Voting should, in Sternberg's view, also be used by the shareholders to approve all directorial appointments, remuneration schemes, and for re-election of boards by rotation. Moreover, company votes could also be made more valuable if the shares voting rights were separated from their other rights and traded separately.

In relation to directors, Sternberg envisages several improvements that are needed. They must be properly qualified to perform the role in terms of experience and capability, and they must also have a minimum shareholding in the company to give them a personal interest in its fate. Directors should compete against each other in terms of their strategic and tactical plans for the company. They should be required to inform shareholders of their reasons for resigning, if they are relevant to matters of corporate governance. Directors should be independent of the management and the board, if necessary, could be made up of all non-executive directors, and possibly even with professional directors appointed to guard the interests of shareholders. Companies should be able to offer financial and structural support for independent directors who should be entitled to full access to company information and company staff.

Directors could be charged with providing to shareholders interim as well as annual reports and these might cover a wide range of subjects such as risk assessment, environmental and social audits and even a governance audit to show shareholders that directors are performing in their interests. To compile the latter report a governance committee could be charged with the duty to ensure that the company is strictly adhering to its avowed purpose. It could also act as a conduit for concerns about the conduct of the company including those of shareholders and those that flow through the company's internal information systems. On the whole, better information flow from management to shareholders is one of the key ways to improve the accountability of the corporate governance system.

The case for employee capitalism

Jeffrey Gates is the author of the book *The Ownership Solution* which maintains that capitalism is good at creating capital but poor at creating capitalists. The solution therefore is to create more capitalists.[10] He suggests that opportunities for ownership of a company should be extended to as many as can benefit from it. He is critical of the notion of stakeholders' rights because they are nebulous and inchoate until they are consolidated into contractual relationships that embody the rights and responsibilities associated with the ownership of company shares. In many ways he has picked up the theme of Peter Drucker that the institutional ownership of shares has brought about a social revolution in share ownership. Gates's proposal is to extend this still further by creating more employee share ownership plans (ESOP). He suggests that ESOPs can be made to pay for themselves, not out of employees after-tax income, but out of the pre-tax earnings of the company they work for. The law is changed to allow for the creation of an ESOP which allows the company to borrow money for the purchase of shares for the employees. The loan, which attracts tax relief for the company, is then repaid from the company's future earnings. Employees then have an asset which pays for the cost of its own purchase. In the USA, he estimates there are more than 10,000 ESOP schemes which cover ten million workers, with an average ownership level of 15 to 20 percent. Avis Inc., the large car rental company in the USA, is an interesting example of a self-financing ESOP. It became 100 percent ESOP-owned in 1987 through a buy-out transaction which enabled its previous owners to end their investment in Avis and reinvest their capital gain on a tax-free basis. He does not suggest that this is the only method of broadening share ownership that should be used. He thinks many kinds of scheme should be experimented with but that they should be tested against the following principles. First, as many participants as possible should be included whether they are direct employees or employees of related enterprises or indeed consumers. Second, some limit must be placed on the relative shareholdings, otherwise experience suggests that this ownership opportunity will, in time, be monopolized by a few. Thirdly, rewards and incentives need to be included in the plans so that participants do not sell their shares immediately and pocket the proceeds; longer-term ownership and participation need to be induced by the design of the scheme. In terms of the UK, Gates claims that many opportunities were missed in the privatization programmes to generate a wider share ownership culture. He is, though, a firm believer that, if share ownership can be made more extensive and meaningful to the ordinary worker, capitalism, as a system, will become much more accountable and productive. The problem is that property ownership has not spread widely enough to make everyone a stakeholder.

This theme of improving the accountability of the board to shareholders and the sharper pursuit of greater shareholder value is a theme of some commentators in the USA. Most notably Robert Monks and Nell Minow who both side with Hayek in arguing that the interests of society are best served when management's efforts focus exclusively on the enhancement of shareholder value.[11]

Monks and Minow: Watching the Watchers

In the USA, at the forefront of shareholder activism for many years, is an investment company called Lens Inc., operated by Robert Monks and Nell Minow. They have pushed for better shareholder value from many large companies and have written several books expounding their position. In *Watching the Watchers* they put forward a set of proposals for improving the shareholders' position in corporate governance matters, entitled the re-empowering of shareholders. Their main point is that this will only happen when there is an meaningful level of accountability between the company and the shareholders. After all, the purpose of corporate governance is to find a way to maximize wealth creation over time, in a manner that does not impose heavy costs on third parties or on society as a whole. In their view, an effective governance system requires a set of checks and balances, assuring that the right questions are asked of the company management. They are explicit about the principle behind their approach which is that the greatest benefit to the greatest number will come from a governance system in which each person profits according to their contribution to the company. Accordingly governance has to focus upon performance and competitiveness and the minimization of agency costs. Whilst investors and management have different interests, there is much that can be done to align those interests on many issues of company activity. There has to be a system of checks and balances between the freedom of the company to create wealth and the protection of members of society who are vulnerable or of society itself in the face of externalities.

In their view, corporate managers have been given too much power without proportionate responsibility and, apart from some spectacular abuses, the market has shown a reluctance to respond appropriately to performance failures and managerial shortcomings. They are particularly critical of the weakness of the corporate response to environmental issues and of governmental attempts to regulate the behavior of corporations. They advocate an approach which starts with the corporation itself and, importantly, the participation of an informed and much broader base of shareholders. Great strides have been made in this direction with the growth of institutional investors in pensions funds and insurance moneys. These institutions need to have a long-term perspective on investments and, importantly, they are urging them to become much more active investors than they hitherto have been. In the past they have been reluctant to exercise shareholder voice on their investment portfolios, preferring instead to exercise their exit rights and move or churn investments for better returns. Monks and Minow are urging these institutions to play a more collective and active part in putting voice pressure on underperforming companies and claim that this can lead to substantial improvements in returns to these institutional shareholders. They are also urging regulators of the investment institutions to encourage the relaxation of rules restricting such collective voice and to encourage the fund managers to interpret their remit in a more interventionist manner.

The creation of a stable and long-term class of institutions shareholders is the first requirement of a better corporate governance system. Next measures are required that will make it possible for shareholders to monitor the performance of the companies they invest in more closely. Shareholders, in their view, need to monitor certain key factors: director nominations, evaluation of director performance, executive and director compensation plans, overall company performance and structure. They should not concern themselves with the ordinary business decisions of the management. The structure of the governance process is the next requirement. Large investors should share information and resources and develop policies regarding poorly-performing companies. Shareholders should try to take control of the proxy voting systems, either as institutional investors or as employee investors, and vote together to ensure unity of purpose and action in the company general meetings. They should submit shareholder resolutions and competitive proposals to the management in a meeting. This would require the designation of company or shareholder resources to be effective, and could be organized through shareholder committees.

Monks and Minow would like to see the chairman of the company as a separate director from the CEO, and the chairman should appreciate that they owe their job to the shareholders, not matter how large their personal investment. They would like to see rights and responsibilities reflecting different shareholder needs and abilities. Whilst some investors value the ease of transferability and liquidity that presently accompanies shareholding, others, perhaps the institutional investors, would prefer more infrastructure to be able to monitor and nurse their investments. They suggest that different types of share could be offered: ownership shares which give up some liquidity in return for greater ownership rights, and trading shares which give up some ownership rights in favor of liquidity. The example of Warren Buffett is instructive here, as he was able to persuade several companies to create a new class of shares in their companies, usually convertible preference shares, that ensure him an increased return compared with the common shareholder but secure for the company his participation and commitment to holding the shares for a long period. In effect, long-term owners need to have insider status, full access to information, influence with management, and seats on the board.

Appropriate performance criteria to measure company performance are also required. In Monks' and Minow's view, the only shareholders who can provide the necessary normative standards for company performance are the long-term owners. They would also support the view that a new kind of professional director should help to bring about these changes in corporate governance. Such directors should be fully-conversant with their legal powers and responsibilities, be led by an independent chairman, be prepared to commit the necessary time and effort to fulfill these duties, maintain their independence from the company's management, be competent and trained to understand and use the information made available to them, and have an equity stake in the company's performance. In essence, the principal-agent theory at the heart of this model of corporate governance has to be made to work more effectively and attention has to be paid to the shareholder role of principal and the principal's job of holding a professional management accountable to a broad and participative shareholder base. Shareholders should and can rule, OK!

Conclusions

The company's role in generating or recovering social capital is largely ignored by this position. The generation of wealth by companies is considered very important for social well-being, but it is not the job of companies to interfere with the personal, political and charitable decision of others about the distribution of this wealth. These are considerations that lie outside the economic sphere. After all, the company is not a church, state, welfare agency or a family. It is, according to this position, an economic association with specific and limited responsibilities which, simply by being what it is, serves the common good of the community. The weaknesses of this position will be explored in chapter 11. Before then, a consideration of another scenario within the liberal view of property needs to be examined, but one that does draw upon a high level of social capital for its efficient functioning.

References

[1] Novak, M., (1997), *The Fire of Invention: Civil Society and the Future of the Corporation*, New York, Rowman and Littlefield, p 93.

[2] Gray, J., (1986), *Liberalism*, Milton Keynes, Open University Press.

[3] Friedman, M., (1962), *Capitalism and Freedom*, Chicago, Chicago University Press.

[4] Hayek, F., (1969), 'The corporation in a democratic society: in whose interest ought it and will it be run?', in Ansoff, l., *Business Strategy*, Harmondsworth, Penguin.

[5] Sternberg, E., (1998), *Corporate Governance: Accountability in the Marketplace*, London, Institute of Economic Affairs.

[6] Ibid, p 60.

[7] Ibid, p 61.

[8] Ibid, p 74.

[9] Ibid, p 93.

[10] Gates, J., (1998), *The Ownership Solution: Toward A Shared Capitalism for the Twenty-First Century*, London, Penguin.

[11] Monks, R. A. and Minow, N., (1996), *Watching the Watchers: Corporate governance for the 21st Century*, Oxford, Blackwell.

chapter ten

Replace the Company

'If there is a postbureaucratic world, it will not be one in which bureaucracy is eliminated...the positive functions and moral worth of bureaucracy cannot be ignored. Rather, the new, nonbureaucratic forms will be essential leaven in the bureaucratic dough.''

Introduction

This chapter will consider the final scenario in the trajectory model; this is the position that can envisage the company becoming less and less important as an institutionalized form for conducting business transactions. This will either be the result of large businesses being undermined or replaced by smaller ones, or as the result of new business forms slowly replacing the company form altogether. Much will depend upon whether social capital can be preserved and regenerated so that business transactions can be maintained on the basis of wider and richer networks of norms and values. Whilst these two possibilities might seem to be contradictory, if the legitimacy of the company is increasingly called into question, the option for companies to remain as they are, in the long run, might not be open and it could mean that they are, in fact, entering a period of decline. This chapter will explore these two possibilities.

Will the need for the company form decline?

The history of the company has been, until this point, one of growth and ever larger increases in size and scope of operation. The principal influence which has brought this about is the advantage of producing on a large scale. New ways of producing on a large scale have continually been invented, and some of them have offered great gains in efficiency; thus in many industries the size of company has had to keep on growing in order to take advantage of these more productive methods. In the 18th century a company which employed a few tens of men was a large firm; by 1815 there were a few large concerns who employed a few thousand men; in the 19th century may firms employed tens of thousand of men; in the 20th century we got to the point where some large firms employed hundreds of thousands of men. However, we appear to have reached the point where firms, in terms of employment, are beginning to get smaller and are increasingly employing fewer workers in their direct labour forces. This of course begs the question of whether firms are in decline. The answer to this question is perhaps best pursued if it is split into two parts. Will the company form disappear as a legal category, and will the large company survive and prosper in the informational age?

The company form is likely to be a necessary feature of a capitalist society for the foreseeable future primarily, because this is a superb vehicle for the management of risk inherent in the 'creative destruction' of the business enterprise. Prior to the Companies Acts businessmen, if they did not have enough capital to run their business, had to resort to borrowing and partnerships to increase their capital. Partnerships did not tend to work smoothly if they had more than a dozen members; and the amount that could be borrowed by a partnership depended upon the amount of money the partners had themselves put into the venture. This put limits on the growth of business and made lending to business difficult and risky. The formation of joint stock companies with limited liability was a great innovation for both inventors and entrepreneurs.[2] The shareholders' investment was at risk but only up to the limit of the paid-up share capital, not in an unlimited way when involved in a partnership. The entrepreneur was also given greater capital to work with, but the company was limited in terms of its liabilities. The history of company law is a long story of cat and mouse between the law (cat) and fraudsters (mouse), whose activities form the shady side of company promotion. The shareholder has the protection of limited liability, but in many respects puts himself into the hands of the company directors who will mange his property and hopefully deliver a return. If the shares are traded on the stock exchange they can, of course, be sold and the investment liquidated; this is another way of limiting the shareholders' risk. However, the ability to sell will be dependent upon the state of the market and a company in trouble may find buyers of its shares in short supply. For business transaction of any size and volume, the basic protections and encouragements to take risks is shared by this institutional mechanism. It is therefore unlikely that this will become redundant in the near future unless there is a radical transformation of the nature of economic activity in society. Firms are a necessary institution in the conduct of business and so are likely to remain a feature of the business environment for a long time to come. In fact, the question many governments in Europe are facing is how to promote and simulate the creation of businesses and make the company form more attractive as a vehicle for entrepreneurial activity. In

Europe, a large share of economic activity is carried out by organizations other than large profit-seeking companies with quoted shares, these range from professional partnerships to employee-owned companies, non-profit making trusts, the self-employed and small and medium-sized enterprises. These organizations account for 66 percent of all EU non-agricultural market sector employment.[3]   The USA has generated a tremendous number of new firms in recent years and thereby reduced its unemployment levels dramatically in the 1990s, but Europe has not, so far, found the right recipe to generate sufficient quantities of new firms. Relaxing the regulatory conditions that govern small businesses is thought to be one solution, along with making the laws of bankruptcy less stringent and discouraging to the failed entrepreneur. Much will depend on whether the bankruptcy law can be drafted to make the distinction between culpable and non-culpable bankrupts; the former will be punished more harshly and the latter less so in an attempt to encourage a risk-taking business culture.[4]

Will large companies survive and prosper ?

With regard to the second question about the survival of big companies, the outlook is less clear. There undoubtedly is a trend towards smaller firms in term of the numbers employed, if not in terms of capital employed or global reach. Some profound changes may be influencing the economics of the firm in the informational age. Industrial economists have indeed pondered the question of why are there firms, and of what will happen to them.

After all, if the theory of the price system is to be believed, then the market should be the supreme allocator of resources and opportunities, so that firms are seemingly unnecessary to these transactions. The traditional economic explanation for the existence of firms was a technological one. Factors of production are needed in certain combinations, and some scales of production are more efficient than others, so there is a role for the firm to coordinate these factors. However, there is, on closer analysis , no good reason why all the individuals involved in a production process should not operate their own firms, buying and selling their semi-assembled components with each other as the product is produced. The technological theory of the firm as a manager of the process is rather a weak explanation, because the providers of specialist inputs could simply contract for managerial services from other specialist providers.

A better hypothesis to explain the firm was put forward in 1937 by Ronald Coase.[5] He pointed out that, when economic agents interact with one another, they incur 'transaction costs' that vary with the mode of interaction. In the market, he argued, agents interact by negotiating exchanges, with prices serving as signals of the opportunities facing each supplier of a service or demander of a product. In a firm, on the other hand, a central coordinator or manager organizes the allocation of resources such as machinery owned by him and the workers he employs. Were the production process to be undertaken through the market interactions alone, notes Coase, the interacting parties would have to negotiate new actions and new terms of exchange each time a change in market or technological conditions made profitable a change in the activity being undertaken. Owners of the semi-manufactured parts would have to determine prices at which to exchange their products, a difficult task in the absence of external markets for such goods and because these prices would be subject to change in response to changes in factor supply, technical conditions and other variables. Any changes or problems in the production process would require that the negotiation of contracts begin again. The costs of these re-negotiations, and the 'price discovery process' could be handled by what Coase calls a firm, a set of relationships under which a central coordinator is granted authority to organize tasks and payments.

This analysis, after years of neglect, was further extended by the American economist Oliver Williamson, in to what is now called 'transaction cost' economics.[6] Market and firms are treated as discrete modes of organizing economic activity, and the choice among these modes is thought to be dictated by minimizing decisions with respect to the cost of transactions among the different parties involved. Williamson's emphasis in this theory is upon the problem of investment in assets specific to a given enterprise. He suggests agents contemplating investing in assets face the problems of contracting. These transaction costs are the cost of drafting, negotiating, and safeguarding the contract. They also include the costs of maladaption as the contract progresses, the costs of corporate governance, and the bonding costs of effecting secure commitments. Williamson recognizes that transaction costs may assume particular importance in situations where agents make relationship-specific investments in a firm. There may have been plenty of competition to buy this asset before the specific commitment was made, but after the investment is 'sunk' they are to some extent locked together, and external markets will not provide a guide to the agent's opportunity cost once the relationship is under way. Bringing a transaction into a firm from the market (integration) mitigates opportunistic behavior and improves the investment incentives. Firms exist when these costs are lower than those that prevail in the market, and when the costs of organizational contracting grow to be higher than those that would prevail in the market, then organizations go into decline. However, it might be some time before this is realized and acted upon. Williamson's theory suggests that firms will be larger in those industries where products pass through more stages as intermediate goods without outside markets, or where the ability to flexibly redeploy resources is of greater importance. For example, the railway companies devised line and staff structures when coordination of an end-to-end system of contract broke down and older and simpler structures were unable to manage the resulting networks. The M-form organization structure of General Motors and du Pont helped them handle the internal contracting more efficiently and so was then eventually adopted by many firms in industry.

The trend towards globalisation is changing business conditions in many ways. Behind the growing integration of the world economy lies the decline in the costs of transport and communications. Between 1930 and 1990 average revenue per mile in air transport fell from 68 US cents to 11 cents in 1990 US dollars.[7] The cost of a three minute telephone call between New York and London fell from $244.65 to $3/32. Between 1960 and 1990, the cost of a unit of computing power fell 99 percent. Trade liberalization is also very important. Under the agreement reached at the end of the Uruguay round of multilateral trade negotiations, average advanced country tariffs on imports of manufactures will be reduced to under four percent Tariffs of developing countries are set to fall from 34 percent between 1984 and 1987 to 14 percent. Between 1970 and 1997, the number of countries that eliminated exchange controls affecting imports of goods and services jumped from 35 to 137. Restrictions on investment have been reduced virtually everywhere. Around the world there have been some 570 liberalizing changes in regulations governing foreign direct investment since 1991. Some 1,330 bilateral investment treaties involving 162 countries are now, in effect, a threefold increase in half a decade. These technological changes and movements to deregulate are working together to change the transaction costs in business, and to date they have often favoured the development of multinational companies and internal trade between their affiliates. According to the World Bank, the share in world output of multinationals and their affiliates jumped from 4.5 percent in 1970 to 7.5 percent in 1995. Their share in manufacturing output was put at 18 percent in 1992, up from 12 percent in 1977. The largest 100 multinationals, ranked on the basis of their foreign assets, own $1,700bn in their foreign affiliates, one-fifth of global foreign assets. All but two of the companies are from advanced countries, 30 from the USA alone. The big change in recent years, is a shift in the reasons why companies move production overseas. Historically, companies have located production abroad in order to overcome natural or artificial barriers to trade. If production efficiency were the only criterion, it would have made sense for many companies to locate all their production at a single base, to maximize economies of scale. In practice, however, governments in consuming countries have pushed them to spread production more widely. Other barriers to centralization of production were often inherent in the nature of the business, for example many services needed face-to-face contact. Fear of fluctuations in real exchange rates encouraged the spread of production capacity across frontiers. Many of these trends are now changing. Trade liberalization makes traditional protection avoiding production unnecessary. Improvements in communications are eliminating natural barriers to long-distance transactions. Services can now be produced in one country and exported to another just like manufactured goods. Multinationals may, therefore, be able to locate production sites wherever it is most efficient, and create networks of research, component production assembly and distribution.[8] However, as we saw in chapter 6, the structure of organization that is most appropriate for the informational age is moving towards the network model, which is reducing the size of firms and changing their internal structures away from the mutidivisional structure. The structures that will prosper might well be dependent upon how they interact with factors outside of themselves, such as the preservation and generation of social capital in society.

Network enterprises based upon social capital

In fact, as we noted above, Castells argues that the large company will be replaced entirely by the new form of organization, the network enterprise. With the advent of the computer, the transaction costs involved in market relationships have been reduced and so the incentives to build large companies is reduced. Indeed, the Internet is seen not merely as a communications network but also as the shape of the new organizations of business.[9] Many companies now realize that if they do not seize the opportunity to remodel their businesses around the Internet, then they are likely to be outflanked by existing rivals with more vision. The Internet does not just represent an opportunity to cut costs and shorten supply chains, but importantly the opportunity to expand revenues and build stronger customer and supplier relationships. Business-to-business electronic trading has an enormous potential beyond that of electronic retailing, which is the focus of attention at the moment. The Internet is thought to have changed business transactions is a number of ways already: new channels are changing sales and brand management; the balance of power is shifting towards the customer; the pace and competitive element in business is increasing; information and knowledge are becoming key assets. To thrive in the world of Internet business, companies may need to reinvent themselves, their business models and processes, their interactions with customers, suppliers, network partners, and examine how they use knowledge as a strategic asset. Companies on the Internet have the opportunity to become regional and global players.

Large corporate hierarchies often cannot process the information they need to be as market focused and simple as smaller networked businesses. Market information is local in nature and cannot be responded to quickly enough if it has to rise up the organizational hierarchy to the decision makers and in any case it can become distorted on the way. To deal with this situation large firms have been trying to decentralize their decision-making power to the lower orders, but the problem then becomes one of coordination across the company. This has encouraged a move into the market and companies are now outsourcing and sub-contracting many parts of their operations that they previously organized within their own organizations. Managing a large number of market relationships can become very difficult. One answer has been to develop networks as an intermediate form of transaction between organizations and market. Fukuyama has defined a network as '...a group of individual agents who share informal norms or values beyond those necessary for ordinary market transactions.'[10]

For a network to be established, a set of informal norms must be created between agents, not based upon the imposition by an authority but upon what has previously been described as a foundation of social capital, the norms and values that bind people together and lead them to trust one another. This means that the nature of economic exchange in a network is conducted on a different basis from that conducted in a market. In a network, people are not as likely to take advantage of one another and the reciprocal nature of the relationship gives it a less instrumental quality and a more meaningful relationship results. Fukuyama is of the view that society is capable of regeneration of social capital in spontaneous ways as the inclination to generate norms and values is a biological necessity in most human beings. In favorable conditions the social capital of a community can begin to flourish and gives rise to the generation of networked business transactions. Some of the social capital regeneration can be aided by the technology and networks created. Home working via the use of information and communications technology allows for the reconnection of place of work and home life as it was in the pre-industrial era. It also allows for the tasks of work to be integrated into the tasks of living in a less divided pattern: work can be done before breakfast, after the school run, and later in the evening. This allows the worker to make and maintain more intimate connections with the family and community and so helps to generate social capital.

Networks can have the advantage, compared to organizations, of helping to overcome some of the principal-agent problems. In an organization, information is often a source of power and influence in the hierarchy and so it does not flow freely or without costs. People often hold onto or filter information, sometimes to the detriment of the purpose of the organizations. In a network, information often flows more freely and, because the other person in the network is seen as a fellow principal, the principal-agent division does not arrive. If the power of the network can be used in business then some of the transaction costs of trading information in an organization can be reduced. Networks are not simple or easy to create; they are often the product of shared patterns of socialization, shared spaces and shared interests and tend to arise in an unpredictable and unintended fashion. The milieu of innovation and the site of many advanced technology industries often is coincidental to university and social facilities in certain regional areas. The example of Silicon Valley in California as the home of the leading edge companies in the information technology industry is often cited as an example of this phenomenon." Beneath the surface of strong competition between small companies is a wide array of social networks linking individuals in different companies, based upon university links, social clubs and lifestyle interests. The social capital in these networks facilitates a number of important exchanges. A great deal of knowledge is tacit in nature and cannot be easily reduced to propositions and sold like a commodity as intellectual property, but it can be exchanged between friends chatting in a bar or club and between people who share common experiences and problems. This type of interaction and exchange is clearly more important for the development of advanced technology industries but as these are the growth industries of the future the importance of networking as a business practice is sure to become more prominent. Despite the trends to globalise markets, local milieu and proximity are likely to remain very important to technological progress in the leading edge industries. The manufacture and distribution of good and services created by these new technologies can, of course, be located any where in the world. Smaller rather than larger firms linked into global networks could be the dominant company forms in the next century.

Smaller companies might employ fewer people directly, but they may have a global reach and remain the key players in the world economy. However, the fact that they will be employing more and more sophisticated knowledge workers is highly significant. If capital is relatively cheaply priced as a world commodity, brains and intelligence are likely to be at a higher premium. This may require firms to share some of their profits with these workers who could, at the highest levels, be in a position to command a very high price for their services. The incentive to become an employee will become less obvious for the talented knowledge worker and, consequently, the company will have to try harder to attract them. This may involve offering remuneration and perhaps security incentives to this type of employee. It may also entail the use of sophisticated management techniques, if the employee is to become loyal to the company and remain highly motivated when at work. Highly participative and empowering models of HRM are therefore likely to be deployed, and the reputation of the company for honesty and fair dealing may become important for employee identification, along with the right corporate profile in the external environment for human and responsible conduct. This could have a knock-on effect for other levels of employee, as the company may not be able to act inconsistently in its operations in different parts of the organization or in other parts of its operations in the world, particularly when there is a global market in communication and information. Therefore, having to accommodate the knowledge worker could be a bonus for all employees, and represent a kind of hidden hand of the market for human dignity. Through this mechanism, the firm becomes a major vehicle for the regeneration and replacement of social capital more generally.

In previous economic periods there were often short spurts of growth and longer periods of stability; these are the conditions under which the large company developed. Today, this process of punctuated evolution is moving towards almost a continuous pattern of change and adaptation. This might be termed punctuated evolutionary chaos. The Asian financial crisis in 1998-9 was an example of how informational flows are changing the world economy; these countries went from boom to bust in a few months and could well have taken others with them. Reaction and adaptation time in business has to be ever-shortened. Companies that can find new ways to do this and compete with each other on this basis are likely to be the dominant forms of business organization with a real competitive advantage. Companies will perhaps still be powerful and pervasive in the global market, but on the whole be smaller, leaner and fitter than they are at the moment.

Having outlined all four positions on the model of future trajectories for the company the final chapter will attempt to evaluate them and draw some conclusions about the future of the company form.

References

[1] Selznick, P., (1992), *The Moral Commonwealth*, Berkeley, University of California Press.

[2] Alborn, T.L., (1998), *Conceving Companies*, London, Routledge.

[3] Ricketts, M., (1999), *The Many Ways of Governance*, London, IEA Social Affairs Unit.

[4] *Financial Times*, (1999), 'Government aims to sift rogues from risk-takers', 13th July.

[5] Coase, R.H., (1937), 'The Nature of the Firm', *Economica*, 6, pp 386-405.

[6] Williamson, O. E., (1993), *The Nature of the Firm: Origins, Evolution and Development*, Oxford, Oxford University Press.

[7] *Financial Times*, (1997), 'The Global Company', 3rd October.

8   Dicken, P., (1998), *Global Shift: The Internationalization of Economic Activity*, New York, Guilford Press.

9   Gates, W., (1999), *Business @ the Speed of Thought: Using a Digital Nervous System*, London, Penguin.

10   Fukuyama, F., (1999), *The Great Disruption*, London, Profile Books, p 199.

11   Saxenian, A. L., (1994), *Regional Advantage: Culture and Competition in Silicon Valley and Route 128*, Cambridge Mass., Harvard University Press.

chapter eleven

Evaluation and Conclusions

'It is perhaps the biggest job of the modern corporation as the representative institution of industrial society to find a synthesis between justice and dignity, between equality of opportunities and social status and function.'[1]

Introduction

This chapter will attempt to bring the threads of this study together and make an evaluation of the four trajectories for the company form outlined in each of the last four chapters. All the four scenarios have strengths and weaknesses in political and economic terms; what will make them more or less likely is whether they match the turn of events unfolding in the global economy, and whether they can offer business enterprise a legitimate position in society. Once the legitimacy question is settled for a certain period then the normal determinancies of economics can more comfortably be relied upon to predict the course of events.

An evaluation of the four scenarios
Reform of the company

The notion of reforming the institutional form of business is an idea with a long pedigree. Boswell gives an interesting account of some of the business leaders who advocated changes in this direction (the reconstructionists) in earlier periods in British industry.[2] Many of these were industrialists with social views influenced by Christian beliefs or socialist thinking along the lines of Ruskin, Morris and Tawney. Their proposals for the reform of business were not against capitalism but aimed at changing its course in the direction of internal structural reform, increased external constraints and more countervailing power for trade unions and the state. George Goyder was an early and persistent advocate of a reconstruction of the governance structure of the firm, calling for a general objects clause in company law that would enshrine multiple responsibilities and also legislation to provide workers with equivalent rights to shareholders. In his books, starting with *The Future of Private Enterprise* ,he proposed a shift of power away from shareholders and advocated in large firms dividend limitations, effectively making the shareholders creditors of the business.[3] Companies would become public trusts and those that refused to do so would be forced to do so after 50 years. In other books, Goyder refined his proposals adding worker-directors to unitary company boards, greater use of the AGM as a forum for deliberation and decision, periodic social audits and greater accountability to stakeholders.[4]

An interesting parallel should be drawn between the legitimization crisis of the inflation boom in the early 1970s when business legitimacy was once again in question. An inquiry under Lord Watkinson was set up by the CBI to review the 'Responsibilities of the Public Companys' in 1972-3.[5] The Committee flirted with the idea of establishing an ethical code of conduct to encourage greater social responsibility on the part of the company. However, the proposal ran into considerable criticism and was eventually dropped. A second idea was to try to involve the institutional investors more actively in company monitoring, but again the intentions of the CBI membership to embrace the idea were misread and it was dropped in the face of opposition. The third approach the committee considered was to introduce independent directors onto company boards. This was eventually taken up but its implementation was largely voluntary. Employee participation proposals were almost a none starter in the opinion of the committee, as was the suggestion put to them of including worker directors on the boards of companies. The Committee favoured instead the creation of company-wide joint councils with information disclosure on similar lines to those operated by ICI at the time. Again the final recommendations of the Committee were rather vague on this front which left it a matter for members' voluntary initiatives. Sort shrift in the final Report was also given to the continental idea of supervisory company boards, as these were seen to weaken the link between executives and shareholders and the notion of managerial responsibility. In many respects this is a similar package of reform proposals to that submitted by the advocates of the stakeholder company today. Many of these suggestions are echoed in the work of Kay and Parkinson considered above and so can perhaps be labeled ahead of their time. It is therefore instructive to analyze the reasons why these reconstructivist proposals failed to find favour in the 1970s.

First, there were few wider political projects that would support and sustain this approach. The Labour Party was dominated by trade unions who were reluctant to become partners in industry and saw itself as a loyal opposition to management instead. There was no well-developed lobby for industrial democracy as there was in Scandinavia at this time. Second, the reconstructionists did not coin an attractive title or slogan to represent their proposals; their approach was somewhat vague and difficult to articulate in a wider arena. Third, there was strong, articulate and forceful opposition from the peak organizations of business to contend with: the CBI, BIM and others were beginning to embrace a liberationist ideology in the face of the Labour Government's corporatist tendencies in the 1970s. Fourth, the economic performance of the UK in the face of a world recession was giving rise to concerns about investor returns and the over-mighty power of trade unions in holding back the productivity of the firm. In short, these ideas fell upon a stony ground in political and economic terms.

However, if the similarity of the reconstructionists' ideas with the reforms of the stakeholder advocates is noted, what of the circumstances for the reception of these new ideas? The soil may now be more fertile for the growth of these seeds of change. The political climate is that of New Labour, a revisionist form of social democracy which has severed many of its socialist roots. The aspiration of its leader, Tony Blair, is to find a 'third way' between liberalism and socialism in politics. Leading theorists of this search, such as Anthony Giddens, are willing to embrace the global market but insist on there being adequate regulation to ensure the a responsible capitalism results.[6] This is a much more receptive ideology for the notions of stakeholder revisions to take hold in and find a wider political umbrella to shelter under. There is also a clear and bold label to be applied to the approach: 'Stakeholding'. Its leading exponent, Will Hutton, has made this so popular that its meaning in company governance terms has now been broadened out to include the whole of society.[7] This has helped to give the notion broad support and widespread legitimacy. The use of the term 'stakeholding' is now heard very often in business circles, and features heavily in the public statements and publications of many leading businessmen and companies. Stakeholder language is so common that it may now be possible for this notion to make its way into company processes and practices. After all, if managers are saying they are stakeholder-orientated, then it can only be a matter of time before managers are expected to act this way as well. As outlined in chapters 4 and 6, the drivers moving companies are those in the field of social and environmental reporting at the moment, because of the need to respond to organized and articulate pressure groups in these fields. The issue of business legitimacy is also pushing many firms in this direction and into embracing stakeholder language. Leading the way, in many instances, is a professional management cadre who, having had MBA educations, are now much more receptive and willing to embrace the latest management thinking and incorporate it into their own company's practice. Public relations functions have also grown markedly in the 1980s and 90s and, in particular, in the newly-privatized industries in the face of often hostile public opinion and publicity. There, too, they are strong advocates of the stakeholder language.

Moreover, the changes in industry that Peter Drucker recognized early on, the increase in knowledge workers as the main population in industry, have been profound. Today, companies are very keen to convince their workers that they are genuine partners in the mission and values of the company, so the language of inclusion is particularly apt in this climate. Other factors making for a receptive atmosphere are the relative weakness of trade unions in industrial relations, the trade unions' own strategy of partnership, and their embrace of the approach of continental Europe in matters of human resource management. Indeed, the growing alignment of the UK with Europe, and the prospect of further legislation to harmonize company law in Europe, is another factor that could lead to the convergence of corporate governance practices. Perhaps, the vehicle to implement greater change will be the company law review set up by the DTI in 1998, which is due to report in 2001, and which has on its steering group many of the leading advocates of stakeholder reform such as John Plender, John Kay and John Parkinson. Of course, the conjunction of such a wide range of favorable factors should not blind one to the degree of opposition that will exist to substantive changes in this direction, but the grounds for some optimism for change along this trajectory do exist.

Radical change in the company form

Whilst the omens might be good for limited change in the institutionalization of business in order to improve its legitimacy, the likelihood of the circumstances being right for a fundamental or radical change in these institutions does not look good at the moment, or even moderately favorable in the medium to long term. The main problem is a lack of ideological debate, and little sign of the generation of political movements upon which these ideas can ride and begin to shape events. Such ideas and movements are up against a massive weight of vested interests in the present system, not least of which are the investments ordinary people have made in insurance and pension funds. There may come a time when the climate is right for a radical change. It need not always be a slow process, as in the case of revolutionary change, but would probably require some catastrophic event or major crisis to generate the disruption and ferment needed to unseat the present structure of interests. Until this eventuality comes to pass, these ideas, whilst provocative and interesting, are unlikely to become the main drivers of change.

Another major weakness in the concept of the radical change theorists is whether they have been able to demonstrate that the stakeholder company would be robust enough to ride the waves of innovation and change at the heart of the capitalist system. Schumpeter is still one of the best exponents on the role of the entrepreneur in business and the constant need for innovation and risk taking that fuels the 'creative destruction' of capitalism. He notes that the entrepreneur is a special character who is willing to go against popular opinion or norms to bring about change, and so, is rare. The problem with self-government in industry and putting the workers in control of the management of the company is that this might put a veto into the hands of those who will be affected by change the most. Employees, instead of facing up to this challenge and the uncertainty regarding the possibility that they might have to resign their positions in the firm, might vote against innovation and change because it might lead to these unpalatable consequences. This could put a brake on the development of the firm and make it uncompetitive in the longer run. The case could be made for a limited veto on the introduction of change into the firm (to allow employees to secure discussions of all the strategies and options available), but a full veto on preventing change altogether is unlikely to be a proposal that will lead to a flourishing business. If innovations and changes are reduced in the self-governing firm because the structure of incentives is not sufficient to bring these about, then again, in the longer term, investors will be reluctant to lend capital and the competition from the non-stakeholders companies will probably overwhelm them. This situation might become apparent to the declining stakeholder firm in the fullness of time, but may not do so in sufficient time for them to be able to take the necessary steps to put the proper incentives in place. They will all go down with the ship for want of a good captain. It is a very real challenge for proponents of the radical stakeholder concept to demonstrate the practical feasibility of managing change and creating innovation in the operation of the these firms.

Restoring the control of the shareholders

The prospects of a movement in this direction with the corporate form are reasonable in that this represents only a small move away from the status quo, by strengthening the present model of corporate governance that is widely entrenched in company law in both the USA and UK. However, this position suffers from two major weaknesses: one conceptual regarding the nature of company purpose; the other practical regarding its chances of implementation.

In much of the governance literature the objective of business is assumed to be obvious and widely accepted, and consequently can be unproblematically posed to employees as a uniting common purpose. What unites commentators such as Sternberg, Hayek and Freidman is the basic contention that business is a specific and limited activity that has to function within the constraints of the law and established ethical norms, but that, apart from respecting these constraints, business is about profits for shareholders and has no other obligations or responsibilities. Sternberg for example argues that business is a very specific, limited activity, whose defining purpose is 'maximising owner value over the long term by selling goods or services'.[8] Consequently, business is not about providing social welfare, spiritual fulfilment or full employment, nor is the company to be thought of as a family, a club, a hobby or a sort of government. Emphatically, 'the purpose of business is not to promote the public good.'[9]   However, if we study business as it is actually practised in society, a different concept can be found. The objectives pursued in business are many and various; its participants may be there to make a profit, to earn a living, to make life interesting, to gain status, or for a multiplicity of purposes which cannot be defined out of the analysis at its outset.[10] As Adam Smith made it plain, prosperity not profit is the goal of the free enterprise system.[11] To single out profit maximisation rather than productivity or public service as the central purpose of business activity is a falsification of many people's motives in business. As the result of which, too narrow a vision of what the purpose of business is about can be adopted and the contribution it makes to other aspects of society such as the development of co-operation, community and integrity may be missed altogether. There is no reason to suppose that corporate governance should be exclusively concerned with the pursuit of one purpose; a company may well be able to pursue several purposes with a reasonable degree of success. Firms may be able to satisfy a balanced scorecard of performance indicators, some based upon profit and investment performance, others related to customers and their satisfaction, and still others related to employee satisfaction and community and environmental contributions.

Despite the fact that many commentators have claimed that the key to reforming corporate governance is to give content to the existing structure of notional accountability to shareholders, there are several reasons for doubting that this is possible. It is doubtful whether shareholders have either the incentive or capacity to provide such monitoring. It is also doubtful whether the system of independent directors and more extensive involvement of shareholders in decision making, even if given fuller information, would really work. This is the type of governance system that was meant to have controlled the old nationalised industries, but was a lamentable failure, because it undermined management responsibility for company performance without providing the stimulus to make the firm more effective. There are also dangers in trying to make work a mechanism that is now a long way adrift from reality. The creation of remuneration committees under the Cadbury reforms are seemingly very weak restraints upon the self-interested behaviour of directors in matters of reward. The independence of the remuneration committee is often a sham, existing not to restrain remuneration but to justify it on the whole.

It is also unlikely that, after a period of shareholder value renewal, or what Boswell labels 'liberationalism' in the 1980s and 90s, a new wave of power building and deregulation will take place. Serious doubts about the viability of this political project are justified in the face of certain trends: the rich are getting richer, large gains in capital values are being delivered by the stockmarket year on year, and the depressed nature of the trade union movement and the relatively low increases in wages and inflation. The liberationist grip on power might be waning, but it still remains considerable. The fortress of shareholder value in semi-regulated privatised industries, low income tax, labour market flexibility, small business entrepreneurial support, and institutionalised capital ownership are likely to take along time to erode, albeit it these walls are not impregnable. Increased shareholder control is unlikely to do much to repair the damaged fabric of business legitimacy that is presently failing to cover the needs of this body. Strengthening the voice of the shareholder may, however, strike a more popular chord in the USA where the holding of shares is more widespread and the active shareholder in an individual and institutional sense is more vocal, articulate and widely-accepted. In Europe and the UK, despite the widespread interest in institutional shareholding, this is weakly perceived as a form of social capitalism (Drucker's phrase) and the legislative trajectory is moving in a different direction towards the regulation of governance matters in even more detail, especially in the case of the PLC.

The end of the company

The proposition that companies might be superseded by networks can be criticized on a number of points. First, the existence of networks and their underlying social capital cannot be taken for granted, and where they do not or cannot exist the hierarchical organization may be the only possibility. Social capital, as such, is much more the property of communities and institutions rather than firms; it cannot necessarily be created by firms, even if they make a conscious effort to do so. In the absence of social capital, an organization can make a lot of sense, and may be the only way a low trust labour force can be coordinated. Taylorism in the USA was a system of management that was able to deal with an immigrant labour force of differing nationalities and languages in the industrializing America of the turn of the century.[12] In situations where the labourforce is poorly educated, ethnically divided, and shares few social norms, hierarchical scientific management is a very appropriate solution. Second, large hierarchical firms are often functionally necessary for businesses to achieve their goals. In some industries the ability to move very quickly can be very important and networks can often frustrate this requirement if a consensus has to be established before movement can be attempted. This can be the case in shipowning and trading where deals are often clinched very quickly and without much consultation. Network coordination can also be very risky at times, especially when the local operator has the power to put the whole company at risk. The case of Nick Lesson and his ruining of Barings Bank is a case in point of fact. The ability to control fraud and corruption in some firms means that formal rules and procedures are needed to prevent such damaging behavior and to oversee acceptable conduct. Social capital cannot only keep some norms and values in place, it can also support and generate crooked ones in some instances, as in the case of the Mafia. Third, it is said by some commentators that people are naturally more inclined to want to work in organizations that are hierarchical than in networks. The informal norms and cultures of many organizations are founded and sustained by leaders who are the guiding personalities of the company.[13] Networks are leaderless and norms are in the background, they have to be generated by the members themselves. If the members of the network are not able to do this the network may well disintegrate. Sometimes charismatic individuals are needed to regenerate these norms and values. They often do so through the creation of new organizations that then socialize their members, and this then becomes a tradition of the organization and its informal networks. People may, at various points, want to rejoin a organization if the networks they are connected to are not sustaining enough. After all, consultants are not always what they seem to be. Sometimes, in truth, they are redundant managers who are looking for new jobs.

Conclusion: the likely trajectory of the company form

From the evaluation of the four scenarios above it can be seen that on several grounds the movement towards a more conditional view of property is a strong possibility in the future. But as Schumpeter wrote, 'this opinion of mine, like that of every other economist who has pronounced upon the subject, is in itself completely uninteresting. What counts in any attempt at a social prognosis is not the Yes or No that sums up the facts and arguments which lead up to it but those facts and arguments themselves.'[14]   The change is unlikely to go as far as the radical reformers would like it to go, but it seems highly likely that it will move to some extent in the reformist direction. This is because of the key importance of the need for legitimacy for the institutions of business. The company is a powerful social formation and it needs to be put to the service of the hopes and aspirations of the great majority of those in society. As Drucker rightly noted of the American corporation in 1946: 'The corporation as a representative institution of American society must hold out the promise of adequately fulfilling the aspirations and beliefs of the American people.'[15]   This applies just as much now in the new millennium in the UK, and perhaps more so, given the greater uncertainties under which we now live.

The factors identified in chapter 2, when taken together, put the legitimacy of business into question. And although companies are moving in the direction of greater social responsibility and accountability, as was noted in chapters 3, 4 and 5, they have a long way to go before they are likely to be in a position to regain this legitimacy. Our present system of company institutionalization has become unbalanced: neither the function of companies as creators and distributors of wealth nor the sense of security which comes from partaking in ownership of the company are as inclusive as they need to be if legitimacy is to be restored. For non-shareowners, it appears as if they have a diminished stake in the system of capitalism; it does not offer them job security, or adequate sources of income on which to live, or a sustainable environment. If the state is unable to cushion the blow of uncertainty, an increasingly divided and unequal society could result. In fact, the social fabric of society could wear very thin if the base of social capital upon which capital accumulation depends is not rewoven. Increasingly, workers are being asked to shoulder the risks of capitalist society without gaining a sufficient share of the rewards of company profitability. It follows that if company legitimacy does deteriorate there could be further deterioration in the moral and social order of society and a growth in property-related crime, and there could be a growth of political pressure for more regulation of industry and the protection of trade and companies that will serve the interests of the home market. These pressures would not bode well for the creation of an open and tolerant society that is able to shoulder its share of international burdens in the turbulent world of the twenty-first century.

Schumpeter's sensitivity to the social environment of industrial society and the growth or decay of social capital is a very important insight of his work. The social in many respects determines the parameters in which the economic factors play themselves out. He was rather pessimistic about the fate of the social institutions of capitalism: kinship, religion and local associations. All these social relationships have become weaker as centres of motivation, security and allegiance. Modern rationalization and impersonalisation are changing irrevocably the customs and traditions upon which capitalism was built. As Schumpeter wrote, this 'shows so well that the capitalist order not only rests on props made of extra-capitalist material but also derives its energy from extra-capitalist patterns of behavior which at the same time it is bound to destroy.'[16] In his view, to divorce economic ends from the contexts of social association within which motivation towards these ends is nourished is fatal. The capitalist system and large companies will not be able to save themselves if their purposes become impersonal and remote, separated from the symbols and relationships that have meaning in peoples lives. If the meaning and vividness of property ownership and its accumulation begin to wane then so will the desire of the businessman to maintain it. The incentives of entrepreneurs are not the products for Schumpeter of instincts but of social relationship and tangible norms and institutions. The capitalism of Schumpeter's day, in his view, was, particularly in the corporate form, tending to steadily weaken the symbolic and normative aspects of economic life.

Schumpeter was very critical of Marx's synthesis but did accept some of his propositions that the economic engine of capitalism had a big impact on the social structures and values of capitalist society and that the logic of the economic system was very powerful and had many unintended effects upon society. He also took from Marx the very important insight that capitalism cannot be stationary. It does not expand steadily but is revolutionized at various points by innovations and changes in the conditions, and methods of production. The conditions of doing business are always in a process of upheaval so economic progress means turmoil. New investments compete with the old; the latter dying, while the former expand in a process of creative destruction. In his analysis, it is not the weakness of capitalism that might bring about its undoing but its very success. This is because progressive capitalist accumulations bring about prosperity and discontentment so that the economic motivations that fuel the process begin to erode and the social supports of capitalism in the community also begin to decline. In his view, this would be the signal for the rise of socialism, as the culture of capitalism is gradually socialized. The movement towards socialism was, in his view, inevitable and, with the victory of the Labour Party in the post-war election in Britain in 1945, this seemed to be a real sign his forebodings were coming true.

Schumpeter could not have foreseen the full turn of events in the post-war years. In the early years, it might have looked like his thesis was to be proven correct, but by the 1950s and 60s the capitalist system was back to strength again and flourishing like never before in the USA, and also to a large extent in a reconstructed Europe. However, whilst his prediction of socialism did not come to pass, his thesis is still a relevant one for an understanding of this period and the events of subsequent years. In the post-war era, in the UK, in particular, the engine of capitalism, whilst still running, was effectively slowed down and was working under a set of formidable constraints. The creation of the welfare state after the war and the nationalization of the commanding heights of the economy, began to reduce some of the entrepreneurial opportunities in industry, and these industries offered working people more security and support in the community. The rise of trade union membership after the war was slow at first, but eventually under full employment policies, their membership density increased as did their bargaining power in industry. This, gradually, put a brake on the accumulation process and the profitability of British capital. It also shored up and helped to rebuild the superstructure of social institutions: families, communities and associations. This restoration was given credence as a political project by the larger conflict between the capitalist west and the communist east, with the countries of east and west Europe somewhere in between . Cold War politics had the effect of slowing unbridled capitalism down, and helped to redistribute the gains and risks under this system. It might be noted that only after an inflation crisis and the world recession triggered in the mid 1970s, did the reconstruction of the capitalist engine and an ideology of liberation begin again. This movement began to flower and bear fruit in the 1980s under the Thactherite and Reganite Governments in the UK and USA, and gradually the tide of social democracy was made to turn in economic and cultural terms in these societies. The USA, of course, did not labour under the twin constraints of trade unions and an elaborate welfare state, but its economic fortunes had been set back by the competitive performance of those newly-developing nations in the far east. The US economy has been considerably reinvigorated in the 1990s, and is now beginning to suffer some of the symptoms of success Schumpeter predicted: the erosion of its communities, kinship patterns and rising crime in its cities.[17] The UK's experience is similar: a resurgence of enterprise and business regeneration in the 1980 and 1990s, although its relationship with the European project sits uncomfortably with this change. Alignment with Europe in matters of welfare and trade union recognition are likely to reverse some of these changes, and possibly slow down the engine of growth once again.

In relation to Schumpeter's thesis, it might be said that, in crude terms, the capitalist system was put on hold and its pace of change was moderated in the period 1945-89, but that with the decline of the communist alternative, and the reinvigoration of the economic liberal perspective in the 1980s, it has been able to re-invent itself again and is now beginning to run faster with accumulation restored. The problem, as Schumpeter reminds us, is capitalism's success; it will not weaken and collapse, although from time to time crises will occur. The problems to be faced continually, therefore, are the unintended consequences of capitalism's success, the impact it has upon social structure, and on the culture that supports and motivates its populations. Fukuyama has in many ways chronicled the nature of the problems in this area in terms of trends regarding the family, crime, education, suicide and loss of community. If capitalism and its representative institution, the company, is to reinvent itself again, and there is no reason to suppose that it cannot do so, then it may have to respond to these concerns and make a real contribution to the alleviation of these problems. In other words, it will have to begin to maintain and rebuild social capital. The mechanisms to do this are not very direct and not easy to engineer, but if the pessimistic thesis of Schumpeter is to be overturned, society must attempt to do so. Socialism may have been, in hindsight, an optimistic outcome; the other option could well be decay and decadence, and a slow decline in civilization similar to that which befell the Roman Empire.

The main conclusion to be taken from this analysis is that economic institutions cannot rest upon a possessive individualist order or upon a disintegrating social fabric. Capitalism as a system of private property will only flourish in areas and spheres where it has been joined to a flourishing community. If the foundations of the community and its relationships, its social capital, becomes weak, then capitalism itself is weakened and it will become moribund. For capitalism to flourish it must be sustained by a system of social and moral trust, resting securely in institutions and organizations, or it will degenerate into a sand heap of disconnected individuals.

An examination of some of the recipes for change in the governance of companies has been attempted in the chapters above. Certain changes are perhaps desirable. One of the problems is to overcome the view of the firm which is presently contained in company law. This regards the company as a disposable and purely instrumental tool for the creation of wealth and ignores its aspects of endurance, community and substantive significance. The law prescribes narrow accountabilities and limited responsibilities; the challenge is to open these up and to broaden our understanding of the social significance of business activity without destroying its wealth-creating processes. Indeed the political process of reviewing these assumptions is underway in the UK. The Department of Trade and Industry's Company Law Reform Steering Group will publish revised legislative proposals in 2001. Let us hope that a more imaginative concept of membership of the company will be recommended, one that is able to restore the legitimacy of the firm in our society.

Modern company law requires a rethink of the relationship to the shareholder and a new definition of what the relationship with stakeholders is to be. In existing company law, shareholders are considered to be the owners, and this confers upon them exclusive rights and absolute control. This masks the power of private property in our society and ignores the wide range of other stakeholder interests that are implicated in company decision making. It also distorts our appreciation of company rationality, which is taken to be that of maximizing long-term returns to shareholders. With limited liability, shareholders have acceptable risk but little responsibility for the business as a going concern. When takeovers or mergers arise, the shareholders need only look to their own self interest as to the decision to sell or hold, and the interests of the company, which may be broken up or closed down with massive social costs, can be ignored. To many people this has become an unacceptable state of affairs, and one the at is increasingly putting business at odds with the greater common good.

It should be acknowledged that the company, owned by institutional shareholders and run by professional managers, is a new kind of person in society. It is not a natural person, so the normal mechanisms for controlling the actions of a person have to be applied in a more imaginative way. New mechanisms for making the company responsible have to be developed: corporate governance could be made more responsible to internal stakeholders by the representation of those interests on the boards of directors, and in other processes of decision making in the firm, such as collective a bargaining and works councils. The pragmatic issue here is to ensure that the effective representation of employees' interests does not seriously impair the economic efficiency of the firm and its competitive performance. Empirical evidence on this in other countries suggests that workable solutions are possible. Mayer's study of the literature concerned with the link between governance structures and company performance concluded that the systems of corporate governance in Germany and Japan seemed to be superior in handling and implementing strategies involving wider stakeholder relationships, compared with the governance models that predominated in Anglo-American companies.[18]

Making the company more responsible to stakeholders outside the firm is more challenging and uncertain in terms of proven institutional mechanisms. Putting representatives onto the company board from interests outside the company is difficult: who should represent the environment or the local community? A more pragmatic solution may be to make the company more accountable through its audit process to a wider range of stakeholder interests: consumers, communities, and the environment. The law with regard to company accounts and reports could be changed to make much more information available about the social impact of the company in its environment. Another solution is to use tax and regulatory incentives to induce the company to take greater account of other stakeholder interests. Companies found to have seriously infringed other stakeholder interests in terms of health and safety, human rights abuses, or serious environmental pollution should be placed under stricter regulatory and taxation regimes, and likewise firms that show an exemplary record in these matters should be offered tax and regulatory rewards for good company citizenship. For both natural and corporate citizens in a democracy, virtuous conduct should be esteemed, and vice should be punished. The institutionalization of the company should try to reflect these principles. The challenge for the new politics of corporate governance was perhaps best set down by Peter Drucker.

> The large-scale organization of the business enterprise is very new. It is therefore highly probable that we are not very good as yet in organizing and managing this social institution. That it has great potential has already been proved. The realization of this potential demands hard work on problems of order and structure, individual self-development, and community values and beliefs. It demands above all that our large corporations and their managers take the largest view of their functions and make the greatest demands upon themselves. [19]

References

1   Drucker, P., (1964), *The Concept of the Corporation*, New York, Mentor, p 131.

2   Boswell, J. and Peters, J., (1997), *Capitalism in Contention: Business Leaders and Political Economy in Modern Britain*, Cambridge, Cambridge University Press.

3   Goyder, G., (1951), *The Future of Private Enterprise*, Oxford, Blackwell.

4   Goyder, G., (1975), *The Responsible Worker*, London, Hutchinson. Goyder, G., (1987), *The Just Enterprise,* London, Andre Deutsch.

5   Confederation of British Industry, (1973), *The Responsibilities of the British Public Company*, London, CBI.

6   Giddens, A., (1999), *The Third Way*, London, Polity Press.

7   Hutton, W., (1995), *The State We're In*, London, Jonathan Cape.

8   Sternberg, E., (1994), *Just Business: Business Ethics in Action*, London, Little Brown, p 32.

9   Ibid, p 36.

10   Warren, R.C., (1996), 'Business as a community of purpose', *Business Ethics, A European Review*, 5: 2, pp 87-96.

11   Smith, A., (1982), *The Theory of Moral Sentiments*, Indianapolis, Liberty Classics.

12   Taylor, F.W., (1947), *Scientific Management*, New York, Harper Row.

13   Schein, E.H., (1988), *Organizational Culture and Leadership*, San Francisco,Jossey-Bass.

14   Schumpeter, J., (1987), *Capitalism, Socialism and Democracy*, London, Counterpoint, p 61.

15   Drucker, op cit, p 25.

16   Schumpeter, op cit, p 162.

17   Fukuyama, F., (1999), *The Great Disruption*, London, Profile Books.

18   Mayer, C., (1997), 'Corporate Governance, Competition, and Performance', in Deakin, S. and Hughes, A., *Enterprise and Community: New Directions in Corporate Governance*, Oxford,Blackwell, pp 152-176. Drucker, op cit, p 247.

Bibliography

ACCA, (1998), *Environment under the Spotlight*, Glasgow, ACCA.

Accounting Standards Committee, (1975), *The Corporate Report*, London, ICAEW.

Alborn, T. L., (1998), *Conceiving Companies: Joint-Stock Politics in Victorian England*, London, Routledge.

Ansoff, I., (1969), *Business Strategy*, Harmonsworth, Penguin.

Barnes, C. (1992), *Disabled People in Britain and Discrimination*, London,Hurst and Company.

Bellah, R., at al., (1991), *The Good Society*, New York, Vintage.

Berle, A.A. and Means, G.C., (1968), *The Modern Corporation and Private Property*, New York, Harcourt Brace.

Blair, T., (1999), 'Blair praises social responsibility', *Financial Times*, London, 16th July.

Boswell, J., (1990), *Community and the Economy: The Theory of Public Co Operation*, London, Routledge.

Boswell, J. and Peters, J., (1997), *Capitalism in Contention: Business Leaders and Political Economy in Modern Britain*, Cambridge, Cambridge University Press.

Bowen, R. H., (1953), *Social Responsibilities of the Businessman*, New York, Harper.

Bowie, N.E., (1999), *Business Ethics: A Kantian Perspective*, Oxford, Blackwell.

Burchill, F. (1997), *Labour Relations*, London, Macmillan.

Burnham, J. (1941), *The Managerial Revolution*, Harmondsworth, Penguin.

Cappelli, P. et al. (1997), *Change at Work*, Oxford, Oxford University Press.

Carson, R., (1962), *Silent Spring*, Boston, Houghton Mifflin.

Cassis, Y., (1997), *Big Business: the European Experience in the Twentieth Century*, Oxford, Oxford University Press.

Castells, M., (1998), *The Information Age: Economy, Society and Culture*, (3 Volumes: *The Rise of The Network Society; The Power of Identity; End of Millennium*), Oxford, Blackwell.

Chandler, A.D., (1962), *Strategy and Structure*, Cambridge Mass., MIT Press.

Charkham, J., (1994), *Keeping Good Company: a Study of Corporate Governance in Five Countries*, Oxford, Oxford University Press.

Coase, R.H., (1937), 'The nature of the firm', *Economica*, 6, pp 386-405.

Cole, G.D.H., (1938), *Socialism in Evolution*, Harmondsworth, Penguin, pp 97-132.

Coleman, J. S., (1990), *Foundations of Social Theory*, Cambridge, Mass., Harvard University. Press. Jacobs, J., (1992), *The Death and Life of Great American Cities*, New York, Vintage.

Collinson, D. L. et al. (1990), *Managing to Discriminate*, London, Routledge.

Committee of Inquiry on Industrial Democracy, (1977) (Bullock Report), London, HMSO.

Committee on the Financial Aspects of Corporate Governance, (1992) (Cadbury Report) London.

Committee on Corporate Governance, (1998) (Hampel Report) London.

The Company Report Report, (1997), Peter Prowse Associates, London.

Company Reporting, (1996), 'Environmental Reporting', Edinburgh.

Confederation of British Industry, (1973), 'The Responsibilities of the British Public Company', London, CBI.

Cowton, C., (1999), 'Playing by the rules: ethical criteria at an ethical investment fund', *Business Ethics: A European Review*, 8: 1, pp 60-69.

Dahl, R.A., (1985), *A Preface to Economic Democracy*, Berkeley,University of California Press.

Department of Trade and Industry, (1998), 'Modern Company Law for a Competitive Approach'.

Dicken, P., (1998), *Global Shift: The Internationalization of Economic Activity*, New York, Guilford Press.

Drucker, P. (1964), *The Concept of the Corporation*, New York, Mentor Books, p27.

Drucker, P., (1998), *Peter Drucker on the Profession of Management*, Boston, Harvard Business School Press.

The European Board of Directors Study, (1997), London, Korn/Ferry Intl.

Etzioni, A., (1995), *New Communitarian Thinking*, London, University Press of Virginia.

Financial Times, (1995), 'Greenpeace admits Brent Spar blunder', 6th September.

Financial Times, (1996), 'Body Shop challenges Shell to confront new business reality', 31st October.

Financial Times, (1996), 'Fund to target corporate governance', 18th November.

Financial Times, (1997), 'Call for companies league table', 12th November.

Financial Times, (1997), 'Drive to end company law deadlock', 14th May.

Financial Times, (1997), 'The Global Company', 3rd October.

Financial Times, (1998), 'Amnesty questions ethics of multinationals', 22nd April.

Financial Times, (1998), 'Ethical codes of practice not being implemented', 1st December.

Financial Times, (1998), 'Holier-than-thou bank's ethical audit', 15th April.

Financial Times, (1998), 'Interactive annual reports urged', 3rd March.

Financial Times, (1998), 'KPMG and Body Shop link to offer ethical auditing', 7th December.

Financial Times, (1998), 'Oiling the group's wheels of change', 31st March.

Financial Times, (1998), 'Standard to verify business ethics launched', 11th June.

Financial Times, (1999), 'Review of company law should uphold social responsibility', 8th June.

Financial Times, (1999), 'Business in the Community', 16th July.

Financial Times, (1999), 'Companies urged to issue social performance data', 8th June.

Financial Times, (1999), 'Cook plans ethics guide for companies', 2nd January.

Financial Times, (1999), 'Government aims to sift rogues from risk-takers', 13th July.

Financial Times, (1999), 'Greener profit drivers', 28th April.

Financial Times, (1999), 'Measure of progress in the works', 21st June.

Financial Times, (1999), 'Multinationals attacked over child labour', 5th July.

Financial Times, (1999), 'Pension funds end opposition to rules on ethical stance', 2nd July.

Florence, P. S., (1953), *The Logic of British and American Industry*, London, Routledge.

Friedman, M., (1962), *Capitalism and Freedom*, Chicago, Chicago University Press.

Freidman, M., (1970), 'The Social Responsibility of Business is to Increase its Profits', *New York Times Magazine*, pp 32-33, 122, 124, 126.

Freidman, M., (1988) 'The Social Responsibility of Business is to Increase its Profits' in Beauchamp, T. and   Bowie, N. *Ethical Theory and Business*, Englewood Cliffs NJ, Prentice Hall.

Fukuyama, F., (1995), *Trust: the social virtues and the creation of prosperity*, London,Hamish Hamilton.

Fukuyama, F., (1999), *The Great Disruption*, London, Profile Books.

Future Foundation, (1997), *The Responsible Organization*, London.

Galbraith, J. K., (1967), *The New Industrial State*, London, Hamish Hamilton.

Gates, J., (1998), *The Ownership Solution: Toward A Shared Capitalism for the Twenty-First Century*, London, Penguin.

Gates, W., (1999), *Business @ the Speed of Thought: Using a Digital Nervous System*, London, Penguin.

George, H., (1880), *Progress and Poverty*, London, Bell.

Ghoshal, G. Bartlett, C., (1997), *The Individualized Corporation*, London, Heinemann.

Giddens, A., (1999), *The Third Way*, London, Polity Press.

Glyn, A. and Milliband, D., (1994), *Paying for Inequality*, London, Institute for Public Policy Research.

Goodpaster, K., (1991), 'Business Ethics and Stakeholder Analysis', *Business Ethics Quarterly*, 1:1, pp 53- 68.

Goyder, G., (1951), *The Future of Private Enterprise*, Oxford, Blackwell.

Goyder, G., (1963), *The Responsible Company*, Oxford, Blackwell.

Goyder, G., (1975), *The Responsible Worker*, London,Hutchinson.

Goyder, G., (1987), *The Just Enterprise*, London, Andre Deutsch.

Gray, J., (1986), *Liberalism*, Milton Keynes, Open University Press.

Gray, J., (1998), *False Dawn*, London, Granta.

Gray, R., Owen, D. and   Adams, C., (1996), *Accounting and Accountability*, London, Prentice Hall.

Gregg, P. and Wadsworth, J., (1995), 'A Short History of Labour Turnover, Job Tenure and Job Security, 1973-93' *Oxford Review of Economic Policy*, 11:1.

Gregg, P., Machin, S. and Szymanski, S., (1993), 'The Disappearing Relationship Between Directors' Pay and Corporate Performance', *British Journal of Industrial Relations*, 31: 1, pp 1-9.

Guest, D. and Mackenzie, K., (1996), 'Don't write off the Traditional Career', *People Management*, February, pp 22-5.

Habermas, J., (1973), *Legitimation Crisis*, London,Hutchinson.

Habermas, J., (1987), *Theory of Communicative Action*, Vol. II, London, Heinemann.

Hayek, F. A., (1969) 'The Corporation in a Democratic Society: in whose interest ought it and will it be run?' in Ansoff, H. I. (ed.), *Business Strategy*, Harmondsworth, Penguin.

Herriot, P. and Pemberton, C., (1995), *Competitive Advantage Through Diversity*, London, Sage.

Hertz, N., (1999), 'Better to shop than vote', *New Statesman*, 21st June.

Hirst, P., (1994), *Associative Democracy: New Forms of Economic and Social Governance*, London, Polity Press.

Hirst, P. and Thompson, G., (1996), *Globalisation in Question*, London, Polity Press.

Hobson, J.A., (1987), *Imperialism: a Study*, London, Unwin Hyman.

Hoffman, A.J., (1997), *From Heresy to Dogma: An Institutional History of Corporate Environmentalism*, San Francisco, The New Lexington Press.

Hume, D., (1963), *Essays, Moral, Political and Literary*, Oxford, Oxford University Press.

Hutton, W., (1995), *The State We're In*, London, Jonathan Cape.

Institute for Fiscal Studies, (1994), *Update: the changing face of inequality*, London, IFS, Autumn/Winter.

International Survey Research, (1997), *Tracking Trends: Employee satisfaction in Europe in the 90's*, London, ISR Ltd. pp 1-12.

Jeremy, D.J., (1998), *A Business History of Britain: 1900-1990s*, Oxford, Oxford University Press.

Kanter, R. M., (1993), *Men and Women of the Corporation*, 2nd Edition, New York, Basic Books.

Kay, J., (1986), *The Role of Mergers*, London, Institute of Fiscal Studies Working Paper No 94.

Kay, J., (1996), *The Business of Economics*, Oxford, Oxford University Press.

Kelly, G., Kelly, D., and Gamble, A., (1997), *Stakeholder Capitalism*, London, Macmillan.

Kempner, T., Macmillan, K., and Hawkins, K., (1974), *Business and Society*, Harmondsworth, Penguin.

Kennedy, P., (1993), *Preparing for the Twenty-First Century*, New York, Random House.

Krugman, P., (1994), *Peddling Prosperity*, London, W.W. Norton.

Lane, T., (1987), 'Economic democracy: are trade unions equipped?', *Industrial Relations Journal*, 18: 4, pp 322-329.

Likert, R., (1967), *The Human Organization*, New York, McGraw Hill.

Lindblom, C.E., (1977), *Politics and Markets*, New York, Basic Books.

Lyall, D., (1982), 'Disclosure practices in employee reports', *Accountants Magazine*, July, pp 246- 248.

Maine, H., (1903), *Ancient Law*, London, John Murray.

Mandeville, B., (1970), *The Fable of the Bees*, Harmondsworth, Penguin.

Marsden, D. and Richardson, R. (1994), 'Performing for Pay? The effects of merit pay on motivation in a public service', *British Journal of Industrial Relations*, 32:2. pp 243-261.

Marx, K., (1865), *Capital III*, London, Lawrence and Wishart, 1959.

Mayer, C., (1997), 'Corporate Governance, Competition, and Performance', in Deakin, S. and Hughes, A., *Enterprise and Community: New Directions in Corporate Governance*, Oxford, Blackwell.

Maynard-Smith, J., (1993), *The Theory of Evolution*, Cambridge, Cambridge University Press.

Mill, J.S., (1914), *Utilitarianism, Liberty and Representative Government*, London, Dent.

Millward, N., (1994), *The New Industrial Relations?* London, Policy Studies Institute.

Mitchell, N.J., (1997), *The Conspicuous Corporation*, Ann Arbor, University of Michigan Press.

Monks, R,A. and Minow, N., (1995), *Corporate Governance*, Oxford, Blackwell.

Monks, R. A. and Minow, N., (1996), *Watching the Watchers: Corporate governance for the 21st Century*, Oxford, Blackwell.

Morse, G., (1987), *Charlesworth's Company Law*, 13th Edition, London, Stevens and Sons.

Murray, C., (1994), *Underclass: the crisis deepens*, London, IEA.

National Power Report and Accounts (1999), London.

New Statesman, (1997), 'Interview: John Browne', 4th July.

Nohria, N. and Eccles, R., (1992), *Networks and Organizations: Structure, Form, and Action*, Boston, Harvard Business School Press.

Nonaka, I. and Takeuchi, H., (1995), *The Knowledge-Creating Company*, London, Pitman.

Novak, M., (1997), *The Fire of Invention: Civil Society and the Future of the Corporation*, New York, Rowman and Littlefield.

Nozick, R., (1977), *Anarchy, State, and Utopia*, New York, Basic Books.

Observer, (1999), 'Canny companies come clean', 27th June.

Parkinson, J., (1994), *Corporate Power and Responsibility: Issues in the Theory of Company Law*, Oxford, Oxford University Press.

Peters, T. and Waterman, R., (1982), *In Search of Excellence*, New York, Harper Row.

PIRC, (1998), *Environmental and Social reporting: a Survey of Current Practice at FTSE 350 Companies*, London, PIRC.

Plender, J., (1997), *A Stake in the Future*, London, Nicholas Brealey.

Plender, J., (1997), *Financial Times*, 7th July.

Putnam, R., (1993), *Making Democracy Work: Civic Traditions in Modern Italy*, Princeton, Princeton University Press.

Putnam, R., (1995), 'Bowling alone: America's Declining Social Capital', *Journal of Democracy*, 6, pp 664-682.

Railtrack Group PLC, Annual Report and Accounts (1999), London.

Rawls, J., (1971), *A Theory of Justice*, Oxford, Oxford University Press.

Redding, S.G., (1990), *The Spirit of Chinese Capitalism*, Berlin, de Gruyter.

Reich, R., (1991), *The Work of Nations*, London, Simon and Schuster. Chapter 17.

The Report of the Committee on Directors' Remuneration, (1995), (Greenbury Report), London.

Ricketts, M., (1999), *The Many Ways of Governance*, London, IEA Social Affairs Unit.

Roslender, R. and Dyson, J., (1992), 'Accounting for the worth of employees: a new look at an old problem', *British Accounting Review*, 24:4, pp 311-329.

Royal Society of Arts, (1995), *Tomorrow's Company*, London.

Ruskin, J., (1860), *Unto this Last*, London, Dent.

Ryan, A., (1984), *Property and Political Theory*, Oxford, Blackwell.

Sacks, J., (1997) *The Politics of Hope*, London, Jonathan Cape, p 170.

Sampson, A., (1995), *Company Man: the Rise and Fall of Corporate Life*, London, Harper Collins.

Sandel, M. J. (1996), *Democracy's Discontent*, Cambridge MS, Harvard University Press.

Saxenian, A. L., (1994), *Regional Advantage: Culture and Competition in Silicon Valley and Route 128*, Cambridge Mass., Harvard University Press.

Schein, E.H., (1988), *Organizational Culture and Leadership*, San Francisco, Jossey-Bass.

Schumpeter, J., (1961), *The Theory of Economic Development*, New York, Oxford University Press.

Schumpeter, J., (1987), *Capitalism, Socialism and Democracy*, London, Counterpoint.

Scott, J. (1997), *Corporate Business and Capitalist Classes*, Oxford, Oxford University Press.

Selznick, P., (1992), *The Moral Commonwealth*, Berkeley, University of California Press.

Senge, P. M., (1990), *The Fifth Discipline: The Art and Practice of the Learning Organization*, New York, Doubleday.

Shaw, G.B., et al., (1890), *Essays in Fabian Socialism*, London, Fabian Society.

Shell Report, (1999), *People, Planet and Profits: an act of commitment*, London.

Smith, A., (1976), *An Inquiry into the Nature and Causes of the Wealth of Nations*, Oxford, Clarendon Press.

Smith, A., (1982), *The Theory of Moral Sentiments*, Indianapolis, Liberty Classics.

Stapledon, G.P., (1996), *Institutional Shareholders and Corporate Governance*, Oxford, Clarendon Press.

Sternberg, E., (1994), *Just Business: Business Ethics in Action*, London, Little Brown, p 32.

Sternberg, E., (1998), *Corporate Governance: Accountability in the Marketplace*, London, Institute of Economic Affairs.

Tawney, R.H., (1921), *The Acquisitive Society*, London,G.Bell and Sons.

Taylor, F.W., (1947), *Scientific Management*, New York, Harper Row.

Tricker, R.I., (1994), *International Corporate Governance*, London, Prentice Hall.

Trades Union Congress, (1991), *Greening the Workplace*, London, TUC.

Warren, R.C., (1996), 'Business as a community of purpose', *Business Ethics: A European Review*, 5: 2, pp 87-96.

Weber, M. (1968), *Economy and Society Vol 3*, London, Routledge, p 953.

Welford, R. (1995), *Environmental Strategy and Sustainable Development*, London, Routledge.

Wells, H. G., (1967), *A Short History of the World*, Harmondsworth, Penguin.

West, J. (1982), *Work, Women and the Labour Market*, London, Routledge.

Wheeler, D. and Sillanpaa, M., (1997), *The Stakeholder Corporation*, London, Pitman.

White, J.B., (1985), 'How Should We Talk About Corporations? The languages of Economics and of Citizenship', *Yale Law Journal*, 94, pp 1416-1425.

Williams, A. P. (1994), *Just Reward? the truth about executive pay*, London, Kogan Page.

Williamson, O.E., (1993), *The Nature of the Firm: Origins, Evolution and Development*, Oxford, Oxford University Press.

Index